ROUTLEDGE LIBRARY EDITIONS: SOCIOLOGY OF EDUCATION

Volume 33

TEACHERS' CAREER AND PROMOTION PATTERNS

TEACHERS' CAREER AND PROMOTION PATTERNS
A Sociological Analysis

RUPERT MACLEAN

LONDON AND NEW YORK

First published in 1992 by The Falmer Press

This edition first published in 2017
by Routledge
2 Park Square, Milton Park, Abingdon, Oxon OX14 4RN

and by Routledge
711 Third Avenue, New York, NY 10017

Routledge is an imprint of the Taylor & Francis Group, an informa business

© 1992 R. Maclean

All rights reserved. No part of this book may be reprinted or reproduced or utilised in any form or by any electronic, mechanical, or other means, now known or hereafter invented, including photocopying and recording, or in any information storage or retrieval system, without permission in writing from the publishers.

Trademark notice: Product or corporate names may be trademarks or registered trademarks, and are used only for identification and explanation without intent to infringe.

British Library Cataloguing in Publication Data
A catalogue record for this book is available from the British Library

ISBN: 978-0-415-78834-2 (Set)
ISBN: 978-1-315-20949-4 (Set) (ebk)
ISBN: 978-0-415-79034-5 (Volume 33) (hbk)
ISBN: 978-0-415-79036-9 (Volume 33) (pbk)

Publisher's Note
The publisher has gone to great lengths to ensure the quality of this reprint but points out that some imperfections in the original copies may be apparent.

Disclaimer
The publisher has made every effort to trace copyright holders and would welcome correspondence from those they have been unable to trace.

To Professors Eric Hoyle, P.W. Musgrave and Sir William Taylor — three excellent teachers who have taught me much about the social contexts of schooling.

Teachers' Career and Promotion Patterns:
A Sociological Analysis

Rupert Maclean

Foreword by
Professor Sir William Taylor

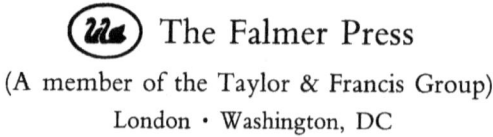 The Falmer Press
(A member of the Taylor & Francis Group)
London · Washington, DC

UK The Falmer Press, 4 John Street, London WC1N 2ET
USA The Falmer Press, Taylor & Francis Inc., 1900 Frost Road, Suite 101, Bristol, PA 19007

© R. Maclean 1992

All rights reserved. No part of this publication may be reproduced, stored in a retrieval system, or transmitted in any form or by any means, electronic, mechanical, photocopying, recording or otherwise, without permission in writing from the Publisher.

First published 1992

British Library Cataloguing in Publication Data
A catalogue record for this book is available from the British Library

Library of Congress Cataloguing-in-Publication Data is available

Jacket design by Caroline Archer

Typeset in 10½/12pt Bembo by
Graphicraft Typesetters Ltd., Hong Kong

Printed in Great Britain by Burgess Science Press, Basingstoke on paper which has a specified pH value on final paper manufacture of not less than 7.5 and is therefore 'acid free'.

Contents

List of Tables and Figures   viii

Acknowledgements   xii

Foreword   xiii
Sir William Taylor

Chapter 1: Introduction   1

    Background: The Sociological Study of Work and
        Occupations   1
    The Content of Occupational Sociology   4
    Why Study Occupations?   5
    The Sociological Study of School Teachers   6
    Studying Promotion and Career Patterns in Teaching   7
    Purpose of this Research Study and Theoretical Orientation
        Adopted   10
    Main Findings of the Study   12
    Organization of this Book   12
    Conclusion   13

Chapter 2: Ways of Conceptualising Occupational Careers   14

    Occupation, Profession and Career   15
    Careers in Context   18
    The Career Structure   20
    The Attributes of Individuals   27
    Perceptions of the Career Structure   35
    Conclusion   36

Chapter 3: The Teaching Career   38

    Occupation, Profession and Career as they apply to School
        Teachers   38

Contents

The School Teaching Career in Context	42
The Career Structure in School Teaching	43
Attributes of School Teachers as an Occupational Group	55
Teacher Perceptions of the Career Structure	59
Conclusion	62

Chapter 4:   Opportunity Structure of Tasmanian Teachers   63

Changing Structure of the State School System	64
Number, Description and Size of Schools	64
Changing Structure of the Promotions System	66
Hierarchy of Promotion Positions	67
Number and Distribution of Promotion Positions	69
Appointments and Promotions Procedures within the Opportunity Structure	71
Conclusion	73

Chapter 5:   Case Study of Teachers' Careers:
              Research Design and Procedures   74

Research Framework	75
Drawing Parts of the Framework Together	79
Methodology	80
Conclusion	86

Chapter 6:   Personal and Professional Characteristics of
              Promoted Teachers   88

Personal Background Details	88
Academic and Professional Qualifications	94
Factors and Views Related to Promotion	99
Conclusion	117

Chapter 7:   Career Patterns of Teachers   118

Methodology for Analysing Teacher Career Patterns	118
Teachers in Primary Schools	121
Teachers in Secondary Schools	124
Teachers in District Schools	129
Teachers in Non-school Advisory, Supervisory and Administrative Positions	133
Mobility between Work Locations	133
Horizontal vs Vertical Mobility	136
Teachers in Different Sectors of the Education Department	139
Distribution of, and Competition for, Promotion Positions	141

Rate at which Promotion Occurs	145
Career Pathways of Directors and School Principals	149
Conclusion	153

Chapter 8: Teacher perceptions of the Teaching Career — 154

Teaching as a Career	154
Stages in the Teaching Career	159
Why do Teachers Seek Promotion?	160
Career Contingency Factors	163
Career Anchorage Perspectives	171
The Promoted Teacher: A Composite Picture	172
Teachers Who do not Seek Promotion	173
Operation of the Promotion System	174
Horizontal Mobility	176
Teachers Who do not Seek Mobility	178
Changing Opportunity Structure in Teaching	180
Chances of Gaining Further Promotion	182
Reduced Promotion Opportunities, Teacher Behaviour and Morale	183
Conclusion	186

Chapter 9: Teachers' Careers: Summary, Discussion of Results and Conclusions Drawn — 187

The School Teaching Career	187
Career Maps, Strategies and Timetables	193
Career Anchorage Perspectives	194
Vertical and Horizontal Mobility, and Career Contingency Factors	196
Structural and Phenomenological Perspectives in Studying the School Teaching Career	208
Concluding Comments	209

Bibliography — 213

Appendices — 231

1	Propositions Tested	233
2	Stage 1 Data: Information from Education Department Personnel Files	240
3	State 2 Data: Questionnaire	243
4	Stage 3 Data: Interview Schedules	254
5	Career Profiles of Promoted Teachers: Statistics	258

Index — 263

List of Tables and Figures

Tables

5.1	Status of full-time teachers and personnel engaged in supervisory, advisory or administrative duties	84
6.1	Distribution of respondents according to gender	89
6.2	Distribution of respondents according to age	90
6.3	Age characteristics of respondents according to promotion position	91
6.4	Distribution of respondents according to marital status, by gender	91
6.5	Distribution of respondents according to number of children, by gender	92
6.6	Distribution of respondents according to relatives who are, or have been, teachers, by gender	92
6.7	Distribution of respondents according to whether or not they would encourage a son or daughter to become a teacher	93
6.8	Father's occupation of respondents at the time teachers completed secondary school	93
6.9	Mother's occupation of respondents at the time teachers completed secondary school	94
6.10	Distribution of respondents according to age group of pupils trained to teach during initial teacher training	95
6.11	Distribution of respondents according to years of pre-service teacher training	95
6.12	Distribution of respondents according to whether they were studying for a qualification relevant to their career	96
6.13	Distribution of respondents according to graduate/non-graduate status, by gender	96
6.14	Distribution of respondents according to graduate/non-graduate status, by sector of employment	96

List of Tables and Figures

6.15	Distribution of respondents according to graduate/non-graduate status, by promotion position	97
6.16	Main subject specialisms of respondents with degree qualifications	98
6.17	Teaching-method areas of respondents	98
6.18	Subjects taught by respondents employed in schools	99
6.19	Respondents' views regarding relative importance to overall personal satisfaction of pursuing a career	100
6.20	Respondents' main satisfactions with teaching in schools	100
6.21	Respondents' main dissatisfactions with teaching in schools	101
6.22	Female respondents' main satisfactions with teaching in schools	101
6.23	Male respondents' main satisfactions with teaching in schools	102
6.24	Female respondents' main dissatisfactions with teaching in schools	102
6.25	Male respondents' main dissatisfactions with teaching in schools	103
6.26	Satisfactions with current promotion position of respondents employed in non-school advisory, supervisory or administrative positions	103
6.27	Dissatisfactions with current promotion position of respondents employed in non-school advisory, supervisory or administrative positions	104
6.28	Distribution of respondents according to whether they would feel (or have felt) loss or gain if they were to (or have) left the classroom for an administrative type promotion position	104
6.29	Number of times respondents moved place of residence as a result of gaining promotion, by gender	105
6.30	Number of times respondents moved place of residence as a result of gaining promotion, by promotion position occupied	106
6.31	Respondents' estimated chances of gaining further promotion, by gender	106
6.32	Respondents' views regarding estimated chances of gaining promotion, according to promotion position occupied	107
6.33	Respondents' views regarding pursuit of a career in the Education Department in or outside schools, according to promotion position occupied	109
6.34	Respondents' views regarding pursuit of a career in the Education Department in or outside schools, according to gender	110

List of Tables and Figures

6.35	Distribution of respondents according to preference of teachers to work in city rather than country schools	110
6.36	Distribution of respondents according to preference of teachers to work in large rather than small schools	111
6.37	Distribution of respondents according to preference of teachers to work in schools in 'middle class' rather than 'working class' areas	111
6.38	Respondents' views regarding factors that currently favour promotion	112
6.39	Female respondents' views regarding factors that currently favour promotion	113
6.40	Male respondents' views regarding factors that currently favour promotion	113
6.41	Respondents' views regarding factors that ought to favour promotion	114
6.42	Male respondents' views regarding factors that ought to favour promotion	114
6.43	Female respondents' views regarding factors that ought to favour promotion	114
6.44	Principals' views regarding factors that affect promotion	115
6.45	Superintendents' views regarding factors that affect promotion	116
6.46	Principals' views regarding factors that ought to affect promotion	116
6.47	Superintendents' views regarding factors that ought to affect promotion	116
7.1	Number of times senior masters/mistresses and senior teachers had moved between schools/work locations during teaching career, by gender	137
7.2	Number of times promoted teachers in non-school positions moved between school/work locations	137
7.3	Proportion of principals' moves between schools/work locations over teaching career associated with vertical rather than horizontal mobility	138
7.4	Proportion of senior masters'/mistresses' and senior teachers' moves between schools/work locations over teaching career associated with vertical rather than horizontal mobility	139
7.5	Proportion of moves by non-school promoted teachers between school/work locations over teaching career associated with vertical rather than horizontal mobility	139
7.6	Promotion positions advertised according to school/branch type	144
7.7	Promotion positions advertised according to urban, country or isolated location	144

List of Tables and Figures

7.8	Average number of applicants for promotion positions advertised according to gender of applicant	146
7.9	Average number of applicants per post for promotion positions advertised in different types of schools	147
7.10	Average number of applicants per post for promotion positions advertised in urban, country and isolated locations	147
7.11	Principals in different types of schools: years of teaching experience when first promotion awarded, in five year time spans 1940–1974	148

Figures

4.1	The school system of Tasmania	65
7.1	Promoted teachers in primary schools	122
7.2	Promoted teachers in primary schools, by gender	123
7.3	Promoted teachers in primary schools, by graduate/non-graduate status	125
7.4	Promoted teachers in secondary schools	126
7.5	Promoted teachers in secondary schools, by gender	127
7.6	Promoted teachers in secondary schools, by graduate/non-graduate status	128
7.7	Promoted teachers in different types of secondary schools	130
7.8	Promoted teachers in district schools	131
7.9	Promoted teachers in district schools by graduate/non-graduate status	132
7.10	Promoted teachers in non-school positions	134
7.11	Number of principals' moves between school/work locations	135
7.12	Principals in different types of schools by size of school	140
7.13	Vice-principals and principal education officers in different sectors of the education department	142
7.14	Senior masters/mistresses, senior teachers and senior education officers in different sectors of the education department	143
7.15	Pathways in the promotion of directors	150
7.16	Pathways in the promotion of secondary principals	151
7.17	Pathways in the promotion of primary principals	152

Acknowledgements

I wish to first and foremost acknowledge my debt to the hundreds of teachers employed in the Education Department of Tasmania who gave so freely of their time and effort to this research by completing questionnaires, and by attending individual or group interviews. Without their generosity and interest this research would not have been possible.

Administrative and library staff within the Education Department of Tasmania, and in particular Director-Generals Mr. B.G. Mitchell and Mr. K. Axton, were very helpful in providing full access to information on the career histories of teachers. The Tasmanian Teachers Federation, and its Research Committee, contributed generously to research costs, the balance of finance being provided by the University of Tasmania, through its Centre for Education. To all these persons and institutions I wish to express my thanks.

Professor P.W. Musgrave and Dr. F.J. Hunt of the Faculty of Education, Monash University, Professor K.F. Collis, of the Centre for Education at the University of Tasmania, and Dr. Gary Easthope, of the Sociology Department, University of Tasmania, provided helpful comments on earlier draft sections of this book. I thank them for having given their time and experience so freely during the course of this research.

Finally, I express my gratitude to Noelene Hale, Margaret Wood and Cate Lowry for their assistance in preparing the typescript.

Foreword

This is an important book on an important subject. On the basis of numbers alone, detailed examination of the occupation of teaching is amply justified. In many countries teachers and other education workers now constitute one of the largest single employment categories. But there is more to it than that.

The influence that teachers exert on the life chances of individuals, on the values of society and on economic success is difficult to quantify; it is nonetheless real. Witness the reluctance of governments to hand over responsibility for admission, training and discipline to self-governing professional organisations. These days, education rates as too important to be left to the educators.

Rupert Maclean shows that despite appearances and beliefs to the contrary, teachers go in for career planning just as systematically as the members of any other occupation. In his own words, 'the career movements of teachers...are patterned and not random' (p. 191). Status and rewards matter, but so do teaching locations and conditions; the costs and benefits of both vertical and horizontal mobility are carefully calculated.

These are findings of more than academic interest. The implications for policy extend far beyond the state in which the research on which this book is based was undertaken. Explicit and defensible criteria for appointment and promotion are important in maintaining and enhancing teacher morale and effectiveness — both of which assume significance in the context of studies which demonstrate that as far as student outcomes are concerned, teachers do indeed make a difference.

In addition to reporting comprehensively on the outcomes of his own research, the author offers a wide-ranging review of the relevant literature which will interest and benefit anyone concerned with the sociology of occupations. His book has much to teach us not only about teachers but much else besides; it deserves to be widely read.

William Taylor
February 1992

Chapter 1

Introduction

Background: The Sociological Study of Work and Occupations

The interest of sociologists in work, occupations and employment-related areas is long-standing and has existed since the beginning of the discipline's history in the mid-nineteenth century. For example, Emile Durkheim, in his first major work entitled *The Division of Labour*, published in 1893, examined the relationship between employment in modern industrial society and the creation of social order. It would appear to be both natural and logical that this should be the case, because work is a central activity in the lives of most people and all societies. However, it is only since the research undertaken at the University of Chicago, particularly by Everett Hughes and his associates from about the mid 1940s, that occupational sociology has achieved independent status as an area of study within sociology. Before this time, despite the large and often rich body of empirical studies that had been accumulated over the previous century, the content of this area was decentralized amongst a wide range of subject areas within sociology such as industrial sociology, rural sociology and demography.

In Britain and Europe interest in sociological aspects of the world of work can be traced back over approximately two centuries, an examination of important aspects of this area being found in the writings of various social philosophers, economists, historians and (later) sociologists. In 1776, for example, the father of classical economics, Adam Smith, published a book called *An Inquiry into the Nature and Causes of the Wealth of Nations* in which he explored the effect of the division of labour on the productivity of labour. As part of his analysis, Smith examined the social impact of changed production methods on various occupational groups and the broad society.

Some early sociologists, such as the founding fathers of the discipline, Marx, Weber and Durkheim, examined work in a relatively broad sense, largely focusing upon a study of the labour force and alienation, which they regarded as being particularly important. Only to a limited extent did they undertake a study of any particular occupation or profession. Emile Durkheim (1933, orig. 1893), in his seminal work *The Division of Labour in Society*, examined and emphasized the importance of changes in the division of labour and the effect this would have upon the move from a state of mechanical solidarity to that of organic solidarity within a society; Karl Marx (1961, orig. 1846; 1954, orig. 1867) stressed the fundamental importance of labour in human history and in helping to define man's humanness and identity; and both he and Max Weber (1947, orig. 1922) examined the relationship between work and alienation, Marx being primarily concerned with the alienation of factory workers while Weber expanded the concept to include other occupational groups. Weber was particularly interested in the notion of work in connection with his concept of rationalization; and also undertook a detailed study of particular occupations, including the political, the scientific, the professional, and the Chinese literati.

Some other precursors of modern sociology who showed a particular interest in the study of work and/or occupations include: Frederick Le Play (1877–79) who in his mammoth six volume work entitled *The European Working Classes* undertook empirical studies of the life and working conditions of various occupational groups; Charles Booth (1902) who organized investigations into the *Life and Labour of the People of London;* De Mann's (1929) studies of the manual worker; and, Dreyfuss' (1938) work on the salaried employee.

In the United States, the development of the sociology of occupations appears to have occurred almost as a by-product of the work of Robert Park (1925) and his associates at the University of Chicago in the 1920s and 1930s. As part of their major interest in the ecological and social integration of various groups living in the inner-city, ghetto type areas of Chicago (see Wirth, 1928), Park and his fellow researchers studied a variety of low status, often marginal occupations such as the hobo (Anderson, 1923), prostitute (Donovan, 1920), taxi-dance-hall girl (Cressy, 1932), and professional thief (Sutherland, 1937); and generally adopted a social-psychological and social-interaction approach to the occupations studied. They were interested in what Everett Hughes calls 'the dirty work in society', and the ways in which the practitioners of such work were able to overcome or control the problems and tensions associated with such types of work.

Some went beyond this narrow focus on low status work to study various more respectable occupations whose practitioners were not concentrated in the inner city areas. Examples are the studies undertaken on sales-staff in shops (Donovan, 1930) and the school teacher (Donovan, 1938).

At a later date, the studies undertaken by Mayo and Lombard (1944), and by those involved with the famous 'Hawthorn studies', widened existing approaches to the study of work and occupations. Both these studies were concerned with important aspects of industrial sociology such as the study of work organizations, industrial relations and human relations in industry; and they adopted a psycho-sociological approach to the study of men and women working in groups.

Academic interest in, and research about, the sociology of work and occupations waned in both Europe and America from the late 1930s until after World War 2. Although there are no doubt many reasons why this eclipse occurred, one could speculate that it was partly due to a reduced interest in and confidence about the value of the empirical, largely descriptive studies of occupations that had been generated; and was also due to the fact that despite the large number of studies accumulated, no truly satisfactory theoretical framework for the study of work and occupations had been developed. It was not until the work of Everett Hughes, a major intellectual figure at the University of Chicago whose influence was substantial from about the 1940s onwards, that a coherent sociological approach and theoretical framework within which occupational groups could be analysed was developed. This framework evolved as a result of many diverse types of work being compared in order to identify the common denominators.

It was only after a plausible theoretical orientation was accomplished that occupational sociology achieved the academic status of becoming a sub-field of sociology, being taught as a separate field of study in many European and American universities. More recently, the growing importance of and interest in this area was clearly indicated when a new international journal, *Sociology of Work and Occupations*, was founded in 1974.

Everett Hughes (e.g. 1937, 1949, 1952, 1958a, 1958b, 1971) is the pivotal figure in occupational sociology. Hughes states his goal as being 'to learn about the nature of society itself from the study of occupations', the more immediate purpose of his study being to describe and understand the behaviour of the people who are involved in different kinds of work (Soloman, 1968). Hughes' influence on this area of study has been enormous, for apart from his own insightful and voluminous research output, virtually all of the major figures in occupational sociology, such as Oswald Hall (e.g. 1948), Howard Becker (e.g. 1952), William F. Whyte (e.g. 1943), Blanche Geer (e.g. 1966), Julian Roth (e.g. 1963) and Dan Lortie (e.g. 1975), were either students of Hughes or were clearly influenced by his ideas and theoretical approach to the study of work and occupations. Hughes, and those influenced by his approach to the study of work, were responsible for extending and diversifying the body of studies on occupations to include doctors, lawyers, teachers, dance musicians, white collar workers, railroad workers, soldiers, ministers, cleaners, nurses, librarians, salesmen, boxers, quacks and real estate agents.

The Content of Occupational Sociology

As a field of study, the sociology of work and occupations may be defined as the application of the principles and concepts of sociology to a particular social phenomenon, that of occupational life and people at work. Nosow and Form (1962, p. 3) say that as a sub-discipline within sociology, the sociology of work and occupations is organised around five substantive themes. These are: the social nature of work and related phenomenon such as leisure activities; the analysis of occupational structure and the causes of changes within it; the study of individual occupations in terms of such matters as recruitment, training and careers; the ways in which the occupational structure and individual occupations articulate with other segments of society, such as in the case of occupations and systems of social stratification; and, the study of a particular occupation in order to highlight a problem in the broader society, such as those who are employed in the mass media and the operation of the political structure. These five areas are, of course, not totally self-contained, for there are substantial areas of overlap between them.

The research study reported upon in this book is primarily concerned with probing important aspects of the third major theme in occupational sociology as outlined by Nosow and Form (1962): the study of individual occupations. Occupations may be viewed as either a cluster of skills, or as a group of people who have similar skills and who also perform similar roles. The thing which identifies the occupational role, and separates it from other roles, is that it is a specific activity with a market value which people are paid to perform.

The research study reported upon in this book focuses on state school teachers as an occupational group in society, and in particular on career patterns and promotion within teaching.

One of the main problems associated with undertaking a study of various aspects of work careers, including promotion at work, is that despite the fact that many people appear to be curious about and interested in this area, it is one which is rarely openly discussed. The reason appears to be that many people do not want to talk about their careers except under the most exceptional circumstances, perhaps because they do not want to acknowledge the self interest that is implied by anyone who pursues a work career and promotion (Glaser, 1968). As Glaser puts it: 'In a sense, a person's own career is a sensitive or taboo topic. Discussions occur only under the most private and discreet conditions.' (p. 1). It is probably due to this reluctance on the part of many people to talk about their work careers that the ethnographic approach has been so popular amongst those who have studied occupations.

Introduction

Why Study Occupations?

Several interrelated reasons may be advanced to explain why the study of work and occupations warrants the serious attention of sociologists.

Work is an important and highly pervasive activity in the lives of many people, for a substantial part of men's, and an increasing percentage of women's lives, are spent in work related activities. In view of this, many people have an interest in and curiosity about the occupational world. In addition, since work consumes so large a part of the waking hours of many people, it follows that it should be of major interest to our understanding of human behaviour (Pavalko, 1972). The task of the sociologist is to develop concepts and categories which will assist in an explanation of the organization of society, and the behavior of people within it, and so the study of work and occupations is of importance if this is to be achieved.

Occupations are also social roles. As such, specific occupations serve to locate their incumbents in a matrix of other social roles, and links them to others through work patterned interaction. When Hughes (1958) refers to the 'social drama of work' he draws attention to the fact that just like the playing of other social roles, work involves the process of social interaction with others.

Occupations are a fundamental link between individuals and the larger society, because occupational roles are an important element of social structure, and so affect one's participation in other segments of society. A person's occupational status is, for example, the main factor in Western industrial societies like our own that serves to affect their entry into and location within the social structure and stratification system of their society (Chinoy, 1955).

It can also be clearly demonstrated that occupational roles are a major source of personal identity, particularly in industrialised societies like our own, for the nature of work leaves a deep and lasting influence on the lives and personality of people. Hughes (1958a) emphasizes that the social relationships into which the practitioner's work throws him has a great influence on the occupational personality; while Waller (1961, orig. 1936), in reference to the work of the professional, puts it this way:

> Those who follow certain occupations are continually thrown into certain kinds of social situations. These social situations call for, or are best met by, a certain kind of reaction on the part of the professional ... long practice in the social techniques enjoined upon one in a profession makes these the deepest grooves, and at length they grow so deep that there is no getting out. (p. 376)

Following on from the previous point, it should be noted that occupational groups represent distinctive sub-cultures which have a variety of shared norms and values into which the individual is likely to be socialized. The occupational culture can have a substantial effect on the individual's outlook and identity. Sorokin (1947), in referring to the socialization of the individual into the culture of their particular occupation, says that each occupation tends to remake its members in its own image, the longer the individual stays in the same occupation the deeper being the transformation. Thus, an individual's occupation can be a good indication, in broad terms, of the individuals likely social construction of reality, for a wide variety of attitudes, values and behaviour are correlated with a person's occupation.

The study of work also assists us to understand how social life is possible, because occupational differentiation and interdependence help to explain how order is maintained in the social structure. Work is an important basis of social cohesion and integration in society, and results in what Durkheim (1933; orig. 1893) has called organic solidarity.

Finally, it may be said that many of the theoretical issues and concepts in sociology can be examined within the context of work. For example, the concept social role, which is one of the conceptual building blocks of traditional sociology, is basic to most studies of occupations.

For all the reasons that have been outlined above, the study of work and occupations is an area of considerable importance which is of both theoretical and empirical interest.

The Sociological Study of School Teachers

Both in terms of their sheer numbers, and the important contribution they make to the effective operation of school systems, school teachers constitute a major occupational group in society. In Australia, there are more teachers than any other occupational groups which have a professional or semi-professional status in society. For instance, 210,000 of the employed civilian population in Australia are teachers, which is greater than the combined numbers of lawyers, medical practitioners, dentists, and nurses employed throughout the country (Australian Bureau of Statistics, 1990).

Teachers also represent an important occupational group in society in the sense that it is widely recognized that the nature and functioning of any school system largely depends upon the characteristics of those employed as teachers; and the enormous contribution school teachers make to the advancements of society was well expressed by the educationalist Henry Adams when he said 'A teacher affects eternity for he (or she) can never tell where his influence stops'.

However, despite the large number of personnel involved, and the fact that it is widely recognized that teachers play a major role in schools, they have (until recently) attracted surprisingly little sociological

Introduction

study, particularly in Australia. As a result, the extent of the available knowledge about school teachers as an occupational group is rather meagre.

The research study reported upon in this book sought to help correct this situation by adding to the theoretical and empirical knowledge available about school teachers through a study of teacher promotion and career patterns.

Studying Promotion and Career Patterns in Teaching

It is speculated here that one of the main ways of achieving a deeper understanding of the behaviour, perceptions and occupational culture of school teachers as an occupational group is to study promotion and career patterns in teaching.

The reason is that the promotion system is likely to be of central importance and concern to many teachers because it is the means by which highly valued things such as money, status, prestige and power are allocated between individuals. As such it can be said to have a dominant influence upon such matters as the way in which teachers direct their energies, perceive their roles, and develop an occupational identity. In addition, as the American sociologist Everett Hughes (1937) has so effectively argued, the study of career patterns is also important in providing valuable insights into the occupation, the individual and the society.

Job mobility, occupational careers and organizational careers are important and complex phenomena, yet in spite of this the study of the career patterns of various occupational groups has received relatively little recent sociological study. As indicated earlier, those studies that have been undertaken mainly investigate an unrepresentative range of occupations such as doctors (e.g. Hall, 1948), lawyers (e.g. Ladinsky, 1963) and businessmen (e.g. Dalton, 1951), as well as marginal occupations such as the hobo (e.g. Anderson, 1923), professional thief (e.g. Sutherland, 1937) and prostitute (e.g. Donovan, 1920). In addition, much of this research was conducted quite some time ago.

The studies which examine teacher careers are especially limited in range and number. In Britain, examples are the study by Marsland (1975) into the early career mobility of teachers; that by Smith (1975) who examined the career structure of head-teachers in one Midlands city; the research by Hilsum and Start (1974) which is a more comprehensive study of promotion and careers in teaching; research by Lacey (1978) which focuses attention upon the socialization and career patterns of teachers during their induction into the occupation; and Lyons' (1981) study of teacher careers and career perceptions in the secondary comprehensive school. Some interesting more recent research being undertaken in Britain provides new insights on teachers' careers. Of particular value are those studies focusing on the professional life cycle of teachers, such

7

Teachers' Career and Promotional Patterns

as the books of readings by Sikes, Meason and Woods (1985) and by Ball and Goodson (1985), which examine aspects of teachers' lives and careers with particular reference to the interplay that occurs between the determinants of their career behaviour, both within and outside the particular institution and context in which they work; and the longitudinal study by Nias (1989) in which primary teachers reveal their perceptions of the teaching career.

In the United States the most famous studies are those by Waller (1936) on the sociology of teachers and teaching, Becker's (1952) study of the careers of a small sample of Public school teachers in Chicago, and Lortie's (1975) sociological portrait of the American school teacher.

Other useful insights into the teaching career are provided by Willett and Singer's (1989) examination of the methodological issues surrounding the analysis of career-path data, and Guskey's (1989) research into the attitudinal and perceptual changes among teachers over the length of their teaching career.

In other countries Huberman (1989) has examined the professional lifecycle of teachers in Switzerland, while Prick (1989) in the Netherlands has examined career development, satisfaction and stress among secondary school teachers.

Very little research has been undertaken on the career patterns of school teachers in Australia. One of the most comprehensive works to date is that by Jecks (1969) who traced the careers of a group of male and female teachers who graduated from Claremont Teachers College, in Western Australia, from 1947 onwards. Other works include a study by Carlson (1979) of teachers' careers in NSW and Western Australia; Bassetts' (1980) study of the characteristics of teachers in Australian schools; the work by Sampson (1985) on the factors affecting the promotion of women and men teachers in Australian state education systems; the research by Connell (1985) on various aspects of teachers' work; Ingvarson and Greenway's (1984) portrayals of teacher development; and the recent Australian College of Education Census Study (Logan, Demster, Berkeley and Warry, 1990) which develops a profile of the Australian teaching service. In fact, much of the research on teachers in Australia concentrates mainly on examining the world of the beginning teacher and teacher induction (e.g. Tisher *et al.*, 1978; McArthur 1981).

The main study in New Zealand (Department of Education, 1982) on teachers' careers places particular emphasis on the promotion and careers of women teachers.

The research study reported on in this book provides more recent, comprehensive information on the various career patterns and pathways of Australian state school teachers. It also moves beyond the descriptive level to explain consistencies associated with career movements, in terms of available theory, and in so doing seeks to develop a conceptual framework for the analysis of occupational career patterns and mobility.

Introduction

The main stages in a teaching career are said to be:

1 Choice of teaching as an occupation.
2 Pre-service teacher education.
3 Induction into the occupation.
4 The teaching career proper.
5 Exit from the occupation.

Although all stages in the teaching career will be referred to, this study is mainly concerned with a detailed examination of the fourth stage: that of the teaching career proper.

This book comes at a time when there is a heightened interest in, and concern about, promotion and careers in teaching on the part of Education Departments, teacher unions, and individual teachers (Department of Education, 1982; Maclean *et al.*, 1984; Maclean 1989). The reason is that stabilizing participation rates in schools and falling numbers within the relevant age cohorts have led to a reduced demand for teachers. One result is that, given a stable teacher/pupil ratio, there is an over supply of persons seeking employment as teachers, and this is likely to have a substantial effect upon teacher career patterns in terms of such things as a reduced level of recruitment to and wastage from the occupation. In addition, one legacy of the rapid expansion of school systems that occurred during the 1950s, 1960s and 1970s is that a significant proportion of the positions at various levels within the promotions hierarchy are occupied by relatively young teachers, and so this, coupled with a lack of growth in the teaching service, has dampened down the career and promotion opportunities available in teaching. We are still uncertain about the likely effect of these reduced opportunities for advancement on teacher behaviour and the teaching profession.

This book also comes at a time when problems are occurring with regard to recruitment into teaching, declining numbers of young people (especially the ablest of each cohort) wanting to enter this occupation. Much of this reluctance to enter teaching is said to be caused by the poor career and promotion opportunities currently available to those in the occupation, and by the poor image of teachers and teaching in the community. (Karmel, 1985; Abbott-Chapman, Hull, Maclean and McCann, 1990.).

Although the main focus of the book is upon certain aspects of teachers as an occupational group, the research findings and conclusions should also help enhance our understanding of the operation of school systems. For example, it could be argued that an improved knowledge and understanding about teacher career patterns, and how the promotion system operates (or is perceived by teachers to operate), will not only help explain the behaviour of teachers within the occupational group but also within the school and classroom.

Purpose of this Research Study and the Theoretical Orientation Adopted

Using a research framework derived from the sociology of occupations, the research reported upon in this book aimed to achieve an improved understanding of teachers as an occupational group internationally by examining the promotion and career patterns of a group of state school teachers in Australia. The theoretical assumption upon which the study is based is that the career movements of teachers, in both the horizontal and vertical mobility sense, are not random. Rather, teachers move in patterned ways between competing positions, and this equally applies to those in administrative and services positions in an Education Department's head-office, as it does to those who are employed in schools.

If this assumption is valid, it should be possible to identify and compare the career pathways adopted by various individuals and groups within teaching, for identifiable career pathways are used (and made) by those who do, or attempt to, achieve access to various positions within the promotion hierarchy. There are also likely to be similarities between the pathways pursued by teachers who currently occupy the same type of status position. Some pathways are, for a wide variety of reasons, open to some teachers but closed to others; some will be dead-end, while others lead onto further career opportunities.

In addition to the identification of the various types of career patterns that exist, it should also be possible to identify the factors that appear to affect the actual and likely career patterns and career pathways that occur for any given individual or group of individuals within teaching. Those who occupy a common status position, for example, are likely to share the same types of professional, academic and social characteristics which may not be common to other groups in the occupation.

The study seeks to describe and explain differences and similarities in the career patterns of those occupying different promotion positions (men and women teachers, graduates and non-graduates, and those employed in different types of schools and sectors of the school system); and to ascertain their perceptions regarding a career and promotion in teaching.

In terms of research methodology, the research reported upon in this book could have been approached in a number of different ways. For example, teaching careers could have been viewed exclusively in terms of the actual work behaviour of individual teachers, or it could have been largely conceived of in terms of the 'career perceptions' rather than the 'career behaviour' of individuals in teaching.

When deciding upon the most suitable approach to adopt, the research was conceptualised in the following way. Teacher careers and promotion occur in systems, and so a structural description is necessary; but individuals also make careers within systems, and so it is necessary to tap their perceptions of the opportunity structures within which they

Introduction

operate and negotiate. Thus, there are two levels to the study, both of which are important: the first is the structural dimension, and the second may be described broadly as phenomenological. In view of this, the research methodology adopted is one which blends together both quantitative and qualitative data and analysis. It was therefore necessary to obtain information about the actual career patterns and promotion achieved by various groups of teachers, as well as data about the context within which careers are established. As was the case for earlier researchers, this information was best obtained from sources such as Education Department records and through administering questionnaires to teachers.

However, in addition, information on teacher perceptions was obtained through a questionnaire and through conducting semi-structured interviews with a smaller number of teachers than those who were surveyed through the use of official records and the questionnaire.

To summarize, the research undertaken sought to accomplish the following things:

- To achieve an improved understanding of teachers as an occupational group by exploring career patterns and promotion in teaching;
- To describe and compare the career patterns of various groups of teachers in terms of both vertical and horizontal mobility;
- To explain differences and similarities in the career patterns of various groups of teachers, who occupy differing positions within the promotions hierarchy, by seeking to identify the factors that influence teacher careers and promotion;
- To survey the opinions, and probe the perceptions, of teachers regarding important aspects of career patterns and promotion within teaching;
- To test empirically the validity of existing theories and commonly held views (some of which are part of the folk-lore of occupations) that relate to mobility, career patterns and promotion, particularly in reference to school teachers; and
- To develop a research framework which facilitates the meaningful analysis of teacher career patterns in a more comprehensive way than has hitherto occurred. This model will take account of the strengths and weaknesses of the various theories that currently exist to explain career patterns. It is believed that such a framework and theory needs to blend together effectively aspects of both structural and phenomenological analysis.

The research sought to achieve the aims outlined above through a case study of the career and promotion patterns of state school teachers in one Australian state, that of Tasmania. In addition to limiting the study to state school teachers in one state, it was also decided to limit the research to examining full-time teachers who occupied promotion positions in the education system being examined.

Main Findings of the Study

In essence, the main findings of the study are:

- the career movement of teachers, in both the horizontal and vertical mobility sense, are not random but generally planned and patterned;
- both horizontal and vertical mobility are important features of the school teaching career;
- there are substantial differences in the career patterns and perceptions of teachers according to their age, level of experience, gender, marital status, academic and professional qualifications, promotion position occupied and sector of the Education Department in which they are employed;
- teachers conceive of the teaching career as consisting of a number of distinct stages these differing markedly in both number and content to those identified in other studies;
- school teaching is an occupation that offers a number of different types of careers;
- the most successful teachers in gaining promotion develop a career map, strategy and career timetable;
- teachers develop a 'career anchorage perspective' which influences the level of promotion that satisfies their career needs, this perspective being reassessed and readjusted by the individual at different stages in their career;
- teachers develop a career perspective which recognizes that there is both an internal (phenomenological) and external (structural) aspect to an individual's working life.

The chapters which follow examine and elaborate upon each of these matters (plus other related concerns) in detail, and indicate the implications of these findings for the functions of school systems and for effective policy making with regard to improving the quality of schooling received by children.

Organization of this Book

In Chapter 2, the research and related literature relevant to ways of conceptualizing work careers is reviewed. This establishes a framework of sociological concepts that are appropriate for a study of occupations. Chapter 3 reports on what is known about the school teaching career with regard to the framework developed in Chapter 2. Because school teaching careers usually (although not always) occur in government organized education systems, it was necessary to provide a description of the structural context within which the teachers surveyed in the study reported upon here are employed. This is presented in Chapter 4 'Opportunity Structure of Tasmanian Teachers'. Chapter 5 outlines the research design and procedures adopted.

The next three chapters report on the results of the study. Chapter 6 presents information on the personal and professional characteristics of promoted teachers, which was largely gathered through a questionnaire; Chapter 7 analyses the career history information on Tasmanian teachers obtained from Education Department records; and Chapter 8 describes teacher perceptions about the teaching career, which were obtained from semi-structured individual and group interviews. In Chapter 9 the results reported in the previous three chapters are discussed with reference to the research framework adopted, and propositions to be tested. This chapter also draws the various threads of the book together by providing a summary of the main findings, policy recommendations, and suggestions for further research.

Conclusion

This chapter provides a background to the sociological study of work, maps the content of occupational sociology, and presents a case as to why the study of occupations warrants the serious attention of sociologists. It then provides an introduction to, and brief overview of, the research study reported upon in this book.

The primary purpose of the research reported upon is to add to the theoretical and empirical knowledge available about school teachers as an occupational group in society through a study of teacher promotion and career patterns in one state education system in Australia, that of Tasmania.

Chapter 2

Ways of Conceptualising Occupational Careers

The purpose of this chapter is to identify and discuss briefly important sociological concepts associated with the study of work careers because these formed the basis from which the conceptual framework for the study reported upon in this book was developed.

There are several important characteristics of the literature reviewed in this and the next chapter which warrant mention. First, the stress in this and the next chapter is upon examining that literature which is essentially of a sociological nature. However, there are research studies and literature in a wide variety of disciplines such as economics (e.g. Sjaasted, 1962; Bowman, 1966, Ahamad and Blaug, 1973; Greenberg and McCall, 1974; Burke, 1979); geography (e.g. Lansing and Muellen, 1967; Keown, 1971; Mann, 1973; Greenwood, 1975); and psychology (e.g. McLeish, 1970; Morrison and McIntyre, 1973) that are also of relevance to the study of teachers' careers, and so a broader range of literature than that which is just sociological will be referred to (albeit briefly) in developing the research framework.

Second, as will be demonstrated in this chapter, in Australia research on occupational sociology is meagre. As a result, most studies to which reference is made mainly refer to the situation in the United States and Britain. In view of this it should be borne in mind that the results from these studies may not necessarily hold true for all countries; and that the findings from different countries are not necessarily comparable.

Third, since about the early 1930s, there have been several waves of interest in various aspects of the sociology of work and occupations. One result is that in order to cover adequately the range of ideas that are important to this field of scholarship one frequently needs to refer to studies that were undertaken up to forty years ago. There is therefore a need to interpret these studies cautiously for, although they may provide useful theoretical and empirical insights into the topic being examined, and many of their concepts are likely to be still illuminating, it cannot be assumed that they are necessarily directly comparable with more recently conducted studies: this needs to be empirically tested rather than assumed.

Fourth, although the focus in this book is upon the career patterns of teachers, in this chapter research that refers to a variety of occupational groups will be examined. These studies are important in that they serve to sensitize one to potentially important ideas and concepts; but it cannot be assumed that the findings that refer to one particular occupation are necessarily transferable to another (such as school teachers) since this is something which needs to be tested empirically.

Occupation, Profession and Career

In any discussion of work and occupations in society it is important that key terms such as 'occupation', 'profession' and 'career' are defined precisely, because these have meanings and evoke connotations which are often at variance with the way in which they are used by sociologists. Consider the term 'career'. In popular usage this is often taken to mean a person's commitment to full-time employment over an extended period of time, an instance of the term being used in this way being when a woman is described as being a 'career woman'. However, in sociology the term means more than this: it implies a long term commitment on the part of a person to obtaining promotion, through the status hierarchy that exists in their occupation, according to some time schedule (Pavalko, 1971).

Occupation

Occupations may be defined as 'relatively continuous patterns of activities that provide workers with a livelihood and define their general social status' (Form, 1968, p. 245). Occupations are social roles which are generally performed by adult members of society and which directly and/or indirectly yield social and financial consequences that represent a major focus in the life of the adult (Hall, 1949). In view of this, an occupation 'identifies a category of persons ... who behave or can be legitimately expected to behave in the same or similar ways in given situations' (Solomon, 1968, p. 6).

Although the sociologists' main interest is in occupations as social roles, this is not their only source of interest. Occupations are not simply constructs that are external to the individual, but become internalized in important ways which have an effect on a person's identity and world view. People are also able *to make* as well as be *made by* their particular occupation.

Profession

Some occupations are said to be professions, which are occupations that involve the identification of a body of knowledge or theory that defines an area of expertise; the development of professional associations which help to increase group identity; appropriate codes of behaviour for those in the occupation; and a commitment to clients.

More specifically, if one adopts an 'ideal-type' model, professions are said to possess the following characteristics (Purvis, 1973, p. 57):

(a) Gives a specialized, unique service which is essential to society;
(b) possess intellectual techniques;
(c) offers a long period of training and professional socialization;
(d) enjoys a high degree of group and individual professional autonomy;
(e) exercises its own means of social control through the enforcement of a code of ethics;
(f) commands a high level of commitment in which work and leisure hours are not easily demarcated;
(g) offers a life-time calling within a career structure;
(h) encourages the pursuit of research, the diffusion of knowledge, and in-service training.

When the criteria listed above are used to judge whether or not a particular occupation is also a profession, one finds that only a relatively small proportion of occupations would be classed as professions, although this changes through time. Examples are the ministry, university teaching, medicine and the law. Certain other occupations, such as school teaching, nursing, librarianship and social work, are classed as being 'semi-professions' or 'aspiring professions' (Etzioni, 1969) because they only display some and not all of the attributes of the traditional professions, as listed above.

The study of professions and professionalization is a murky and controversial area because there are major differences of opinion over such matters as the criteria and the approach that should be adopted when judging whether or not a particular occupation is a profession (e.g. Jackson, 1970; Johnson, 1972). In view of this, plus the fact that the concept is not central to the research reported upon in this book, it will be only be referred to in passing.

Career

Many occupations, and all professions, offer their recruits the opportunity of pursuing a career: that is, the possibility of moving over their working life between various work activities, which are of a related type, in a patterned rather than a random way:

> A career may be defiend as being a succession of functionally related jobs which are arranged in a hierarchy of prestige and through which persons move in a more or less ordered sequence. (Ladinsky, 1963, p. 50)

Put another way, work careers consist of a sequence of roles appropriate to the various stages of the career in question, and embody the notion of upward social mobility. They are 'continuous and conspicuous work in which notable achievement can be won' (Hughes, 1952).

Some occupations offer their incumbents a career in the sense that individuals can be promoted through a clearly delineated promotions hierarchy. This aspect of a career is referred to as its *vertical mobility* dimension. It is also possible for individuals to move between work locations of a similar status, not only in the pursuit of promotion but also in order to find work environments which, for some reason or another, are more to their liking. This second aspect of a career is referred to as its *horizontal mobility* dimension (Becker, 1952; Caplow, 1954; Hughes, 1958, 1971).

Some have argued (e.g. Wilensky, 1961) that the term career should primarily be used to refer to the vertical mobility of white collar workers; however, the term will be used here in the broader sociological sense, as advocated by others (e.g. Nosow and Form, 1962; Ritzer, 1972), to mean any pattern of occupational change, whether vertical and/or horizontal, of any occupational group. Ritzer (1972) says:

> Every individual in every occupation follows a career pattern, and if he looks back over his career he can chart the sequence of upward, lateral and downward moves. Although there is considerable individual variation, each occupational level has rather distinctive career patterns caused by the structure of the occupation. (p. 42)

In considering work careers it is important to recognize that they have both an objective/external and subjective/internal aspect to them, both of which may be studied (Hughes, 1958a; Guba, Jackson and Bidwell, 1959; Lyons, 1981). Taking up this point, Friedman (1972) notes:

> Objectively and externally, a career indicates the succession and series of work roles, ranks and offices that a person occupies during his life. Such career histories of occupational groups ex-

hibit, in varying degrees, discernable patterns of orderliness and regularity. (p. 225)

The subjective and internal aspects of a person's career reflects the individual's picture of his work life, and image of self. It includes the values and aspirations that interplay in every phase and change of career history (Becker and Strauss, 1956; Champoux, 1975). The nature of the career pattern that develops for any individual over his working life is the outcome of the often subtle interplay that occurs between the objective and subjective aspects of his career (Hall, 1949; Hughes, 1958a; Lyons, 1981).

A small but increasingly influential body of feminist literature (e.g. Sampson, 1985) has questioned the appropriateness of such a definition of career. These researchers argue that the definition does not enable a meaningful analysis of the working lives of women. They also argue that what is embedded in such a definition of career is the male-centred concept of 'promotion' and a male dominated ideology with regard to what counts as useful and worthwhile work, and that this acts to devalue the distinctive way in which women organize their working lives. For example, when applied to a consideration of the work of teachers many of the definitions of career given above almost inevitably imply the need for the career-committed employee to move out of the classroom. It also does not take account of the fact that many women do not view 'worthwhile work' in such conventional terms. Many women, for example, adopt a collegial model of *power sharing* rather than a hierarchical and bureaucratic model of *personal power*, the latter being the approach adopted by many career oriented men.

Careers in Context

Occupational and Organizational Careers

The term career may be used to refer to the characteristic pattern of particular occupations (e.g. the medical career) or it may be used to refer to the patterned work activities that occur in particular organizations (e.g. a career in the public service). The former are called *occupational careers* and the latter *organizational careers* (Glaser, 1968).

One of the main ways in which organizations recruit people to work for them, and obtain a work commitment, is by offering individuals the possibility of building and developing a career within their organizational structure (Glaser, 1968). In order to encourage people to develop a commitment to their work, and the notion of pursuing a career, 'organizations distribute rewards, working conditions and prestige to their members according to career level, thus these benefits are properties of the organizational career' (Glaser, 1968, p. 1). Many occupational careers are undertaken within formal organizations. When this occurs, an occupational career may be seen as coinciding with an organizational career, so that the occupational career is also an organizational career.

When occupations exist within formal organizations, it becomes important to examine the reciprocal effects of organizational structure on occupational life (Ritzer, 1972). Slocum (1966) says:

> Only individuals have careers, but they have them as they pursue career lines established by work organizations. Sociologically a career line can be thought of as a structural aspect of organization. As such it consists of hierarchally related occupational positions in the organization that require successively more responsible performance of occupational skills. (p. 6)

Although career lines typically exist in particular organizations, they also exist within occupations, regardless of whether or not these are undertaken in organizations. Within all occupations there is an occupational culture which, amongst other things, indicates the consensus that exists within the occupation regarding what is seen as being the appropriate sequence of work activities and positions, for those who are concerned with developing a work career. With reference to this point, Charters (1970) says that any specialized occupation in society confronts its practitioners with more or less standardized ways for them to pursue their career within it.

Opportunity Structure

The opportunities available for a person to pursue a career within a particular occupation often vary over time (Hughes, 1958; Glaser, 1964). For example, in an expanding and developing organization or profession a great many opportunities are likely to exist for career development. Those who are building their careers at such a time benefit from being 'in the right place at the right time'. Conversely, at a time of contracting career opportunities, restrictions may occur which reduce the possibilities for promotion available within the occupation and work organization. Thus, in any occupation, work organization or profession there exists an 'opportunity structure' which has a considerable affect on the career patterns and pathways that develop for the individuals involved. Career 'opportunity structures' are not static, but generally develop and change over time (Maclean et al., 1984).

The Career Structure

Stages in a Career

It is possible to conceive of careers in terms of their possessing a number of distinct stages. Hall (1948), for example, has identified four separate stages in the medical career. These are:

1. The generation of an ambition;
2. Gaining admittance to the various medical institutions, which refers to both the period of training, and to the work career itself;
3. Acquiring a clientele, retaining and improving it, and perhaps transferring it to a successor; and,
4. Developing a set of informal relationships with colleagues which facilitate the above steps in some suitable fashion.

He argues that the stages of a medical career, as he has conceived of them, are by no means unique to the medical profession, and could be usefully investigated in areas such as law, the academic world, engineering and the ministry, a view which is also supported by others (e.g. Caplow, 1954; Pavalko, 1972). Although the content of each of the stages Hall (1948) has identified differs substantially, he argues that, for the purposes of analysis, they are fundamentally alike.

However, the career stages that apply to any particular occupation can vary enormously (Pavalko, 1972), depending upon factors such as: the nature of the work activities involved; the institutional arrangements within which the work is undertaken; whether or not the occupation is also a profession; and, the features of the typical career patterns of those who are members of the occupational group. For example, although, 'acquiring a clientele' and 'developing a set of informal relations with colleagues' (stages 3 and 4 in Hall's model) may be very important stages in the careers of musicians, authors, prostitutes, accountants, lawyers and doctors, they may be less important for other occupational groups such as airline pilots, public servants, or school teachers.

Vertical Mobility (promotion and demotion)

Caplow (1954) has suggested that there are three main ways in which vertical mobility can occur. The first occurs when an individual moves from one occupation to another occupation which is of higher or lower status; the second occurs when an individual is promoted or demoted within the same occupation; and, the third occurs when a person accumulates increasing seniority within an occupation which leads to a substantial change in their status. Pavalko (1971, p. 112) has suggested a fourth form of vertical mobility which occurs 'when those in the occupation as a whole experience mobility in the sense that they are 'carried along' by the change occurring in the status of their occupation'. An example would be when the professionalization of an occupation occurs.

Various factors affect the extent to which, and the rate at which, an individual gains vertical mobility (promotion) within their occupation (Hughes, 1958). In the most general sense we could say that the more capable a person is at their chosen work, the more likely it is that they will rise upwards through the promotions hierarchy. However, such an explanation is too simple, for although ability is clearly an important factor in affecting vertical mobility, it is not the only (or even necessarily the main) factor that operates, for there are many other variables, often of a very subtle nature, involved. In fact, the means by which individuals rise in their occupations, or in the organizations in which they pursue their careers, is largely a matter of dispute (e.g. Sorokin, 1947; Glaser, 1968; Tronc and Enns, 1969; Lyons, 1981).

When the occupations concerned are in formal organizations, the formal processes of selection and the criteria that are said to be used when deciding upon whether or not a particular individual gains initial selection or promotion, are usually set out in the form of explicitly stated rules and regulations (Hall, 1946; Glaser, 1964; 1968). This is especially the case in organizations that adopt the bureaucratic form of formal structuring.

Promotion Criteria

In occupations which offer individuals a career, and thus vertical mobility, promotion criteria are generally set out explicitly. Such *formal criteria* usually refer to factors such as a person's formal qualifications, type and level of experience within the occupation, and suitability for the promotion position in question (Caplow, 1954; Hughes, 1958).

Even when promotion criteria are not set out explicitly, a widespread expectation is that a formal pattern of selection and promotion exists within an occupation or the organization in which people are employed. In many cases this is based upon a combination of factors such as tradition, logic and notions of natural justice. Thus it is to be expected that certain regular and recurrent promotion patterns would occur, according to objective criteria such as an individual's age, length of service, level of experience, and number and type of qualifications (Pavalko, 1972). Thus one would expect to find that individuals usually do not reach various status positions in the occupation or organization unless: they first accrue certain qualifications; are above a particular age; and, have an acceptable work history within the occupational group (Hall, 1949). However, as shall be demonstrated in the study reported upon in this book, this is not always the case.

In addition to (or instead of) the formal processes and criteria which are likely to affect the shape and time patterns of an individual's career, certain *informal factors* have been found to be also of importance (Hall, 1946; Dalton, 1951). These are *ad hoc* or unordered promotion factors. As Glaser (1968) points out most organizations state that promotion depends upon a combination of factors such as seniority, ability, competence and merit, but many employees will believe that informal processes and factors are also involved, often in a very influential sense.

This latter point is well illustrated by Dalton's (1951) study of careers in a particular managerial hierarchy which revealed that factors such as age at entry, rate of advancement, occupational experience, and type of education were less important than informal processes of selection, with criteria such as a person's religion, ethnicity, political affiliation, and participation in accepted organizations, also being important. He found that selection was to a large extent carried on informally, with personnel occupying the lower positions in the promotions hierarchy or strata achieving promotion by conforming to the social characteristics of those in the upper strata, the main criteria varying as dominant groups of personnel changed through time.

Hall (1946; 1948) found the same type of system operating in the medical profession, for informal organizations and associations were particularly important in affecting an individual's advancement through the status structure of the occupation. He found that in the city examined, the established specialists constituted a social group that was the 'inner core' or 'inner fraternity' of the profession. This group largely determined the structure of the profession by controlling appointments to the medical institutions, excluding or penalising intruders, distributing patients, enforcing rules and controlling competition. Vertical mobility within the profession was dependent on what has been called 'sponsored' rather than 'contest' mobility.

Like Dalton (1951), Hall (1948) found that personal qualities were as important as were levels of technical proficiency, when it came to appointment to certain positions. He says:

> It became clear that appointments are not made on the basis of technical superiority. The appointee must be technically *competent*, but after that level of competence is reached, other factors take precedence over sheer proficiency. At this level personal factors become important. (p. 332)

In addition, he found that the ethnic, religious and social class characteristics of recruits to medicine were very important factors in affecting their career patterns, mainly by influencing whether or not they gained admittance to the various high status medical institutions, upon which the slope and length of career lines largely depended. Once they had gained admittance to a hospital, at the commencement of their medical careers, it was then necessary for them to adopt certain career tactics in order to climb within or among the appropriate range of institutions. Hall (1948) found that as a general rule doctors sought to move to the more prestigious hospitals which were generally the ones which had above average medical care facilities and which mainly treated what the doctors regarded as 'satisfactory clientele', the criteria for determining this being the patients' social origins and income level.

Hall (1946) found that sponsorship was a very important facet of the medical career, which was the means by which the 'inner core' controlled its members. Others have examined the ways in which and extent to which sponsorship functions in many of the professions, Epstein (1970) advancing the view that this is one of the major constraints which operate against women's entry into, and success within, the professions.

Horizontal Mobility

According to Caplow (1954) there are two main ways in which horizontal mobility within a career may occur: the first occurs when an individual changes occupations, moving to one which has the same or a similar status; and, the second occurs when an individual remains in his particular occupation but moves between different work locations at the same status level in the promotions hierarchy.

One of the dominant features of the career patterns of some occupational groups is horizontal mobility (e.g. Morris, 1957; Havighurst and Neugarten, 1957; Greenberg and McCall, 1974). A key research study which drew attention to, and stressed the importance of, horizontal mobility as an important dimension of the school teaching career was that undertaken by Howard Becker (1952). Although Becker was not the first to identify and study the significance of horizontal mobility as part of a work career, he was the first to systematically analyse this phenomenon. Briefly, Becker argues that in the past most researchers (e.g. Hughes, 1937; Hall, 1948; Dalton, 1951) had almost exclusively focused their attention upon examining the vertical aspect of career movement. Due to this emphasis, the importance of what Becker calls 'the horizontal aspect of career movement' (which refers to changes in work activity that do not involve changes in status or income) had been largely overlooked by researchers.

In his study of mobility amongst school teachers, Becker came to the conclusion that although teachers may move between positions which are at the same level in the status hierarchy, these positions are not strictly interchangeable, or equal, in all ways, because they may not be equally easy or rewarding places in which to work. Becker argues that it is largely an individual's search for what they regard to be favourable work circumstances that give rise to occupational mobility and standardized career patterns of a type that stresses horizontal rather than vertical moves.

Becker's study has only been referred to here in précis form because it is examined in greater detail in the next chapter.

Career Timetables

Roth (1963) argues that people will not accept uncertainty in most areas of life, including their work activities. He says:

> One way to structure uncertainty is to structure the time period through which uncertain events occur. Such a structure must usually be developed from information gained from the experience of others who have gone or are going through the same series of events. As a result of such comparisons, norms develop for entire groups about when certain events may be expected to occur. When many people go through the same series of events, we speak of this as a career and of the sequence and timing of events as their *career timetable*. (p. 136)

Roth identifies two conditions which appear to be necessary for timetables to develop: first, the series of events must be thought of in terms of a career (that is, a series of related and definable stages or phases of a given sphere of activity that a group of people goes through in a progressive fashion on the way to a more or less definite and recognizable goal or series of goals); and, second, there must be an interacting (not necessarily face-to-face) group of people with access to the same body of clues for constructing timetable norms.

Career Pattern

Because most job moves are not random, it is possible to identify career patterns which emerge as individuals seek out and follow the career lines that are available within their particular occupation or work organizations, and as they also develop new career lines. People often follow these career lines according to a self-imposed and/or system-imposed *career timetable* (Roth, 1963).

Friedman (1964, p. 73) defined a career pattern as being 'a series of adjustments made to the institutions, formal organizations and informal social relationships involved in the occupation, or sequence of occupations, which made up the work history of a person or group of persons';

while Wilensky (1961) defines it as a succession of related jobs that are arranged in a hierarchy of prestige, and through which people move in an ordered and predictable way. Occupations are characterised by typical, orderly career patterns, although individuals within occupations may have career patterns which vary greatly and which range from the orderly to the highly disorderly.

Some occupations offer their incumbents highly structured and orderly career patterns. This is particularly true when work careers are built within bureaucratic-type organizations (Glaser, 1964; 1968). However, only about a third of the labour force are thought to experience such a type of career (Wilensky, 1961) for orderly careers are most characteristic of those in the traditional professions and other relatively high status occupations (Jackson, 1970). For individuals in low status occupations, such as unskilled workers, disorderly career patterns are the norm (Flittie and Nelson, 1968). If an individual's career pattern is to be labelled as being orderly, a significant proportion of their working life must be spent in jobs that are functionally related (Ladinsky, 1963).

Although each type of occupation is characterised by a general type of career pattern, not all individuals in a given occupation conform to this type of career pattern because many variations are possible within each occupational level (Ritzer, 1972).

The speed at which and the way in which an individual progresses through the various social roles that exist in an occupation or work organization is usually regarded as being an important indication of the extent to which they have been successful in pursuing a work career (Lyons, 1981). One of the main ways in which the work careers of individuals, and their movement from one job to another, can be analysed is in terms of: their *direction* and *distance*; their movement in and out of the occupation; and in terms of their *pattern*, whether it be stable, fluctuating or highly fluctuating (Ladinsky 1963). As was noted earlier, another is by identifying the patterning that occurs, in terms of horizontal and vertical mobility.

Career patterns can also be analysed, as they are by geographers, in terms of the extent and pattern of the geographical mobility associated with job moves. For example, Mann (1973) has suggested that in analysing employee migration one can identify two very broad groups: 'spiralists' and 'locals'. *Spiralists*, or *career transients* as Keown (1971) prefers to call them, are those individuals who display a willingness to move between various geographical areas in an attempt to secure promotion in their employment, or to obtain a more attractive work environment; while *locals* are those who are not willing to move between geographical regions in the pursuit of career advancement (Gouldner, 1957).

Although there is some variation between occupations, the tendency is for people to change from being spiralists early in their careers to become locals at later stages in their working lives (Gouldner, 1957; Stevens, 1978; Lyons, 1981). For example, a person who has just completed his or her formal qualifications is likely to be a spiralist for at least the first few years of their career, but as they get older, marry and have children, they are likely to become tied to a particular locality, and so become a local. This is, however, a general rule of thumb, for within the same occupation individuals vary considerably as to whether they are spiralists or locals at various stages in their career. For example, an ambitious person who is concerned about reaching the top promotion in their particular occupation is likely to be a spiralist for a longer period of time than will be the person who is not as concerned about maximizing their promotion prospects. (One unfortunate repercussion of Mann's use of the term 'locals' to describe non-movers, is that it could be confused with the same term that is used in a different way by Gouldner (1957) when he draws a distinction between 'cosmopolitans' and 'locals'.)

Handling Failure ('Career Crunch')

So far the focus has been upon either those who gain vertical mobility within their occupation, or else the factors that are likely to have a bearing upon the characteristics of a person's career pattern. However, not everyone seeks promotion; and for those who do seek promotion, not all their attempts to achieve promotion may be successful. Lack of promotion, and in some cases demotion, is likely to be painful and awkward for the individual involved as well as for others in the occupational group or organization with whom they work (Pavalko, 1971).

The person who does not gain promotion, or whose rate of promotion is much slower than that which is achieved by his age peers, may come to view himself, and be seen by others, as being failures within their occupation (Hughes, 1958). One way in which individuals adapt to this failure is to seek to redefine their situation by developing a set of rationalizations which serve to justify their current position, and any misfortune or lack of promotion in their occupation or work organization (Goffman, 1952).

Pavalko (1971) refers to *career crunch* as being an important career contingency factor. Career crunch occurs when an individual's career expectations, and the kinds of alternatives open to him in building his career, are out of step. According to Pavalko (1971) this may occur for three main reasons: first, individuals may be ignorant or misinformed about the types of career options available in their occupation, or they may have misjudged the career openings that are likely to be available to them so that their career expectations do not coincide with the available pattern of activities within the occupation; second, there may be changes in the pattern of work activities that make up the occupation, due to such things as technological change; and, third, there may be changes in the organizational context within which the work is performed which prove disruptive to the career expectations.

However, in looking at success and failure in a work career, it is important to note that success or failure are not simply defined in 'objective' terms. It must be remembered that the 'subjective' or internal aspect of a person's career is also important. Individuals are likely to judge success and failure differently. For example, a person who adopts an *unlimited success* view of their career, and so focuses upon the level of ultimate possible achievement when evaluating his or her career success, may judge himself as being unsuccessful unless he gets to the very top promotion position available (Wilensky and Edwards, 1959); while the person who adopts a *limited success* orientation, and so uses the origin of his career line as his point of reference when evaluating his career, may judge himself as successful, even though in terms of objective judgment he has not progressed a long way up the status hierarchy (Mills, 1956; Tausky and Dubin, 1965). Becker and Strauss (1956), in commenting upon this matter, say:

> ... failure is a matter of perspective. Many positions represent failure to some but not to others. For the middle class white, becoming a caseworker in a public welfare agency may mean failure, but for the negro from the lower middle class the job may be a real prize. (p. 257)

A person's judgment regarding success and failure in their work therefore very much depends on the 'occupational horizon' of the individual concerned (Swift, 1967).

Little research has been undertaken which explicitly examines demotion or lack of promotion in occupations. One of the reasons for this may be that this area is likely to be very sensitive and so it is difficult to obtain suitable empirical evidence through means such as the use of questionnaires and interviews. However, in order to develop a satisfactory theory of occupational and organizational careers, this is an area which is of considerable interest and importance (Glaser, 1968).

The Attributes of Individuals

Having examined several important sociological concepts associated with conceptualising work careers in terms of both their 'static' (occupation, profession and career; careers in context) and 'dynamic' (the career structure) aspects, attention will now be directed to examining the attributes of individuals, such as age and gender, which relate to their occupational and organizational careers.

When promotion criteria were referred to earlier in this chapter it was noted that certain informal attributes of individuals, in addition to the formal criteria and processes for determining who will gain promotion, were often important in affecting a person's occupational career. These informal criteria include a person's social class, religion, ethnicity and political affiliation. In this section of the chapter several important career contingency factors will be examined. In addition to factors such as age, gender and marital status, attention will also be focused upon motivational factors linked to work careers.

There are several contingency factors which can have a considerable effect on the career patterns of individuals both between and within occupational groups (Hughes, 1958; Pavalko, 1972). Three particularly important *career contingency factors* are age, gender and marital status, because in all societies these variables have a far reaching affect on the role differentiation that occurs between individuals in many areas of social activity (Hutt, 1972; Oakley, 1972). It is for this reason that regularities exist between age and work activities in most occupations; why women are underrepresented in some types of work, and at the higher levels of the promotion structure in most occupations; and why marital status influences an individual's career and promotion aspirations.

Age

This is a factor which is of special importance, for as Pavalko (1971) puts it, 'careers exist through time, and so age becomes an important consideration in understanding them' (p. 159). The most obvious examples of the link between chronological age and work activities is the fact that in western societies like Australia there is legislation against children joining the labour force on a full-time basis until they are at least 15 years of age; and it is also widely accepted that most women and men should retire from full time employment by (respectively) the ages of 60 and 65 years.

In some occupations, particularly those that occur in bureaucratic organizations, formal rules are laid down which help establish norms regarding the amount of time an individual must spend in a particular status position before being eligible for promotion (vertical mobility) to another position. These norms help define the relationship that develops between age and appropriate work activities in an occupation or organization, and so influence the career patterns of individuals. They serve to create an *age-grade system*, or career timetable, so that it becomes highly unlikely (if not impossible) that an individual will achieve certain positions in the promotions hierarchy until they have reached a particular chronological age, or accumulated a minimum number of years experience (Roth, 1963; Glaser, 1968).

In addition to the established formal regulations that influence the vertical mobility of individuals, certain informal norms and practices develop regarding what are thought to be appropriate career patterns and promotion positions for those in different age groups. Thus certain practices or norms develop indicating the amount of time it is likely to take for an individual to achieve various promotion positions (Dalton, 1951). These formal and informal norms are partly a reflection of the cultural norm that, in general, there should be a positive correlation between an individual's level of power and status in a society and his or her age (Oakley, 1972).

It could be speculated that the norms that become established serve certain important functions. One could be that they increase the likelihood that only those individuals who have proven their loyalty to, and competence in, the organization or occupation, over a prolonged period of time, are given access to key positions of power and influence. Another is that they provide a useful yard-stick against which members of the occupational group can judge the progress of their own career, and those of colleagues. In addition they help individuals establish realistic career expectations, and draw up attainable career timetables (Roth, 1963; Lyons, 1981).

It could also be speculated that the reason why so many of the norms that influence the age-grading system within occupations or organizations are informal rather than formal is that this gives the occupants of positions of power some latitude in deciding whether or not a particular individual should be promoted. For example, in many occupations a small number of individuals achieve rapid promotion at a rate which violates age-grade norms. This situation would not be possible if all of these norms were formalized in terms of regulations. This type of situation may also serve to provide additional work motivation for the younger members of an occupation, because if age-grade norms are not fixed in the form of formal regulations, it remains theoretically possible that a person can move upwards through the promotions hierarchy in a very short period of time. As Parsons (1958) has put it, it is a truism of organizations that administrators need a degree of autonomy and authority to carry out their responsibilities.

The individual who is promoted rapidly, and who therefore violates or deviates from the established age grade norms, is likely to face certain problems (Fogarty, 1971; Hall, 1975). The main one is that of *marginality*, because they will not fit into the age peer group of others who occupy similar positions. They are also likely to attract resentment from other members of the occupational group, both from older members of the occupation who have not been promoted and from those of the same age who may feel that they themselves have been treated unfairly.

Gender[1]

An individual's gender is also an important career contingency factor, for although change is occurring, gender still is one of the most pervasive influences on likely work roles, occupational promotion and career patterns in society (Jacobs, 1975; Department of Education, 1982). In most societies certain widely held beliefs exist regarding whether or not, and the extent to which, women should engage in paid work activities outside the home; and, if they do join the labour force, there are norms about the types of work activities that are appropriate for women (Hutt, 1972; Oakley, 1972).

In Western industrial societies like Australia, ideas have changed substantially since the end of the second world war about the role of women in the labour force (Oakley, 1972). These changes are reflected by the fact that a greater percentage of women are remaining in, or returning to, the labour force than ever before; and women are now engaged in a wider range of occupations than has previously been the case (Caplow, 1954; Fogarty et al., 1971; Freeman, 1975). However, despite these types of changes, gender remains one of the most influential career contingency factors. Women continue to be underrepresented in the higher status occupations, and are less likely than men to achieve access to higher level promotion positions (Fogarty, 1971; Sampson, 1985).

There are many conflicting views as to why gender is such an important work related variable, but this is not the place to become embroiled in issues such as the factors that affect the career aspirations and decisions of women, or the nature/nurture controversy as it affects women's occupational careers (see, for example, Oakley, 1972; Hutt, 1972; Bardwich, 1972; Maclean, 1974; and Duberman, 1975, for an examination of such issues). However, some of the characteristics of work that affect the degree of vertical mobility achieved by women compared to men will be examined.

One of the main features of work, particularly in the professions, is that individuals are expected to display a long-term commitment to, and participation in, their occupation or the organisation within which they work, if they are to have available to them the opportunity of gaining access to the career lines that are typically open to recruits. Because they tend to leave the labour force at various times, for child-bearing and child-rearing activities, women often have highly disrupted work histories (Bassett, 1980). One result is that they are not seen by employers as displaying, in the traditionally accepted way, the high degree of career commitment and persistence that is usually a prerequisite for promotion (Rabinowitz and Crawford, 1960; Kelsall, 1960, 1963; Etzioni, 1969; Morris, 1974). It has been shown that many women are more family orientated than career orientated; and they largely judge an occupation according to the convenience with which it may be integrated with the demands of family life (Duberman, 1975).

McIntosh (1974) found that a lack of women applicants is a major reason why women are under-represented in the various higher status occupations and promotion positions; and that women tend to have a low level of career aspirations. The crucial thing which separated the women who did seek promotion from those who did not was that they viewed work activities outside the home as being as important as, or even more important than, their activities in the home. This finding agrees with those arising from the studies of women in top jobs, which have shown that women who are highly successful in their work careers generally find it necessary to adopt a career orientation which traditionally is more typical of the male than the female career (e.g. Fogarty, et al., 1971; Kundish, 1974; Jones and Montenegro, 1983).

After examining many aspects of the relationship between gender and promotion, particularly as they relate to the occupational careers of women, Fogarty et al. (1971) found that the central issue which needs to be examined is not whether women should be admitted to existing work structures, but how existing work structures can be adapted and modified in order to accommodate women's presence in them. In terms of the teaching careers available to women this could mean changing the promotions system in order to ensure that women are not substantially disadvantaged, in any bid they may make to gain promotion, because they have gaps in their work histories, or because they are not able to move freely between various geographical areas in the pursuit of promotion.

Marital Status

Whether or not an individual is married has an important potential influence on their likely work roles, career and promotion patterns (Caplow 1954; Fogarty et al., 1971; Duberman, 1975). Much of the literature dealing with the relationship between marital status and participation in the labour force focuses upon women (e.g. Hutt, 1972; Oakley, 1972). It is argued that once many women are married they tend to put family considerations before the pursuit of a work career or promotion in their occupation. One result of this attitude may be the under representation of women in the higher status occupations, and at the higher levels within the promotion hierarchy of any given occupation (Fogarty et al., 1971).

Although there is some evidence that the situation described above has been changing in recent years (e.g. Oakley, 1972; Department of Education, 1982), much of the available research evidence indicates that women who are career minded, and especially those in top jobs, are more likely to be unmarried than married (e.g. Fogarty, *et al.*, 1971; Department of Education, 1982). The reason for this is that it appears to be difficult for a woman to combine the focus and dedication required to maximize promotion in their occupation with the responsibilities associated with marriage and motherhood (Epstein, 1975).

Marital status also has an important influence on the nature of men's work careers but the effect appears to be very different to that which occurs for women (e.g. Hughes, 1958). It appears that many men only become concerned about their career, and applying themselves to the pursuit of promotion, after marriage. The reason appears to be that along with the responsibilities of marriage and children comes a concern about achieving success in their occupation, particularly in terms of promotion, because of the effect this has upon the welfare and standard of living enjoyed by their family.

It is clear from the research literature examined that marital status is an important career contingency factor for both men and women, although the emphasis in the literature is on the influence of marital status on the career patterns of women.

Career Perspective and Career Saliency

A person who identifies closely with his or her work, and so has a work career in the subjective as well as the objective sense, is said to have ador 'd a *career perspective* (Champoux, 1975). The adoption of such a perspective involves two distinct phases: first, a recognition on the part of the individual that his occupational life is part of a career; and, second, the practice of judging his occupational position in terms of relative position within the status structure of the occupation.

Career saliency is a term which is used to refer to the extent to which an individual is committed to an occupation. It may be defined as being (Masih, 1967):

1   the degree to which a person is career motivated;
2   the degree to which an occupation is important as a source of satisfaction; and,
3   the degree of status ascribed to the occupation and any other source of satisfaction.

Career saliency is an important career contingency factor. The reason is that those who have a high career saliency are more likely than are those who do not to commit themselves, to the pursuit of a work career, and the achievement of vertical mobility, in their occupation (Tausky and Dubin, 1965; Pavalko, 1972).

Ways of Conceptualising Occupational Careers

Motivation: Career Anchorage Perspectives

Two principal viewpoints are represented in the literature regarding the career perspectives and orientations adopted by individuals within their particular occupation.

One view is that most people direct their energies at trying to achieve advancement (or promotion) in their career over the length of their working life. The main aim is to reach a promotion position which is as close as possible to the peak of the promotions hierarchy. If a person does not reach such a high promotion position, it is believed that their self esteem suffers as a result. Parsons (1954), for example, expresses the view that one of the main ways in which people achieve the respect and recognition of others, which they value highly, is by achieving promotion in their occupation. They are careerist in orientation in that their key aim is to reach the top of the hierarchy as fast as possible, in order to have power and control, and in order to better their general social condition and rank. This view is particularly popular in countries such as America, where it has been widely believed for some time that most adult males, and especially those in the professions, are 'strivers' (Wilensky and Edwards, 1959) in their orientation to work. This theory, which is called the 'unlimited success model', has been advanced and illustrated by a variety of researchers such as Parsons (1954), Lipset and Zettberg (1956) and Lipset and Bendix (1959).

A second, opposing viewpoint, which is referred to as the 'limited success model', has been explored and illustrated by researchers such as Hughes (1949), Whyte (1956) and Mills (1956). They argue that individuals are satisfied with either maintaining their current positions within the promotion structures, or with gaining some modest advancement within their particular occupation or organization. No self esteem is lost because the degree of promotion achieved is of modest proportions.

Tausky and Dubin (1965) have argued that these two models are in fact complementary, because both are concerned with considering the same motivational mechanism, that of a 'career anchorage perspective'. A career anchorage perspective involves two things:

> First, a recognition that one's occupational life is part of a career; and, second, the identification of a point against which present or future occupational positions may be evaluated. (Tausky and Dubin, 1965, p. 210)

They argue further that while some individuals do value top-level occupational positions, and strive to achieve these throughout the length of their occupational life, others mainly value the progress they have already made in their occupation. Thus, figuratively speaking, the people with the 'unlimited success' perspective look upwards through the promotions hierarchy to the highest positions that are attainable (an upward career orientation), and experience a feeling of dissatisfaction with the current position they occupy. In view of this they feel a strong need to continue striving for further promotion. In contrast, the person with the 'limited success' perspective looks downward through the promotions hierarchy to where they started their career (a downward career orientation) and feel satisfied about their current status and the promotion position they have achieved. Satisfaction, and dissatisfaction, according to Dubin (1958), are the individual's subjective responses to incentives.

Tausky and Dubin (1965) constructed a *Career Orientation Anchorage Scale* (C.O.A.S.) which they administered to a sample of middle level managers in order to test their hypothesis that the 'unlimited success' and 'limited success' models are complementary. They found that:

1 Contrary to popular belief, only a small minority (10 per cent) of managers were committed to an 'unlimited success' career perspective.
2 The remainder were ambivalent about their careers, for although they valued high rewards they were unwilling to commit themselves to the playing of the roles that were necessary if they were to achieve this.

They also found that career anchorage perspectives are not fixed, but are re-assessed and re-adjusted by the individual at various stages in their career. Age was found to have the greatest affect on the career orientations of individuals, the tendency being that the older a person became, and/or the greater the occupational distance travelled in building a career, the greater the likelihood that he would re-adjust his career perspectives to accept the 'limited success' model. It was also found that an individual's level of formal education did not affect his career orientations and chosen anchorage points; and that, controlling for level of education, those from middle class backgrounds were the ones most likely to adopt an upward career orientation. Goldman (1978) replicated the Tausky and Dubin (1965) study and came to the same conclusions.

One weakness of both the Tausky and Dubin (1965) and Goldman (1978) studies is that neither of them took account of a sufficiently wide range of personal and social characteristics, such as gender, that are likely to have an effect on the career orientations of various occupational groups; and a further limitation is that both confined their attention to examining middle level business managers in the United States. As a result there is no evidence that the findings would be applicable to high level or low level managers, to other occupational groups or to the same occupational groups in other countries. In addition, these models only seek to account for vertical mobility, and make no provision for explaining horizontal mobility, which in some occupations is a particularly important aspect of an individual's career pattern. The Career Orientations Anchorage Scale would be more useful for the analysis of mobility if it took account of career anchorage on the horizontal as well as the vertical plane.

However, despite these weaknesses and limitations, the studies by Tausky and Dubin (1965) and Goldman (1978) are important for at least two reasons. First, they demonstrate that the 'unlimited success' and 'limited success' models may be complementary; and, second, they show that the widely held view that a substantial percentage of professional workers (particularly males) are committed to maximising advancement in their work careers is problematical.

Perceptions of the Career Structure

Careers and promotion occur within systems, and so it is important to be aware of the structural features of the system within which individuals operate, in terms of such things as the characteristics of the promotions hierarchy that exists and the official criteria or rules laid down to help determine who actually gets promoted. However, individuals also make careers within systems, and so it is important to take account of their perceptions of the structures within which they operate and negotiate, and to examine the extent of the match that occurs between the structural and the phenomenological dimensions.

Little is contained in the research and related literature on the sociology of work and occupations that deals with employee perceptions of the career structures within which they operate and negotiate their occupational and organizational careers (e.g. Hughes, 1958; Pavalko, 1972). That literature which does exist mainly relates to teachers (Hilsum and Start, 1974; Lortie, 1975; Lyons, 1981; Guskey, 1989; Nias, 1989), and will be referred to in the next chapter when research on the teaching career is surveyed.

This gap in the research literature is an important one because what people perceive to be the situation regarding promotion and careers in a particular occupation (rather than what actually is) is likely to be a very powerful influence on their work related behaviour. It is especially interesting to know the extent to which and ways in which employees perceptions regarding the functioning of career structures coincides with what actually does happen.

Most occupations, and all work organizations that offer individuals a career, establish what may be called 'official' rules and norms to determine and regulate who gets promoted. However, at the same time an occupational folklore often develops regarding the functioning of the career structure: this may or may not match the officially stated situation, and what actually occurs, when it comes to careers within a particular occupation.

Conclusion

This chapter has sought to identify and discuss briefly key sociological concepts associated with the study of work careers, and in so doing has reviewed the available research on a range of occupations in society. In setting about to achieve this purpose it was decided that both this and the next chapter (on the teacher career) should not attempt to refer to most of what has been published in this area, but should instead seek to convey the essential flavour of the research identified.

A number of conclusions can be drawn about, and gaps identified in, the literature on the sociology of work and occupations reviewed in this chapter. Much of the research was conducted some time ago, in the 1920s, 1930s and 1950s, mainly as a result, and due to the influence, of the work undertaken by Robert Park and his associates at the University of Chicago. In addition, little research on occupational sociology has been conducted in Australia.

There is a paucity of recent research within occupational sociology which relates to many of the concepts reviewed in this chapter. In addition, much of the literature that is available focuses on an unrepresentative range of occupations, these mainly being either high status (e.g. medical practitioners, lawyers) or marginal/low status (e.g. jazz musicians, prostitutes) types of work.

Several important gaps exist in the literature reviewed. The main ones concern: first, the subjective/internal aspects of work careers; and, second, the impact of what may be called 'informal factors' on an individual's career and promotion pattern. Much of the research that has been conducted is concerned with providing structural descriptions of occupations, relatively little research seeking to tap individual's perceptions of particular occupations and the opportunity structures within which they pursue their careers. Few studies take account of, or blend together, both the structural and phenomenological aspects of working life, some exceptions being the research by Hilsum and Start (1974), Lortie (1975), Lyons (1981) and the New Zealand Department of Education (1982).

Along with this apparent emphasis within the sociology of occupations on structural aspects of work and careers, much of the research that examines promotion concentrates on the more formal personal attributes of individuals, and career contingency factors, that influence vertical mobility. Few studies examine the informal characteristics of individuals and aspects of promotion such as the ability to attract and maintain a sponsor. Yet it could be argued that the informal attributes of individuals may be more powerful than the formally stated ones in determining who gets promoted.

Note

1 The term gender, rather than sex, is referred to throughout this book as being an important career contingency factor. This is in recognition of the part that socialization, rather than simply 'nature', plays in explaining differences in the career and promotion patterns of females and males.

Chapter 3

The Teaching Career

This chapter reviews the research and related literature about the teaching career in relation to the framework developed in the last chapter. What will become clear is that there is a paucity of research within occupational sociology on various aspects of the school teaching career, while that which is available is patchy in terms of coverage. This is especially true about teachers in Australia. In view of this, one of the aims of this chapter is to indicate the gaps that exist, as well as the findings that are available, in the research and related literature on teacher careers.

However, as Huberman (1989) points out, for both conceptual and practical reasons interest in the teaching career as a unit of analysis has greatly increased in the last five to seven years. The increasing interest in teacher careers in the 1980s is indicated by the fact that the *International Journal of Educational Research* (Huberman, 1989) recently devoted a full issue to 'Research on Teachers' Professional Lives'. This interest has occurred in several different countries: in England (e.g. Ball and Goodson, 1985; Sikes *et al.*, 1985), the United States (e.g. Burden, 1981; Adams, 1982; Cooper, 1982); in Australia (e.g. Ingvarson and Greenway, 1984; Maclean *et al.*, 1984; Maclean, 1989), in Canada (e.g. Butt *et al.*, 1985); in the Netherlands (e.g. Prick, 1986); and, in Switzerland (e.g. Huberman *et al.*, 1989; Hirsch and Ganguillet, 1988).

Occupation, Profession and Career as They Apply to School Teachers

School teaching is an occupation that offers its practitioners a *career*, as this term was defined in Chapter 2 (Ladinsky, 1963). For example, the work positions available in a state education department offer individuals a career in the sense that they can be promoted through a clearly delineated promotions hierarchy, from being (say) a classroom teacher to becoming a senior master or mistress and eventually perhaps a principal (A.C.E.R., 1975). There are also a variety of non-school promotion positions available in state education departments involving supervisory, advisory or administrative duties; while some teachers prefer to work for private schools. Thus school teaching is an occupation that offers several different types of careers (Lyons, 1981).

School teaching is also an example of an occupation which offers an orderly career (e.g. Hilsum and Start, 1974; Smith, 1975), especially for those employed in government systems. In pursuing their career, teachers move in a patterned way between competing job locations: that is, their job moves are not random (e.g. Berlowitz, 1971; Lyons, 1981).

In her examination of English primary-school teachers Nias (1989) provides useful insights into the various ways in which the term 'career' can be defined, her study demonstrating that many women conceive of a career in school teaching in ways that can be significantly different to that of men. Nias shows that while many teachers appear to use the term 'career' in its conventional, male-oriented, vertical sense, some (mainly married women) redefine the concept in lateral terms, such as stressing a congenial working life, opportunities for increased self-esteem, personal development, or informal influence. Others treat teaching as one of several 'parallel careers'. In all these cases a successful 'career' in teaching is interpreted subjectively rather than normatively.

However, despite its various limitations in helping to effectively explain the occupational behaviour of teachers, the concept of the teaching 'career' is still a useful tool of analysis, for as Huberman (1989) puts it:

> ... the 'career' construct has several advantages. First, it allows for comparisons between people in different professions. In addition, the construct is more focused than that of a 'life'. Finally, it integrates variables of both a psychological and sociological nature, by studying the interactions of individuals and their work settings over time. The professional life cycle of teachers, for example, allows ways to track the effects of schools as institutions on the commitments, activities and perceptions of teachers spending their lives in different, but fairly homogeneous, work settings. (p. 348)

In their study of school teachers in England and Wales, Hilsum and Start (1974) surveyed teachers' views on various aspects of teaching as a career. When asked to identify their satisfactions and dissatisfactions with the teaching career, few aspects were selected for universal approval or disapproval. The features of the teaching career which teachers found most satisfactory were:

- holidays (50 per cent);
- opportunity to practice one's own ideas (48 per cent);

- economic security (40 per cent);
- staff/pupil relationships (39 per cent); and,
- working hours (37 per cent).

When Lyons (1981) asked his teachers the same question he found that the most chosen factors were: academic subject interest, enjoys contact with children, and enjoys the actual teaching process. However, it must be remembered that these results could be affected by the fact that Lyons only surveyed secondary teachers while Hilsum and Start surveyed both primary and secondary teachers.

Teachers found the most unsatisfactory aspects of their occupation to be (Hilsum and Start, 1974):

- class size (49 per cent);
- status of the profession in society (49 per cent);
- school/classroom accommodation (28 per cent);
- promotion prospects (23 per cent); and
- extent of non-professional work (21 per cent).

These same main satisfactions and dissatisfactions with teaching have also been identified by other studies (e.g. Bassett, 1980; Department of Education, 1982) and appear to be remarkably stable over time (Bassett, 1946).

Prick (1989) has undertaken empirical work on the sources and determinants of career satisfaction among teachers, including an examination of teacher stress and burnout. In his large-scale study in the Netherlands, Prick shows that general job satisfaction among secondary school teachers is primarily determined by the content of the work itself (that is, teaching and other activities which involve direct contact with pupils), and that between the ages of approximately 45 and 55 years, full-time personnel experience a growing dissatisfaction with activities related to teaching. Prick speculates that the most important factor in explaining this situation may be differences in personality characteristics, and so a fruitful area of inquiry would be longitudinal research on teachers' careers, starting from the very beginning of their careers and following them through all the stages of the teaching career until retirement. In addition, Dutch teachers of all ages are shown to be less satisfied with their work than former colleagues who have left teaching, and older teachers feel more 'stressed' than do ex-teachers of the same age. Prick also undertakes some international comparisons which show there are some sharp differences between levels of job satisfaction in different countries.

Butt and Raymond (1989) in their study of teachers in Canada show that throughout their careers teachers seek roles which enable them to closely link working conditions with core personal needs, these needs occurring as a result of significant relationships early in life. In doing this these researchers are concerned with understanding teacher development and school improvement from the perspective of teachers' lives and careers. Their research also adopts an approach to life-course research which attempts to discern the nature and development of teachers' knowledge, as teachers themselves see it, through the use of a form of collaborative autobiography.

Other views of teachers (Hilsum and Start, 1974) relevant to the teaching career were:

- less than 25 per cent said that they would recommend teaching as a career for a son, while more than two thirds said they would recommend it for a daughter; and,
- despite the criticisms they expressed towards teaching, as an occupation, over 50 per cent of those surveyed said that if they had their time over again they would choose to be teachers: only 8 per cent said they would definitely choose not to be teachers.

When teachers were asked by Hilsum and Start (1974) about their career plans and hopes for the future: the majority expected to remain teachers in schools; about 20 per cent hoped to change their career from classroom teaching to a related education field; and, only 4 per cent of all teachers wanted to leave the educational scene completely. In essence, the New Zealand Department of Education's study (1982) found the same types of views amongst the teachers surveyed.

Several studies report that there is a period of self-questioning and 'crisis' for many teachers (e.g. Adams, 1982; Sikes, 1985; Prick, 1986), a type of 'mid-life crisis' when the person involved evaluates their professional life in terms of its satisfactions and dissatisfactions with a view to considering possible other careers before it is too late for them to change to a different occupation.

In recent work (e.g. Prick, 1986; Huberman, 1989; Lightfoot, 1985) it has been found that for many teachers with 20 to 30 years experience there is a tendency for their career ambition to decrease, as does their level of investment in their job, but at the same time teachers express the feeling that they are less vulnerable in their employment in that they feel themselves to be confident and effective. As part of this phase teachers become less concerned with achieving long-term career goals and set themselves more modest objectives.

Although, as we noted in Chapter 2, whether or not a particular occupation is a profession remains an unclear and controversial area, due to differences of opinion over the criteria that should be adopted when judging whether an occupation is a profession, it is frequently argued by researchers that school teaching is a 'semi-profession', (e.g. Etzioni, 1969; Lortie, 1975), rather than a full profession. This view is also widely held by teachers themselves (e.g. Boreham *et al.*, 1976): that is, many of them 'feel' that they belong to a semi, rather than a full, profession.

The School Teaching Career in Context

The structural context within which the teaching career generally occurs is clearly very different to that which typically occurs in many other areas of employment such as medicine, the law or in business, although it is similar to the situation that exists in other semi-professions such as nursing and librarianship (Etzioni, 1969). Most school teachers are employed in public systems of schooling: in large multi-locational, and bureaucratic-type organizations in which many thousands of school teachers are usually employed. One would therefore expect that formal factors would be more important than informal ones in affecting the career patterns of individual teachers and that contest mobility would be more important than sponsored mobility (Smith, 1974; Spaull, 1977).

However, taking up some of the points raised in the studies of other occupations by Dalton (1951) and Hall (1948) it could be speculated that the activities of teachers in various out-of-school organizations, such as a teachers' union, could have either a positive or negative affect on their career patterns. Viel (1971), for example, has argued that in the school teaching career, the ones who gain the greatest promotion are those who involve themselves, in a conspicuous way, in a range of in-school and out-of-school activities that essentially have nothing to do with how well they can teach. The importance of these activities is that they serve to attract the attention of the principal and inspectors, on whom the teacher is reliant for the gaining of promotion. Certainly, many teachers believe that sponsorship, and a willingness to conform to the views of advisors, has an important impact on a teacher's chances of gaining promotion (Hilsum and Start, 1974; Lyons, 1981; Department of Education, 1982).

The *opportunity structure* within which school teachers pursue their careers has varied considerably over time. For example, there was a great expansion in the number of government schools in countries like Britain, the United States and Australia in the 1950s and 1960s due to the effects of the post World War 2 baby boom, and the expansion of secondary education, both of which resulted in increasing school enrolments (e.g. Spaull, 1977; Phillips, 1985). This increased the demand for school teachers, created more promotion opportunities for those within the occupation (e.g. Hilsum and Start, 1974; Lortie, 1975) and extended professional stratification in education through such things as the creation of new salary structures for teachers (Hoyle, 1969). Likewise, the reduction in school enrolments that has been a feature of education systems in Western countries like Australia in the 1970s and 1980s have reduced the opportunities that exist for the career development of teachers (e.g. Department of Education, 1982). We are still uncertain about the long term effect of reduced promotion and mobility opportunities on teacher morale and career patterns (Nadebaun, 1984).

Other researchers, such as Warren (1989), are concerned with building up an historical perspective on the development of schooling systems over the years, in order to identify the changing characteristics of schools over time, because they believe that the 'shape' of schools as workplaces can have an important influence on teachers' careers, both in terms of their actual behaviour in an educational system and their perceptions of what it means to have a career in teaching. An additional benefit of such research is that it provides an 'insiders' view of the development of school systems, from those who have actually participated in the operation and functioning of schools. As such these studies take account of the perceptions of key factors in the schooling system. An important supplementary issue arising out of Warren's work is that he draws attention to the value of letting teachers talk for themselves with regard to their career, through the use of diaries, autobiographies and other primary source material.

The Career Structure in School Teaching

Stages in the Teaching Career

A teaching career may be conceived of as being the status passage of an individual through several work-related social roles over the length of their working life as a school teacher. Although there is some disagreement between authors in terms of the literature available it would appear that five main stages may be identified in the teaching career (e.g. Morrison and McIntyre, 1973; Lortie, 1975; Tisher *et al.*, 1979; McArthur, 1981; Lightfoot, 1985; Huberman, 1989).

1 *Choice of Teaching as an Occupation*: This refers to what Hall (1948) calls 'the generation of an ambition'.
2 *The Pre-service Training Period*: This is the period of formal pre-service teacher education, during which time the individual develops a background in the knowledge, skills and techniques they are likely to require as teachers. They acquire an orientation to the occupational group and to the nature of the teacher's work (Auchmuty, 1980).
3 *Induction into Teaching* (approximately years 1 to 5): This refers to the first four or five years of the teaching career, which is a particularly important period in the professional socialization of the beginning teacher into the culture of the occupation (Coulter,

1971; Tisher et al., 1979; McArthur, 1981). The main reason why it is appropriate to separate the induction period from the remainder of the work career is that this is a transition period for the individual, from being a student teacher to (hopefully) becoming a fully fledged member of the teaching service. During this time the person is likely to face special problems in adjusting to his or her work. This is also the period in a person's career when they are most likely to transfer frequently between schools (horizontal mobility) in an attempt to find a work environment in which the problems faced as a teacher are minimized (Tisher et al., 1979; McArthur, 1981).

4 *The Teaching Career Proper* (approximately from year six onwards): This is the period which dates from the time a person is inducted into the occupation after (say) 5 years, until they leave teaching due to retirement or for some other reason. During this period of time the person is likely to gain upward mobility through the promotion hierarchy, and develop a career pattern which is in some ways distinctive. Periods of re-socialization and re-adjustment will occur at various transition points which are in some ways different to the earlier roles played (and made by) the individuals within the occupation (e.g. Hilsum and Start, 1974; Lortie, 1975; Lyons, 1981).

5 *Preparation for and Exit from the Occupation*: This refers to the stage in his career when a teacher may start to prepare for retirement from the occupation. A greater emphasis may be placed upon the importance, and satisfactions associated with, the time devoted to leisure activities during out-of-school hours (Hilsum and Start, 1974).

Other studies conceive of various 'stages' or 'phases' (or normative sequences) in the teaching career in different terms (e.g. Prick, 1986; Huberman, 1989; Lightfoot, 1985). These 'phases' are: career entry; stabilization, when there is a commitment to 'becoming responsible' as a teacher; diversification and change, where (for example) the attempt to consolidate an instructional repertoire leads to attempts to increase one's effectiveness within the classroom, and there is a more high profile attempt to seek out and achieve promotion; 'stock-taking' at mid-career, which involves doubts about having become a teacher and the wish to possibly change occupations while the person involved believes that they are still young enough to have a range of choices available to them; 'serenity' where, after earlier periods of high energy, the teacher with 20 to 30 years of experience moves into a more reflective, self-accepting phase; conservatism, which often is reflected by such things as the teacher complaining about the characteristics of pupils currently attending school, or the declining status of teachers in society; and, lastly, 'disengagement' and withdrawal towards the end of the professional career cycle.

However, these 'normative sequences' do not necessarily apply to all teachers, and the literature indicates that not all teachers experience the same 'phases' or 'stages', since individual trajectories (especially those later in the career cycle) are very diverse.

Within the literature on the subject 'exit from the occupation' is almost exclusively considered in physical terms: that is, in terms of chronological age and retirement. Another way of looking at this, which is largely ignored in the literature, is to also consider 'exit from the occupation' in the psychological sense, which can occur at any time in a person's career due to such things as low morale or reduced commitment to a work career, which (since the mid 1970s) may be occurring because of reduced promotion and mobility opportunities in teaching.

Five teacher career patterns in terms of entry into, and exit from, teaching can be identified (e.g. Morris, 1957; Hilsum and Start 1974; Department of Education, 1982). These are:

- *Early Entrants*: The recruit trains to become a teacher, goes straight into teaching, and remains a teacher for most of his or her working life.
- *Re-entrants*: The person begins work as a teacher, but then leaves and re-enters the occupation at various times over their working lives. This pattern has been particularly popular amongst women;
- *Late Entrants*: The person enters the teaching service, after spending several years in another occupation, or activity such as marriage;
- *Satisfied Leavers*: These recruits work for a period as teachers and enjoy their work but then leave the occupation in order to take up some other work or non-work activity;
- *Dissatisfied Leavers*: These mainly leave because they do not enjoy the work, or are dissatisfied with other aspects of teaching as an occupation.

Until fairly recently, the wastage rate in teaching has been relatively high compared to other occupations which have similar entry requirements (e.g. Spaull, 1977). This is an important feature of the teaching career which warrants investigation because, amongst other reasons, of the possible waste of talent and training resources from the occupation.

In Australia most teachers are employed by state education departments over the length of their teaching career. In view of this it is also useful to conceptualize the teaching career in terms of:

- the *pre-organizational phase*, which involves two of the stages that have been identified above: stage 1, 'choice of teaching as a career' and stage 2, 'pre-service training period'; and
- the *organizational phase* which involves a consideration of the full time span over which the individual is employed as a teacher, typically in a state education department. This phase involves state 3 'induction into teaching' and the period which follows, stage 4 'the teaching career proper'.
- the *post organizational phase* refers to the career patterns of those who leave teaching on a permanent basis, or who interrupt their teaching career for extended periods of time.

Various studies (e.g. Tisher *et al.*, 1979: Auchmuty, 1980) have been undertaken to examine and probe important aspects of the first three stages of the teaching career identified above, but relatively few studies have examined stage 4 'the teaching career proper'. As Lacey (1978) puts it: 'Most of the stages of the teaching career after the probationary years remain unstudied, and there is surely a pressing need for this omission to be remedied' (p. 152). And, Huberman (1989) says: 'Until about 1975, virtually all the research on career progression in teaching stopped at, or shortly after, entry into the profession' (p. 343).

It is beyond the purpose and scope of this chapter to survey the research and related literature available on each stage of the teaching career identified above since the main concern here is upon the career and promotion patterns of the promoted teacher. In view of this, the remainder of this chapter will be largely limited to examining research on important aspects of 'stage 4 — the teaching career proper', in order to ensure that the research study reported upon in this book is located within its appropriate research context.

The Teaching Career Proper

In an earlier section of this chapter we examined several studies which are relevant to an examination of this stage in the teaching career (e.g. Becker, 1952; Rabinowitz and Crawford, 1960; Roth, 1963; Geer, 1966). We will now examine the relatively few studies in existence that describe and analyse the actual career profiles of particular groups of teachers over a period of time. One of the main characteristics of virtually all these studies is that they largely adopt a structuralist approach to the analysis of teacher career patterns (e.g. Hilsum and Start, 1974; Smith, 1975). The research by Lortie (1975) and Lacey (1978), which contain sections on the long-term career patterns and expectations of teachers, and the study by Lyons (1981), which probes the expectations and perceptions of secondary school teachers regarding a career in teaching, are particularly interesting because they stress the importance of also including a

The Teaching Career

phenomenological perspective when studying promotion and careers in teaching. Several of these studies partly collected data on teacher careers through conducting semi-structured interviews.

The most comprehensive study to date of the career patterns of school teachers is the National Federation for Educational Research (N.F.E.R.) sponsored research undertaken in England and Wales by Hilsum and Start (1974). The objectives of this study were similar to the Research Project reported on in this book, which were: to find out what actually influenced teachers' promotion, and compare this to what teachers believed influenced promotion; to discover how teachers gained promotion; to ascertain teachers' opinions about promotion procedures; and, to discover teachers' expectations about the future.

Two other studies, which had similar aims to the Hilsum and Start (1974) research, and which to varying degrees used some of the instruments developed for that study, were: the Teacher Career and Promotion Study undertaken in New Zealand (Department of Education, 1982), and the N.F.E.R. sponsored study by Lyons (1981) on teacher careers and career perceptions in the secondary modern school. In view of its importance and relevance to the research reported upon in this book the study by Hilsum and Start (1974) will be referred to in some detail at various points in this chapter. Amongst other things, they examined and compared the career patterns and promotion prospects of different groups of teachers (e.g. primary/secondary, men/women, graduate/non-graduate); and the opinions of these teachers about the operation of the promotion system. As 'wastage' from teaching was a widely discussed issue at the time the research was conducted, teachers were also asked about their professional plans. And, finally, the researchers sought the views of teachers about teaching as a career. The data was obtained by administering questionnaires to the headteachers of 963 schools (91.5 per cent were returned) and to 10,043 teachers (67 per cent were returned). This information was supplemented by conducting interviews with 135 teachers; and, in addition, information was obtained from Local Education Authorities through the use of questionnaires and interviews.

Another study which is relevant to the research reported upon here is that by Lyons (1981), which was concerned with: 'the individual as he seeks a career within the school, with his perceptions and interpretations of what he believes to be occurring' (p. 33). The findings of Hilsum and Start (1974) and Lyons (1981) will be referred to in later sections of this book.

Horizontal Mobility

The most insightful examination of horizontal mobility amongst school teachers is the study by Becker (1952). In the Chicago Public School

System, Becker (1952) found that few classroom teachers attempted to rise through the school administrative hierarchy in order to attain higher level promotion positions, such as that of principal. Instead, most stressed the importance of obtaining a transfer to the type of school and locality in which they wanted to teach. The purpose of Becker's investigation was to investigate the often subtle interplay that occurs between the demands of the work situation and the teachers' adjustment to these demands through the career pattern they established.

According to various researchers (e.g. Becker), the work related problems which confront teachers largely occur as a result of their relations with four main groups of people within the structure of the school: parents, colleagues, the school principal, and, most importantly, school children. The problems associated with parents, colleagues and the school principal largely revolve around the issue of the teacher's authority. For example, certain groups of parents (particularly those from high socio-economic backgrounds), colleagues, and some school principals, represent a threat to the teacher's authority. The result is that the teacher experiences feelings of insecurity and anxiety in his dealings with these individuals and groups. In moving between schools, one of the things which teachers attempt to achieve, argues Becker, is a reduced threat to their authority by parents, colleagues, and the principal.

However, by far the most difficult range of problems confronting teachers are those which occur as a result of their interaction with school children. Becker claims that the three main problems teachers face in this area are:

1 those associated with being able to teach their students effectively;
2 those associated with disciplining and controlling students;
3 the 'moral acceptability of their students', which refers to the teacher's ability to accept the behaviour, attitudes and values of students which, in terms of the teacher's own standards and values, may be regarded by her as unacceptable.

Becker argues that the extent to which these problems confront any given teacher largely depends upon the socio-economic characteristics of students in the school in which the person is teaching, the greatest problems of work being found in the lower socio-economic status schools.

However, in terms of the problems teachers face in their dealings with other groups, such as parents, the opposite could well be the case. The parents from high socio-economic status backgrounds are often confident, articulate and assertive in their dealings with teachers, and so they may pose a greater threat to the teacher's authority than do the parents from lower socio-economic status backgrounds.

Becker found that depending upon how teachers choose to resolve the problems of work, two main types of career patterns developed. The first career pattern, which was adopted by the majority of teachers, was characterised by an attempt on the part of the teacher to achieve movement from the low status type of school in which the career typically began, to 'better' schools in more 'desirable' neighbourhoods. The second type of career pattern, which was pursued by a small minority of teachers, was characterised by the teacher making a permanent adjustment to the low status school in which he was working.

Other research studies exist (e.g. Becker, 1952; Duggan and Stewart, 1970) which clearly demonstrate that teachers' socio-economic background and ethnic/racial characteristics can have a considerable affect on the type of school in which they seek to teach. For example, teachers from middle class backgrounds are more likely to transfer away from schools in low socio-economic areas than are teachers from working class backgrounds (e.g. Bendix, 1952; Greenberg and McCall, 1974). In addition, a strong relationship appears to exist between an individual's commitment to teaching in inner city schools, which are most likely to have a large proportion of lower socio-economic group and/or ethnic minority groups, and the socio-economic status and ethnic racial characteristics of the teacher in question (Berlowitz, 1971; Gehrke and Sheffield, 1985). In the case of American schools, teachers from working class backgrounds who were also negroes were more likely to remain in these types of schools than were middle class whites (Smith, 1970).

Others argue that any meaningful discussion of horizontal mobility needs to go beyond an examination of teachers' transfers from inner city-type schools to schools in more pleasant, suburban-type areas. There is also a need to take account of teacher transfers between other types of schools, such as between country and city schools. Sasser (1975), for example, claims that many country schools in the United States are similar to inner city schools, in that they have run-down facilities that are inferior to those in many other areas, staff turnover rates are high, and school staffs are mainly made up of young and inexperienced teachers who seek to transfer out of these schools at the first available opportunity.

It is arguable whether the same type of situation exists in many country schools in Australia in as dramatic a form, for although there are some similarities with regard to such things as the relative inexperience of teachers in country schools (Behrens, 1978), the centralised nature of the Australian school system has meant (until recently) that resources are distributed more evenly throughout the education system than is the case in the United States. In addition, country children are seen by many teachers as being easier to teach than are city children (Behrens, 1978; Peart and Dobson, 1980). Others have commented on the tendency for teachers to seek transfers away from smaller towards increasingly larger schools and communities (Peart and Dobson, 1980). For instance, Havinghurst and Neugarten (1957) comment that although teachers move from place to place, for a variety of reasons, the most typical direction of movement has been from smaller to larger communities. When considering these types of research findings it is, however, important to remember that there are some teachers who prefer to work in country rather than city schools, and/or in small rather than large schools, and who establish their career pattern accordingly (e.g. Hilsum and Start, 1974).

Other researchers have sought to better understand horizontal mobility, as both a distinctive and important aspect of the career pattern of teachers' by examining the things that appear to reduce transfer rates between geographical areas. Jay (1966) undertook a study of teacher mobility in the north of England and found that strength of attachment to a particular geographic region, as indicated by birth-place and the place where the person's secondary schooling was completed, had a dominant effect on the location of a teacher's first and subsequent posts. He found that 81 per cent of the teachers examined in the North of England were either born, or had completed their own schooling, in the north.

Studies have been undertaken which seek to explain the reasons why teachers prefer to work in some schools in preference to others. In his study of the career patterns of teachers in an urban area, Berlowitz (1971) argues that Marx's conception of alienated or estranged labour is of value in helping to achieve an understanding of teacher mobility between schools. He believes that a large percentage of teacher mobility occurs because teachers are attempting to obtain the maximum reward from their work (in both the material and non-material sense) for the minimum amount of effort that is possible. As Mills (1951) has put it, in a slightly different way, in his discussion of the ideology of alienated work, they want 'more and more money (i.e. rewards) for less and less work'.

In order to test his hypothesis, Berlowitz speculates that teachers will try to avoid working in those schools where they perceive the teacher's work as being most difficult. Berlowitz (1971) defined a difficult school as one where a substantial percentage of the children were black or Puerto Rican and from low socio-economic status backgrounds, and where the average level of academic achievement amongst fellow students at the school was low. In keeping with the other research studies already cited, Berlowitz (1971) found that teacher turnover rates were higher in those schools he defined as being difficult than they were in other schools, and on the basis of this finding argues that his hypothesis is proven. Berlowitz's hypothesis relates to 'perceptions' rather than 'facts', so that he appears to far too easily prove what he set out to prove; and one needs to treat his conclusion with some caution, for he does not prove that the effort required to teach in what he classes as being a 'different school' is in fact greater than it is in other schools, and this is the key assumption upon which the validity of his study rests. Depending upon how one defines effort (that is, in intellectual, emotional or purely physical terms) it may well be that the effort required of the teacher is less in the so called difficult school than it is in the other schools, because in all-white, high socio-economic status schools, where academic standards are likely to be higher, the teacher may have to work considerably harder in both an intellectual and emotional sense than they would need to in the 'ghetto-type' schools.

In his study of teacher mobility in the metropolitan setting Pederson (1972) adopts a conceptual framework in which teacher mobility (migration) is viewed in terms of the 'human capital approach' (Sjaasted, 1962; Bowman 1966). By adopting this theoretical framework, Pederson assumes that individual teachers employ a decision-making framework which is based upon a consideration of the costs and related benefits (in both economic and sociological terms) when reviewing alternative employment possibilities, and so (in theory) migration flows will increase if the total money and psychic returns exceed the total costs of relocation.

The independent predictors used in Pederson's study were the selected characteristics of both sending and receiving schools, such as the size of school, socio-economic characteristics of pupils, and the age and sex composition of staff. The purpose of the study was to identify the economic and sociological correlates which would be of explanatory and predictive importance in developing an understanding of teacher turnover. The model that was used conceives of teacher mobility as being a form of private investment in which individuals consider the cost-benefit implications of remaining in, or moving to, another school.

The main findings of Pederson's (1972) study were that:

1 The age and sex composition of the staff in a school are highly predictive of teacher turnover rates, high turnover being associated with a high incidence of young, particularly female, teachers. This finding is, says the researcher, supportive of previous research; and,
2 'Push factors' are more important than are 'pull factors' in explaining teacher mobility. That is, findings suggest that teachers move more because of dissatisfaction concerning one or more characteristics of their current position, rather than because of the attraction of other schools.

It should be noted that although the study by Pederson (1970) is conceptually different to all the other studies so far cited, in that it explicitly relates to both economic (relative net-advantages) and exchange theory, it is included here because it may provide a different and fruitful way to approach the study of teacher migration and mobility, a speculation that will be taken up in a later chapter.

The studies referred to in this section on the school teaching career are mainly concerned with analysing various aspects of horizontal mobility, which is an important feature of teacher career patterns. Out of all of these studies, the one undertaken by Becker (1952) is regarded here to be particularly important for although conducted over three decades ago, and based on interviews with only a small sample of sixty teachers in one education system, the propositions developed in his investigation are still important in providing a useful insight into teacher career patterns, in guiding investigations of teacher mobility and career patterns, and in guiding investigations of teacher careers in other settings. The importance of Becker's study lies in the fact that he developed influential hypotheses regarding the relationship between horizontal and vertical mobility in the career patterns of teachers. But, there is a need for further systematic research which tests Becker's ideas to see whether they still hold true, some 30 years after the original research was conducted, in a different country and different times. Although other studies have taken up many of his points, the following questions posed by Becker regarding the relationship that may exist between horizontal and vertical mobility in school teaching careers have yet to be tackled in a satisfactory or comprehensive manner:

1 To what extent, and under what circumstances, will an individual forego actions which might provide him with a better working situation at one level of an occupational hierarchy in the hope of receiving greater rewards through vertical mobility?
2 To what extent will a person give up possible vertical mobility which might interfere with the successful adjustment he has made in terms of horizontal career movement? For example, to what extent will a person teaching in a pleasant school environment not seek promotion because they may have to move to teach in an unattractive schooling environment.

These questions are examined in later chapters of this book with data obtained in an Australian setting.

Distinguishing between Vertical and Horizontal Mobility

As was noted earlier, vertical mobility refers to a change or movement of an upward or downward nature within a hierarchical structure of status or prestige (Caplow, 1954). Within the teaching career, vertical mobility refers to movement between the various levels in the promotions hierarchy. An example of vertical mobility would be when, in Tasmania, an individual is promoted from the position of classroom teacher to that of Senior Master or Mistress, the latter position having additional responsibilities and a higher salary and status within the social structure of the

The Teaching Career

school than does the former position. In comparison, horizontal mobility refers to changes in the work activities of individuals which do not involve any change in their relative status within the promotions hierarchy. The transfer of a teacher from one school to another, at the same level within the promotions hierarchy, would be an example of horizontal mobility.

In order to ascertain whether or not a particular career move is of the vertical or horizontal type, there is a need to draw a map of the various status positions within any promotions hierarchy: that is, the system of stratification that exists. Within the school teaching career there are several possible ways of identifying and then categorizing positions within any promotions hierarchy: that is, the internal system of stratification that exists. It would appear that the simplest way to achieve this would be to rank the various positions according to the relative status and power that incumbents enjoy within the school system. In secondary schools, for example, we can readily identify and locate, descending from the top to the bottom of the hierarchy, principals, vice-principals, senior masters/ mistress and teachers; while in primary schools we can identify principals, vice principals, infant mistresses, senior teachers and teachers. However, to establish the promotions hierarchy simply on this basis is not as straightforward as it may at first seem. If we also rank these positions from highest to lowest paid we discover that this rank order does not necessarily coincide with that which has been arrived at by using the other method.

To illustrate the point we can use the salary scale applicable for state school teachers in Tasmania. The vice principal of a large high school receives a gross salary some 20 per cent higher than that received by the principal of a middle sized primary school and 25 per cent greater than that received by the principal of a smallish district school. The senior master in a largish district or high school is on a higher salary than the principal of the smallest class of district school. The reason is that the salary received by principals and certain other groups vary according to the type and size of school in which they work. This means that if salary level is used as the criteria, a vice principal in a large school would occupy a higher position in the promotion hierarchy than would a primary principal or a post primary principal working in smaller sized schools.

It could be argued that since the principal of a small school receives a lower salary than some vice principals or senior masters/mistresses in larger schools, if the principal of a district school became the principal of a larger district or high school, this would be regarded as a promotion and therefore classed as upward vertical mobility. Also, in terms of an analysis of promotion, it could be argued that the principal of a small school should not be regarded as being a 'real principal'.

To rank positions within the promotion hierarchy solely on the basis of the amount of salary received could be criticised on the basis that regardless of the actual salary received, or the size of the school in which a teacher is employed, the office of principal has a higher status than that of vice principal or senior master/mistress, both in the eyes of the community and also perhaps in the eyes of the occupational group. Thus, in addition to using so-called objective criteria, such as salary received, it is also important to take account of teacher perceptions regarding the relative position of a particular type of teaching job in the status (or promotions) hierarchy. These are speculations which need to be tested empirically.

In addition, the fact that the incumbents of two or more different types of positions receive the same salary level does not necessarily mean that these positions are equal in terms of the future promotion and career opportunities each offers its incumbents. One position may be of a terminal type, or lead to a blocked career line, while another position may open up a wide range of future career possibilities. For example, a principal (class 1), Infant Mistress (class 3) and primary principal (class 4) all receive the same salary. However, while the vice principal and principal positions can be used by a teacher as a stepping stone to many other positions in the promotions hierarchy, the infant mistress promotion position is most likely to be a terminal one, in terms of the future career lines available for the infant teacher.

Career Timetables

As we noted in Chapter 2, Roth (1963) argues that people will not easily accept uncertainty in their work activities and so seek to structure the time period through which uncertain events such as promotion occurs. As a result, norms develop within the occupational group about when certain events within a person's career will occur. The most useful research which examines the career timetables of teachers is the study by Lyons (1981) of teacher careers in several secondary comprehensive schools in England. Using a theoretical model derived from Hughes (1958), Roth (1963) and Becker (1952), the researchers found that the most successful teachers in terms of degree and rate of promotion achieved adopted career timetables, strategies and maps. These things were mainly acquired by observing the behaviour of significant peers and by the individual then adjusting their own career behaviour accordingly.

Career Patterns

The changing structure of available statuses within the promotions hierarchy of school teaching made it impossible for Hilsum and Start (1974) to construct a 'typical' career pattern for an 'average teacher'. In view of this they constructed patterns based on the actual career histories of teachers. Various groups of teachers were compared in terms of such things as the number of years of experience accumulated before corresponding statuses were reached; and it was found that the number of years of teaching experience at which teachers were first awarded a particular status varied enormously.

Hilsum and Start's (1974) main findings regarding this matter were, in summary form:

- the first promotion of men and women came earlier in the secondary schools (after about 3 years) than it did in the primary schools (after 7 years). However this difference between primary and secondary school teachers did not apply when it came to the time taken to reach all other promotion positions. For example, the Head Teachers of both primary and secondary schools achieved these posts after an average of 18 years;
- Women took longer than men to achieve advancement to the various promotion positions;
- In the secondary sector, graduates received promotion more quickly than did non-graduates, but little difference was found between graduates and non-graduates in primary schools.
- In general, comprehensive and grammar school teachers achieved promotions earlier than did their counterparts in the secondary modern school; and,
- When comparisons were made between the ages when different 'generations' of teachers were first awarded specific statuses, the general conclusion was that in both primary and secondary schools, first and second promotions were being awarded about three and six years earlier respectively than during the previous decade.

However, the findings of Hilsum and Start (1974) need to be treated with some caution because theirs is almost exclusively a descriptive study, in which no major attempt was made by the authors to test whether the differences noted were statistically significantly or likely to occur due to chance. Several studies (e.g. Hilsum and Start, 1974; Lyons, 1981; Department of Education, 1982) have also found that women apply less frequently for promotion than do men.

Attributes of School Teachers as an Occupational Group

School teaching is an occupation which offers practitioners vertical mobility. Hilsum and Start (1974) identified the attributes of teachers in England and Wales who were promoted in the following terms:

- Promoted teachers had taught in more schools than had unpromoted teachers, which suggests that variety of schools played a bigger part in promotion than did long service in one school, or put another way it could be said that promotion takes teachers to other schools. Women's prospects were more affected than men's by the number of schools they had worked in. Service in only one, or in four or more schools, appeared less helpful in promotion than did service in two or three schools;
- As one would logically expect, length of teaching experience was positively associated with rise in promotion status. At corresponding status levels, women had had more teaching experience than men, secondary modern teachers more than comprehensive and grammar school teachers, and 're-entrants' more than 'normal' or 'late entrants';
- For teachers following a 'normal' career, age parallels length of teaching experience. The researchers identify the average ages (and range) at which those in various sectors of the school system (and with various academic and other characteristics) achieve various status positions.
- Increase in status seemed to be associated with attendance at in-service and other courses for primary teachers, but not for secondary teachers.
- Increasing status was associated with the number of times a person had moved their place of residence. In both primary and secondary sectors, men had moved their home in search of promotion more often than had women, grammar and comprehensive teachers more often than modern school teachers, and graduates more often than non-graduates.

The findings of various researchers (e.g. Green, 1966; Masih, 1967) is that, in general, those who plan to become, or are, teachers indicate a significantly lower career saliency than do those in other occupations such as engineering, business and the liberal arts. The reasons for this are unclear, but it may be because of the large number of women in teaching and the blue collar backgrounds (especially in the case of men) of many of those who embark upon a school teaching career.

Research studies from both overseas (e.g. Mason, 1961; Pederson, 1970; Orlick, 1972; D.E.S. Reports on Education, 1975) and Australia (e.g. Jecks, 1969; Burkhardt, 1975, 1976; Stevens, 1978) show that if teacher turnover rates are used as one measure of commitment to and persistence in a teaching career, these turnover rates are much higher for females than they are for males. This is particularly true for females in the 20 to 35 year old, child bearing age group.

An age grade system exists in school teaching so that it becomes unlikely (if not impossible) that an individual will achieve certain posi-

The Teaching Career

tions in the promotions hierarchy until they have reached a particular age, or accumulated a minimum number of years experience (e.g. Lortie, 1975). In the Tasmanian Education Department, for example, there is a regulation which states that a beginning teacher must accrue a minimum of five years' teaching experience before being eligible to apply for access to the first promotion position, which in terms of school positions is that of senior master/mistress or senior teacher.

In addition to the formal regulations established which influence the vertical mobility of individuals, it is said that certain informal norms and practices develop regarding what are seen as appropriate patterns and promotion positions for those in different age groups (e.g. Lortie, 1975; Maclean et al., 1984). These practices or norms relate to statistical phenomenon: that is, the amount of time it is likely to take for an individual to achieve various promotion positions.

Despite the types of changes that have occurred in western industrial societies like Australia since the end of the Second World War, regarding the role of women in the labour force, women continue to be under-represented in the higher status occupations, and are less likely than men to achieve access to higher level promotion positions. (Maclean, 1989; Australian Bureau of Statistics, 1990). Several studies (Hilsum and Start, 1974; Lyons 1981; Department of Education, 1982; Maclean, 1989) have examined and tried to explain the under-representation of women in promotion positions in teaching, particularly in the 'top' decision making jobs. It has been found by these studies that women are absent from senior positions because their main commitment is firstly to a family, and only second to a career in teaching (Eberts and Stone, 1985). Some studies have also sought to identify the characteristics of the women who do enter the 'top jobs' in teaching (Fenwick and Shepherd, 1982).

Other studies, such as one in New Zealand (Department of Education, 1982), have found that a lack of women applicants is a major reason why women are under-represented in the various higher status occupations and promotion positions; and that women tend to have a lower level of career aspirations than do men. However, one can criticize the assumptions upon which this study is based, because the researchers never ask, or seek to answer, the question 'why is this so'?

McIntosh (1974), in a study of the differences between women who do and those who do not seek promotion in school teaching, shows that many women who seek and obtain promotion are, like the majority of other female teachers, likely to be married with children. This is a relatively recent change because there used to be a preponderance of single or childless women amongst those women who did manage to gain promotion to administrative type positions in teaching (Spaull, 1977).

Several other studies, including some in Australia (e.g. Anti-Discrimination Board, 1979; Fenwick, 1982; Sampson, 1985) have focused on the careers of women in teaching, and have sought to discover the reasons for the under-representation of women in promotion positions. They have also suggested ways of changing this situation through means such as reverse discrimination to favour women (Duran, 1982).

Hilsum and Start (1974) examined the distribution of promotion positions between different groups of teachers, their main findings being:

- Fifty-seven per cent of all full-time teachers held a promotion position of some kind: 11 per cent were heads, 8 per cent deputy heads, and 38 per cent held positions below deputy;
- Proportionately, far more secondary teachers (71 per cent) than primary (44 per cent) held a promotion position of some kind. However, because of the greater number of primary than secondary schools, far more deputy headships and headships were held by primary than by secondary teachers (10 per cent of primary teachers were deputies and 16 per cent were heads, compared with the corresponding figures of 6 per cent and nearly 5 per cent for secondary teachers);
- There were important differences in the distribution of promotion positions between men and women. In primary schools, about three quarters of men held promotion positions, compared with about 30 per cent of women. In the secondary sector the proportions were respectively about 80 per cent and 60 per cent. In both systems the difference was generally much more noticeable at the higher than at the lower levels of responsibility;
- The aspirations of women were much lower than those of men: 10 per cent of women wished to be heads compared to 36 per cent of men. The authors speculate that one reason why a lower proportion of women than men occupy promotion positions may be that fewer women seek promotion;
- In primary schools there was no difference between graduates in the way promotion positions were distributed, but in secondary schools graduates held proportionately more of the senior positions than did non-graduates.

Hilsum and Start (1974) undertook an analysis of subject specialists in secondary schools and found that the distribution of promotion positions between various subject areas varied according to level of promotion. All subject areas offered reasonable promotion prospects of some kind or another, however some, such as drama and physical education, offered few prospects beyond lower level promotion positions, while others, such as German and music, seemed to offer better prospects, so that the teachers involved could more readily obtain the headship of a small department. At higher levels in the promotions hierarchy, physics, chemistry, English and maths were among the subjects where disproportionately more teachers held promotion positions. Headships were concentrated disproportionately on a few subjects, history in particularly.

In general, teachers who were 'late entrants' were promoted more than 're-entrants'. In primary schools, promotion was awarded more to women who had pursued a 'normal career' than those who had left and returned to teaching. There was no difference in the secondary sector.

Teacher Perceptions of the Career Structure

Although a number of researchers have referred to the way in which teachers look at their careers (e.g. Waller, 1936; Lortie, 1975; Tisher et al., 1979; McArthur, 1981) the most detailed research studies to date that are directly relevant to the research reported upon in this book are those studies conducted in England and Wales by Hilsum and Start (1974), by Lyons (1981) and by the Education Department in New Zealand (Department of Education 1982). The aims of the research undertaken by Hilsum and Start (1974) and the New Zealand Department of Education (1982) were very similar. First, to identify the more subtle factors that, in the eyes of the teachers, appear to influence promotion; and; second, to see how far these opinions coincided with objective findings regarding promotion and careers in teaching. The researchers asked teachers for their views on what affected promotion because they felt that teachers' beliefs about promotion would probably have an important influence on their behaviour regarding this issue, and their overall satisfactions and dissatisfactions with their job. The study by Lyons (1980) entitled *Teachers Careers and Career Perceptions* focused on the careers of a small sample of teachers employed in secondary comprehensive schools in England. By examining how this group of teachers perceived and constructed their careers (or failed to do so, as so often seemed to be the case) the study sought to throw some light on the problems facing schools where the career development of secondary school staff is concerned.

In the studies by Hilsum and Start (1974), Lyons (1981), and the Education Department of New Zealand (1982), teachers were presented with a list of 31 possible factors that could be seen to affect promotion, and were asked to identify the five factors which they felt were most important in influencing promotion. In the Hilsum and Start (1974) study, the ten items most frequently chosen by teachers from the list, with the percentage of teachers who chose each one, were: being a graduate (41.7 per cent); specialism in shortage subject (41.3 per cent); social contacts (that is, being known by the right people) (39.6 per cent); conformity with the views of advisors (29.0 per cent); good relations with School Principal (27.6 per cent); length of teaching experience (24.6

per cent); course attendance (21.5 per cent); variety of schools taught in (19.8 per cent); extra curricula work (19.7 per cent); and, familiarity with new ideas in education (19.6 per cent). Some of the less frequently chosen items were: being a male (12.8 per cent); unwillingness to move area (12.1 per cent); and, service in one school (10.9 per cent).

An interesting finding was that teachers disagreed quite markedly on what they thought favoured promotion; and, that there is not one single factor that half the teachers regarded as being a chief factor favouring promotion. The items 'social contacts' and 'conformity with advisors' were both rated as being of considerable importance. This is interesting, because it could imply that teachers believe that 'sponsorship' is important in affecting promotion prospects. However, one problem associated with interpreting the importance of these types of ideas is that they rely on subjective judgments, and so cannot be readily measured or quantified. It is also of interest to note those items which teachers thought counted for little: these were, concern for the development of individual pupils, good relations with staff, and administrative ability.

Hilsum and Start (1974) also analysed teacher responses according to whether they were primary or secondary teachers, men or women, graduates or non-graduates, and according to age and the present level of the promotion position held. For some groups it was found that differences in emphasis occurred regarding the relative importance of various factors as being more important than others. When the views of teachers on those things that favour promotion were compared with the survey findings on teacher career patterns, it was found that although some variations existed between different groups of teachers in terms of the extent to which these coincided, in general the factors which the teachers believed were of importance closely coincided with those that were actually found to be of importance in influencing promotion. The authors say:

> The survey findings were that length of teaching experience partially favoured promotion, though many long-serving teachers were unpromoted. Variety of schools was helpful in the limited sense that two or three schools favoured promotion, especially for women, but one school and more than three schools had little effect. Subject specialism was an extremely important factor.... One might conclude, therefore, that a correspondence between 'perceived' ... and 'actual' factors was moderately well achieved. There is, however, a large area of doubt concerning factors which teachers thought desirable but about which no objective evidence was gathered, namely, flexibility in teaching methods, ability to control pupils, concern for pupil welfare, good relations with staff and administrative ability. (p. 293)

Teachers were also asked to indicate the factors which they believed *ought* to favour promotion, in order to examine the extent to which their 'ideal' regarding promotion in teaching varied from what they regarded as being the reality about this matter. The ten main items identified were: (1) flexibility in teaching methods (50.1 per cent); (2) familiarity with new ideas (43.8 per cent); (3) ability to control pupils (43.1 per cent); (4) concern for pupil welfare (41.7 per cent); (5) variety of schools (34.1 per cent); (6) length of experience (32.0 per cent); (7) good relations with staff (28.9 per cent); (8) subject specialization (28.4 per cent); (9) administrative ability (26.7 per cent); and, (10) extra curricular work (19.1 per cent). Teachers were more agreed on what ought to favour promotion than they were about what actually did favour promotion. However, despite this, only one factor (flexibility in teaching methods) was selected by more than half the teachers.

Of the nine factors that were considered by over a quarter of the sampled teachers to be desirable promotion qualities, only three can currently be accurately measured (numbers 5, 6 and 8 in the list above), for all the others rely exclusively on teacher judgment. This implies that teachers were willing to accept that promotion should depend upon judgments rather than only upon more easily measurable and quantifiable factors.

Gallop and Gagg (1972) undertook a study of teachers in further education in England and Wales, and amongst a variety of things inquired into their perceptions regarding the factors that affect promotion. These findings are included here in order to provide a point of comparison with some of the findings of Hilsum and Start (1974). However, it is important to keep in mind that the studies were examining different groups of teachers in that the teachers were employed in different sectors of the education system, and so the findings are not directly comparable. The factors chosen by teachers in the Gallop and Gagg (1972) study were: being in the right place at the right time; educational experience; industrial experience; hard work; exceptional personality; conspicuous administrative ability; being a technical expert; exceptional leadership qualities; having the right background; and luck. No information is available in the Gallop and Gagg (1972) study regarding the proportion of teachers who chose each item: just the ten most chosen items. Even allowing for the fact that these teachers are in the area of further or post-secondary education, while those in the Hilsum and Start (1974) study are primary and secondary school teachers, it is interesting to note that only one factor (educational experience) was selected by both groups as being of importance.

There has until now (Maclean, 1991) been, no research study in Australia that has comprehensively examined the ideas of teachers regarding the factors that influence upward mobility in the promotions hierarchy.

Conclusion

This chapter has examined what is known about the school teaching career, in relation to the main sociological concepts associated with the study of work careers that were reviewed in Chapter 2.

What is clear is that research on many aspects of the teaching career is meagre and that there are major gaps in our knowledge about the career and promotion patterns of teachers, especially in Australia. To be more specific, little is known about the operation of the career structure in teaching, and in particular the relationship between various stages in the teaching career. With the exception of Beckers (1954) study, little is known about how teachers perceive their careers with regard to the relationship between horizontal and vertical mobility in the teaching career, or about the factors which influence the career pathways adopted by teachers. Relatively little research exists on the career contingency factors that influence the rate at which and extent to which teachers gain promotion, and in particular the extent to which 'informal' factors such as sponsorship are important in influencing the career patterns of teachers. However, the research by Hilsum and Start (1974), Lyons (1981) and the New Zealand Department of Education (1982) have helped to fill in these gaps.

There is, in particular a shortage of research on Australian schoolteachers. That which is available mainly examines the induction of beginning teachers, descriptive characteristics of Australian teachers, teacher unionism, the development of the occupation in historical terms, and (more recently) the career patterns of women compared to men teachers.

The study by Hilsum and Start has been given particular prominence in this literature review for three main reasons. First, it is the most comprehensive study to date on the career and promotion patterns of teachers; second, it adopts a research framework that is, in important ways, similar to the one used in the research reported upon in this book in that it seeks to blend together both quantitative and qualitative data and analysis; and third, many of the research instruments used by them have been taken up and used by other researchers such as Lyons (1981) and the New Zealand Department of Education's (1982) study. In addition, there are important similarities in the aims of the Hilsum and Start study, and the research reported upon here. In view of this fact a comparison will be made between the results of these studies in later chapters of this research report. The purpose of the research study reported upon here is to help fill some of these gaps in the research literature on the teaching career.

Chapter 4

Opportunity Structure of Tasmanian Teachers

In order to explain adequately teacher career patterns, in this case study of the Tasmanian state school system, it is necessary to be aware of the contextual factors, or opportunity structure, that has existed for teachers in the Education Department concerned over the period being examined, up until the end of 1988. The characteristics of this changing structure determined the range and types of opportunities available to individuals pursuing a career in teaching, and so largely set the boundaries within which teachers operated.

Given the purposes and emphasis of the research study reported upon here, this is not the place to provide a very detailed description of the changes in the Tasmanian School system that occurred over the last fifty years (see Johnston, 1962; Phillips, 1985; Maclean, in press). Instead, those changes in the education system which influenced the opportunity structure within which individuals pursued a career and promotion within teaching will be briefly outlined.

Like many school systems in the Western world, the Tasmanian school system over the past half century, has been dynamic, rather than static. This was a period during which considerable, and often rapid, change occurred. There were significant changes in the structural characteristics of the school system within which teachers work, which were likely to have had an important affect on teacher careers. These changes had an effect on the overall demand for teachers and on the areas within the school system where the greatest or smallest range and number of promotion opportunities existed. It affected the career structure and opportunities available to particular individuals and groups of teachers, such as: men vs. women; graduates vs. non graduates; and, those employed in the secondary compared to those employed in the primary sectors of the Education Department.

Changing Structure of the State School System

Over the period being examined there were several changes in the structure of the Tasmanian school system that had an important effect on the opportunity structure for teachers. The main changes that occurred were: the introduction after 1958 of comprehensive high schools, and the abandonment of the selective, tripartite school system; the establishment of matriculation colleges between 1965 and 1975; the expansion of secondary education in rural areas through the establishment and growth in the number of area schools; and, the development of technical and vocational education, through the expansion of junior technical schools and commercial high schools. In addition, over the same time period there were considerable fluctuations in school enrolments (see Phillips, 1985); and the raising of the school leaving age to 16 years in 1946 resulted in a major expansion of the secondary school sector. There was also a move in policy from a highly decentralized school system, in terms of providing a large number of small schools throughout the state, to one of consolidation through the provision of fewer, larger schools.

As is illustrated by Figure 4.1: *The School System of Tasmania* the structure of the school system is, (and was at the time that data for this study was collected), as follows:

1 Two years of kindergarten and prep. schooling, followed by six years of primary education in a primary, district high or district School.
2 Four years of secondary education in a high school, district high school or district school, which leads to the award of a School Certificate.
3 Two years of schooling in a secondary (matriculation) college, which leads to the award of a Higher School Certificate.

The government system of schooling in Tasmania is now a fully comprehensive one.

Number, Distribution and Size of Schools

There has been a gradual decrease in the number of schools in Tasmania over the past 50 years, while over the same period there has been an increase in the number of student enrolments. The main reason for the overall reduction in the number of schools was the decrease in the number of primary schools operating in the state. Over the same period there was an increase in the number of post primary schools operating in Tasmania. There was also an increase in the size of post primary schools

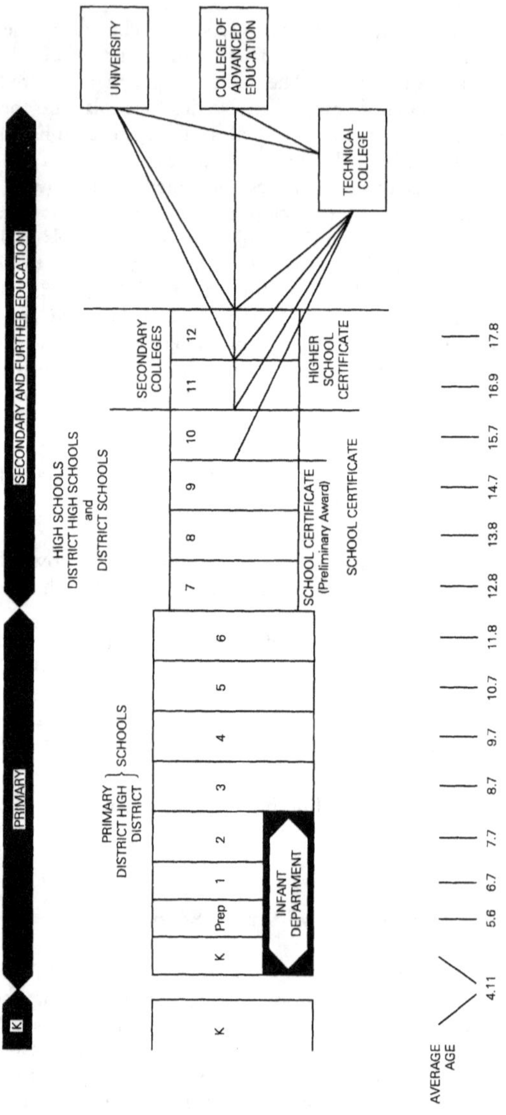

Opportunity Structure of Tasmanian Teachers

Figure 4.1 The school system of Tasmania

NOTES:
1. Average ages in years and months calculated from census.
2. Special schools are not shown.
3. Part-time HSC students not included in age statistics.

65

so that the majority of large schools were high schools and (after 1965) matriculation colleges (Maclean, in press).

The decrease in the number of primary schools mainly occurred owing to the closing down of the smaller one and two teacher schools, and a consolidation of student enrolments. Thus, although there was an overall expansion in the size of the school system in terms of student enrolments, the pattern was for the smaller schools to be closed down, and for schools to generally become larger in terms of student enrolment numbers (Maclean, in press). These changes in the school system resulted in changes in the opportunity structure within which teachers built their careers.

Changing Structure of the Promotions System

Over the period being examined there were significant changes in the promotions hierarchy and nomenclature of positions in the Tasmanian Education Department, the former having an impact on the opportunity structure within which individuals pursued promotion and a career in teaching.

Developing a meaningful map of the hierarchy of promotion positions for teachers in the Education Department of Tasmania was not straightforward for two main reasons: first, changes had occurred over time in the number and relative status of various levels in the promotions hierarchy, and also in the names given to different promotion positions; and, second, if salary is used as the main criteria for locating a particular promotion position in the promotions hierarchy, one finds that there were certain anomolies and a mismatch between the relative status of a promotion position in a particular school and the status of that position within the overall school system. For example, at the current time a vice principal in a large post primary school receives a salary which is considerably more than that received by a principal responsible for the smallest category of post-primary school.

In this study it is generally assumed that salary level indicates the relative status of a particular promotion position within the opportunity structure of the Education Department. Salary level was chosen as the main criteria because there is, in most occupations, a positive correlation between size of salary received and the location of the job in question in the promotions hierarchy: that is, the higher the salary level paid, the higher tends to be the job location in the promotion hierarchy. However, due to some areas of overlap, and several anomalies in the salary structure, some qualitative decisions had to be made regarding the relative position of different groups of teachers in the promotions hierarchy.

Hierarchy of Promotion Positions

The promotions hierarchy that has existed in the Education Department over the period being examined is as follows.

Promotion Positions in Schools

Principal, Head Master/Mistress or Head Teacher: The principal, HM or HT is the highest paid member of the staff of any school, and is responsible to the Director-General of Education for the satisfactory running of that school. He or she is the person to whom all other teachers in the school are responsible. A principal's relative status and salary level, compared to other principals, depends upon the size of the school (in terms of number of student enrolments) for which he or she is responsible. Depending upon the size of the particular school in which they are employed, there are seven 'classes' of primary school principals, while in the post primary sector, there are six principal classes.

Vice Principal, or Deputy Headmaster/Mistress: The VP or deputy headmaster/mistress is second only to the principal in terms of the authority structure within the school organisation and is responsible and accountable to the principal. This promotion position has existed since 1952 for high schools, since 1962 for district high schools and area schools and, between 1954–1957, and since 1967, for primary schools. Prior to these dates most schools appointed a senior master/mistress or senior teacher to undertake, in an unpaid capacity with no salary adjustment, the types of duties now assumed by the vice principal. There are currently three grades of vice principals. Whether or not a VP position occurs within a particular school, and the number of such positions, depends upon the size of the school as defined by the number of student enrolments.

Senior Master/Mistress, Master/Mistress of Subject Department, or Master/ Mistress of Technical Department: This position only occurs in post primary schools, the individuals involved being responsible for the organisation of a specific subject department within his or her school. A recent trend has been for SMs to be appointed to be responsible in other, more general areas of the school curriculum, such as work experience programmes. Up until the end of 1975 there were three grades of SM, while since then there are two grades. In most post primary schools the SMs, together with the principal and vice principal, constitute the senior staff, the main decision making body within the school.

Senior Teacher/First Assistant Teacher: This promotion position only occurs in primary, area/district and district high schools. In terms of salary and status, a senior teacher occupies a position similar to that of a senior master/mistress in a high school, although they generally are not responsible for a particular subject area. Up until the end of 1975 there were three grades of ST, but since January 1976 there have been two grades. With the introduction of vice principals into primary schools in 1954, STs were no longer seen as second-in-charge, except in the smaller primary schools that had no VP position. Senior teachers, along with the principal and vice principal, constitute the senior staff in a primary school.

Assistant Master/Mistress: The position of AM was only awarded in post primary schools between 1930 and 1965. It was not strictly a promotion position as such since it was mainly awarded at the level of an individual school in recognition of a person's competence as a teacher. However, it is referred to here because it was an important step along the way to gaining promotion to the position of SM.

Infant Mistress/Master: The IM is responsible for an infant department which is usually attached to a primary school. There are three grades of IM. Up until 1976, only women occupied this promotion position.

All other teaching positions in schools are occupied by unpromoted teachers: that is, those who have yet to achieve their first advancement within the promotions hierarchy.

Non-School Promotion Positions

If the usual criteria of salary, status and power are used to determine an individual's relative position within a promotions hierarchy then this group of teachers are clearly the ones who occupy the 'top jobs' within the education department. These personnel are engaged in supervisory, advisory and administrative type duties within service branches, and head and regional offices, of the education department. They are a small, select group which consists of (in descending order, from higher to lower status positions): the Director-General of Education, who is permanent head of the Department; his Deputy; the Directors of the various sections within the Department such as Personnel, Primary, Secondary and Technical Education; Regional Directors; Superintendents and Supervisors; and Principal Education Officers. In addition, there are senior education officers and guidance branch personnel who have a status that is roughly equivalent to that of SMs and STs in schools.

The individuals who occupy these positions are, to a greater or lesser extent, the ones involved with overseeing and co-ordinating the professional activities of those who work in the school system, and have the potential to exercise a considerable amount of power over the in-school activities of both teachers and school children.

Number and Distribution of Promotion Positions

The total number of full time teachers employed in the Education Department increased from 886 in 1930 to 4960 in 1989, a more than four fold increase (Peart and Maclean, in press). Over the same period there was a substantial increase in the number, and a change in the distribution, of promotion positions between the various divisions of the Education Department.

Promotion Positions in Schools

Principals: As we noted earlier in this chapter, over the time span examined there was a rapid expansion in the post primary school sector, with many new secondary schools being established throughout the State. The greatest single increase in the number of promotion positions at the principal level occurred in 1941, when there was over a threefold increase in the number of such positions. However, there has been a consistent increase in the number of such positions for most years since 1930 (Peart and Maclean, in press).

In terms of the demand for principals in different types of schools, in the high school sector the period of greatest growth was between 1952 and 1954 when there was a 50 per cent increase in the number of principalships (from 9 to 14) (Peart and Maclean, in press).

For area schools the greatest growth was between 1948 (16) and 1949 (23). Over the rest of the period there was a more gradual increase in numbers, with an occasional downwards fluctuation. The most dramatic increase in the number of principal positions occurred in district high schools, for there was an increase in numbers from 6 in 1972 to 39 in 1973 (Peart and Maclean, in press).

In the case of primary schools, the number of principalships fluctuated substantially over the time span being examined, the periods of greatest growth being between 1931 and 1939, and between 1945 and 1951. Since 1951 there has been a gradual decrease in the supply of school principalships, from 191 in 1951 to 132 in 1989 (Peart and Maclean, in press).

Vice-Principals: In the post primary school sector there has been a consistent increase in the number of VP positions from one in 1952 (when this promotion position was first created) to 52 in 1989. At the current time most of these positions occur in high schools (78 per cent) and district schools (18 per cent), one reason being that it is mainly these schools that are large enough to justify one or two VP positions. There were only two VP positions in primary schools before 1967, but since that time there has been almost a fourfold increase from 6 (1967) to 25 (1989) such positions (Peart and Maclean, in press).

Senior Masters/Mistresses and Senior Teachers: Because these are roughly equivalent positions in the post primary (SMs) and primary (STs) sectors of the school system, they will be dealt with together.

If the current situation is considered in order to illustrate the point, there are less than half as many ST than SM positions in schools, even though a roughly equivalent number of full time teachers are employed in the primary and secondary school sectors (Peart and Maclean, in press).

It is at the 'lower management level' of SMs and STs that there has been the most dramatic and substantial change in the opportunity structure. The greatest increase has occurred at the post primary level, the most substantial increase occurring between 1954 (32 SM positions) and 1974 (357 SM positions). Most of these positions are in secondary (matriculation) colleges and high schools (93 per cent) the remainder (7 per cent) being in district and area schools (Peart and Maclean, in press).

Although there was also an increase in ST positions over the same period in the primary school sector, this was modest when compared with change in the post primary school sector. The greatest increase in the number of middle level promotion positions in primary schools occurred between 1954 (20 STs) and 1974 (59 STs). Almost all of these promotion positions occurred in primary schools, rather than district or other schools (Peart and Maclean, in press).

Non-School Promotion Positions

Very few promotion positions exist in the advisory, supervisory and administrative areas outside schools. At the current time, only 1.5 per cent of the teaching population occupy such promotion positions, and so the possibility of any given teacher gaining promotion to a non-school position has been very slight, and considerably less, for example, than their chances of becoming a school principal. The percentage of the teaching population who have occupied these types of promotion positions has always been relatively low, having fluctuated at around 2 per cent over the 50 year time span being examined (Peart and Maclean, in press).

Although a steady increase has occurred in the number of such positions over time (there were, for example, 19 in 1949, 24 in 1959, 36 in 1969 and 79 in 1989) the rate of growth has not been as great as that which has occurred in the number of promotion positions available in the schools (Peart and Maclean, in press). Thus the number and range of career and promotion possibilities available for teachers in the administration and service areas have been relatively limited over time, and remain at the current time restricted.

Although there have been significant changes over the last half century in the nomenclature of promotion positions in the administrative and services areas, the actual structure and the hierarchy of promotion positions has changed little over this period (see Peart and Maclean, in press).

Appointments and Promotions Procedures within the Opportunity Structure

Having mapped out the opportunity structure that has existed for teachers in the Tasmanian Education Department, and the main changes that have occurred in this structure over time, attention will now be directed to examining the procedures and criteria used (as at 1988) to determine who is selected to occupy the various positions in the promotions hierarchy that applied to the primary, secondary and administrative/services sections of the Education Department. Changes in the appointment and promotion procedures over time will then be documented.

At the time data for the Careers in Education Project was being gathered and analysed the promotion system was organized in the following way:

Promotions Committee

The Promotions Committee had five members. There were three departmental representatives (including an independent chairman) and the Teachers Federation had two representatives who were elected by members.

Promotion Criteria

The criteria used in determining the promotion of teachers were set out in Regulation 66 of the Tasmanian Education Department. These were (in order of importance):

1 general suitability for the position;
2 level of professional skill;
3 professional qualifications;
4 length of professional service; and,
5 present position and status.

In applying these criteria the intention has been that the merit principle should apply.

Promotion Procedures

In order to determine the extent to which a teacher satisfies these promotion criteria, the Promotions Committee has examined the written reports submitted by the applicant's principal and superintendent. In order to adopt a common standard in reports, superintendents have made their recommendation according to the following scale: strongly recommended; recommended; merits consideration; does not merit consideration; and, unsuitable for the position sought. The committee has then submitted a recommendation to the Director of Personnel, who sent out the notification of appointments and promotions.

Appeals Procedure

Any teacher who felt aggrieved by the recommendation of the Promotions Committee could appeal to an Appeals Committee. This could be either against the appointment of another person or against his own non-appointment if no appointment was made to the position.

Appointments

The Director General of Education reserved the right to personally appoint directors, superintendents and some other officers in charge of special branches. These positions were not open to appeal. Other appointments which the Director General may have made, and which were not subject to appeal, were transfers between work locations at the same level in the promotion's hierarchy. For instance, a teacher may have wanted a transfer to enable a member of his family to obtain specialist medical treatment or for some similar reason.

The Director General of Education was appointed by the government of the day on a five year renewable contract.

Changes Over Time

The promotion procedures and criteria described above have applied to secondary teachers since 1963, and primary teachers since 1967. Before that time, and since 1930, the promotion procedures and criteria applied were different to those explained above. There were, for each of the primary and secondary sectors of the system, and for those in different promotion positions, two promotions lists: an *Ordinary Promotions List* and an *Accelerated Promotions List*. Teachers who were regarded as being particularly talented were placed on the accelerated promotions list, while all others were on the ordinary list. These two lists existed for teachers in each promotion position. A person's relative position on the list depended upon their level of seniority, so that those with the greatest years of service were highest on the list. When determining who should get promoted, those who were highest on each list were selected. A ratio of four to two was used, so that if six particular promotion positions needed to be filled, four would be selected from the top of the ordinary list and two from the top of the accelerated list. Under this system, anyone who stayed with the Education Department over a long period of time was virtually assured of gaining promotion.

Conclusion

This chapter has been concerned with discussing the opportunity structure of the Education Department in which state school teachers in Tasmania pursue their careers, and with documenting the main changes that have occurred in this opportunity structure over the last half century. Without a map of the opportunity structure in the Education Department the data on teacher careers and promotion, presented in Chapters 6, 7 and 8 (and the discussion of this data that occurs in Chapter 9) cannot be properly understood and adequately interpreted.

Chapter 5

Case Study of Teachers' Careers: Research Design and Procedures

Chapter 2 examined ways of conceptualizing careers, while Chapter 3 applied the conceptual framework developed to review what is currently known about the school teaching career. Attention was drawn to the various gaps that exist in the research and related literature on the teaching career; and it was noted that one purpose of the research reported upon in this book is to help fill in some of these gaps in the literature by examining the career and promotion patterns of state school teachers in Tasmania.

The present chapter explains the research framework adopted for this study, which developed logically out of the sociological concepts and research literature reviewed in Chapters 2 and 3; and the research methodology adopted for the study. In outlining and explaining the research design and procedures of the project reported on in this book it is important to place this study within its overall research context.

Data for this book on teachers' career comes (in varying degrees) from three research projects undertaken over a ten year period, between 1979 and 1989, all of which have been concerned with examining various aspects of the career and promotion patterns (and career perceptions) of government school teachers employed in Australia's smallest state, that of Tasmania. When taken together these studies provide a comprehensive, longitudinal picture of the careers of the state school teachers surveyed. These three studies are: the *Careers in Education Project*, for which material was collected between 1979 and 1984 on the career perceptions and behaviour of school teachers occupying various promotion positions in the Education Department of Tasmania; the *Teacher Mobility Study* which sought to discover how teachers view their futures in education at a time of declining promotion opportunities, and to ascertain what strategies they believe should be implemented to help make their careers more meaningful and satisfying, data for this study being collected between 1982 and 1984; and the *Women Teachers' Careers Study*, which probed the perceptions and behaviour of women school teachers in Tasmania, with particular reference to explaining why women are underrepresented in promotion positions, information being mainly collected between 1985 and 1988.

In these three inter-related studies data was collected in a variety of ways and from several sources: from Education Department records with regard to the career histories of teachers; through questionnaires being sent out to teachers in their workplaces in order to obtain information on their professional, academic and personal backgrounds, and on their views regarding various aspects of a career in the Education Department; by conducting individual and groups interviews with teachers in order to probe in depth their perceptions regarding teaching as an occupation; from records held by the Tasmanian Teachers Federation; and, from a wide variety of secondary sources.

The intention behind these studies was to gather information on an area of teacher behaviour about which little was currently known, and to examine the extent to which there was a match between the perceptions of individuals with regard to a career in teaching and the actual behaviour patterns of those concerned. The vast majority of the data presented in this book comes from *Careers in Education Project*; the findings of both the *Teacher Mobility Study* (Maclean et al., 1984) and *Women Teachers' Careers Project* (Maclean, 1989) being available elsewhere in published form.

Research Framework

The concepts examined in this research study are:

- Those that relate most directly to school teaching as an occupation that offers its incumbents both an occupational and an organizational *career*;
- The applicability of Roth's (1963) notion of *career timetables* to a study of the careers of school teachers;
- The relevance of the 'limited success' and 'unlimited success' *career anchorage perspectives* in explaining similarities and differences in the vertical mobility (promotion) patterns of teachers;
- The relative importance of what Howard Becker (1952) has called the 'horizontal aspect of career movement' (that is, *horizontal mobility*), compared to *vertical mobility*; and the relative importance of formal and informal 'career contingency factors' in explaining the career behaviour of teachers; and,
- The desirability of using both the *structural* and *phenomenological perspectives* for analysing careers in teaching; and the extent to which there is a 'match' between teachers actual behaviour and perceptions with regard to their occupational and organizational career.

Teachers' Career and Promotional Patterns

For the sake of convenience these concepts will be examined under five main headings, however it is important to remember that there is an important overlap, and interrelationship, between them. They come together into a coherent framework to determine the direction and approach adopted in this study.

Because these concepts were examined in some detail in Chapters 2 and 3, they will only be briefly referred to here when explaining the research framework developed for this study.

School Teaching as an Occupation that Offers a Career

School teaching is taken here to be an occupation which offers its recruits the opportunity of pursuing a career as defined in Chapter 2. The theoretical assumption upon which the study reported upon here is based is that the work related movements of teachers, in both the vertical and horizontal mobility sense, are not random. Teachers move between competing positions in ways which can be seen to form a pattern, and this equally applies to those in administrative and education service positions in head office, as it does to those employed in schools. If this assumption is valid it would be possible to identify and compare the *career patterns* adopted and created by various individuals and groups within teaching, as they seek out and follow the career lines available within their occupation and work organization.

Career patterns can be analysed in several ways, such as in terms of the extent and pattern of the geographical mobility associated with job moves. *Spiralists* (Mann, 1973), or career *transients* as Keown (1971) prefers to call them, are those individuals who display a willingness to freely move between geographical areas in an attempt to gain promotion or a more desirable work location, while *locals* (Keown, 1971) are those who are generally not willing to move between geographical regions in the pursuit of career advancement.

As was noted in Chapters 2 and 3 the term career may be used to refer to the characteristic work pattern of particular occupations (such as the medical career) or it may be used to refer to the patterned work activities that occur in particular organizations (such as a career in the public service). The concern here will be on examining school teaching as an occupation which offers its incumbents a highly structured and orderly *occupational career* and *organizational career* (Wilensky, 1961; Glaser, 1968; Talbert, 1986), within a particular multi-locational organization, the Education Department of Tasmania.

Another basic element of the framework used in this study is the notion of a career in teaching as being composed of a number of stages (Waller, 1936; Hall, 1948; Lortie, 1975), which are sequentially arranged. A teaching career may be conceived of as being the status passage of an individual through several work-related social roles over the length of their working life as a school teacher. The applicability of the five main stages in the teaching career, outlined in Chapter three, will be tested for the population of state school teachers surveyed in this study.

Roth's (1963) Notion of Career Timetables

As we noted in Chapter 2, Roth (1963) argues that in order to reduce uncertainty in their lives most people structure the time period through which uncertain events occur.

In the study reported upon here teachers are viewed as being members of an occupation in which it is likely to be useful to analyse occupational life and career patterns in terms of Roth's notion of career timetables.

In adopting this view attention becomes directed to several related ideas which Roth regards as relevant to the study of career timetables. Thus, in applying the notion of career timetables to the study of the careers of state school teachers in Tasmania, our attention becomes focused on answering the following types of questions:

1 What are the *timetable norms*, and *bench marks*, that develop for the teachers being studied, which serve to allow the teacher to internalize *time perspectives* and measure himself or herself against these?
2 With changes in the career opportunities available in teaching, which are closely linked to periods of growth and contraction in the education system, what changes have occurred in timetable perspectives during the course of an individual's career?
3 What are the *career maps* and *career strategies* adopted by teachers in their attempt to achieve success in their careers?
4 What are the *reference points* that have developed in the school teaching career from which individuals may predict and measure further progress? To what extent are these reference points clear cut and stable, and to what extent must they be discovered and interpreted through observation and interaction with others in the same career group?

Not all individuals are able to achieve the career timetable norms that develop within an occupation, so that the 'normal' career timetable does not apply to them except to show how much they have fallen by the wayside. It therefore becomes important to examine how *failure* is handled by both those who suffer the failure and by others who play a part in the control of their career timetables; and the extent to which *situational adjustment* occurs.

These are the types of questions this study will seek to answer in operationalising Roth's notion of career timetables as an important concept for the study of state school teachers in Tasmania.

Career Anchorage Perspectives

As was noted in Chapter 2, two main views are contained in the research literature regarding the career perspectives and orientations adopted by individuals within their occupation. Those who adopt what has been called the *unlimited success* model (e.g. Parsons, 1954) hold the view that most individuals in the world of work direct their energies at trying to achieve promotion in their career over their working life, the aim being to reach a promotion position which is as close as possible to the peak of the promotions hierarchy. If a person does not reach such a high promotion position it is believed that their self esteem suffers as a result.

An opposing viewpoint called the *limited success model* (e.g. Hughes, 1949; Mills, 1956) argues that most people are satisfied with either maintaining their current position within the promotions structure, or with gaining some modest advancement within their particular occupation or organization. No self esteem is believed to be lost because the degree of promotion achieved is of modest proportions.

Most recently Tausky and Dubin (1965) and Goldman (1978) have argued that these two models are complementary, because both are concerned with considering the same motivational mechanism, that of a *career anchorage perspective*. They argue that while some individuals do value top level occupational positions, and strive to achieve these through the length of their work life, others mainly value the progress they have already made in their occupation.

The applicability of the notion of 'career anchorage perspectives', and the extent to which the limited success and unlimited success model are complementary, will be tested for the group of state school teachers examined in this research study.

Relative Importance of Horizontal vs Vertical Mobility as Features of the School Teaching Career

One of the main ways in which the work careers of individuals, and their movement from one job location to another, can be analysed is in terms of horizontal and vertical mobility. As was noted in Chapter 2, *horizontal mobility* refers to a change of job at the same occupational status level, while *vertical mobility* refers to a job move which results in discernible change in status, prestige, power or other rewards (Caplow, 1954; Pavalko, 1971). In this study it is intended that both the vertical and horizontal mobility patterns of teachers be analysed.

Becker (1952) argues that it is largely the teachers' search for favourable work circumstances that gives rise to teacher mobility, and standardized career patterns of a type that stress horizontal rather than vertical moves. Amongst other things this study will test the applicability of Becker's (1952) results for state school teachers in Tasmania.

One of the concerns of the study reported upon here is with identifying the factors that influence the extent to which, and the rate at which, individuals and groups of teachers gain vertical mobility within their work organization. This interest directs our attention to examining matters such as the formal and informal factors that appear to influence promotion (Glaser, 1968; Tronc and Enns, 1969) including *career contingency factors* such as age, gender, marital status and sponsorship (Pavalko, 1971; Hilsum and Start, 1974; Lyons, 1981; Department of Education, 1982; Sampson, 1985).

Importance of Utilizing both the Structural and Phenomenological Perspectives in Studying Work Careers

As noted in Chapter 2 careers have both an objective/external and a subjective/internal aspect to them (Friedman, 1964; Lyons, 1981; Prick, 1989; Nias, 1989). The nature of the career pattern that develops for any particular individual over his working life is the outcome of the often subtle interplay that occurs between the objective and subjective aspects of his career. Thus, in studying the career patterns of state school teachers in Tasmania there is a two fold interest: first, to describe the actual career patterns of teachers; and, second, to examine the nature of the social reality which teachers construct about their careers out of the phenomena of experience. For instance, the actual characteristics of teachers who gain promotion to the top jobs will be examined alongside teacher perceptions regarding the characteristics of such highly successful teachers.

In view of what has been said this research study has been conceptualized in the following way. Teacher careers and promotion *occur* most commonly in systems, and so a structural description is necessary; but individuals also *make* careers within systems, and so it is also important to tap their perceptions of the structures within which they operate and negotiate. Thus there are two levels to the study: the first is the *structural* dimension; and, the second may be described broadly as *phenomenological*.

Drawing Parts of the Framework Together

In this chapter, five main streams of thought which arose from, or were supported by, the literature reviewed in Chapters 2 and 3 have been referred to. These have been ordered in a way which supports the following logical flow:

1 School teachers move between competing positions in an Education Department in a patterned rather than a random way, and so teaching can be regarded as being an occupation which offers its recruits the opportunity of pursuing a *career*. As they seek out, follow, or reject the career opportunities available to them within their occupation, and the Tasmanian Education Department, teachers adopt and create identifiable *career patterns*;
2 The attitudes and behaviour patterns which teachers adopt towards their careers are generally time related, and so it is appropriate to examine the career patterns that develop in terms of Roth's notion of *career timetables*;
3 In pursuing their careers teachers also develop a *career anchorage perspective* which will have an important influence upon the position in the promotions hierarchy they will seek to achieve in order to satisfy their particular career orientation and needs;
4 An important feature of careers in teaching is that many teachers are particularly concerned with achieving a desirable work location (i.e. *horizontal mobility*), which may be more important to them than gaining promotion. In view of this there is likely to be a close relationship between a teacher's career anchorage perspective and the relative importance they place upon horizontal *versus* vertical mobility. In addition, various career contingency factors exist which influence a teacher's pattern of vertical and horizontal mobility; and,
5 When considering careers in teaching it is important to recognize that they have both a *structural* (objective/external) and an *interpretive* (subjective/internal) aspect to them, both of which need to be examined if an understanding of careers in school teaching is to be achieved.

Methodology

The validity of the results of any research study depend upon the appropriateness of the procedures used to obtain them. The purpose of this section of the chapter is to describe the research methodology adopted in this research in order that the results reported in later chapters can be considered in the light of such things as the nature of the population studied and the instruments used to collect the data.

Basis for the Design

Aims

In terms of research design two aims were identified. The *first aim* was to obtain reliable data on the career histories of teachers employed in schools and personnel engaged in supervisory, advisory and administrative duties in the Education Department of Tasmania, in order that the actual career and promotion patterns of these personnel could be described and compared in terms of such dimensions as their vertical and horizontal mobility. This meant that 'objective' information on the career histories of teachers needed to be collected. The *second aim* was to identify and explain differences and similarities in the career patterns of those occupying various positions within the Education Department's promotions hierarchy, and to ascertain teacher perceptions regarding these matters. The intention here was to build up a picture of how teachers perceive both their own careers and those of others employed in the Department. This was the 'subjective social reality' aspect of careers in teaching.

Both of these aims had important implications for the design of the research study. In order to obtain reliable information on the career histories of teachers it was decided to use the teacher records housed in the personnel section of the Education Department of Tasmania. It was decided to obtain data on how teachers perceive their own career, and those of their Education Department colleagues, in two main ways: first, by administering a questionnaire to all teachers for whom career history data was collected; and, second, by conducting semi-structured interviews with individuals and groups of teachers regarding promotion and careers in teaching and the services areas.

Case study of one Australian State Education System

The research reported upon in this book examines teacher promotion and career patterns in one state education system in Australia, that of Tasmania. It was decided to adopt this approach for the following main reasons: first, as has been noted, there is a paucity of research on teacher careers, the research project reported here being the first major study of its type in Australia. In view of this it was decided that a thorough study of teachers in one education system, rather than a larger scale but more superficial study of a greater number of teachers in more than one state, would be the most appropriate and fruitful approach to adopt; and, some differences exist between the various Australian states and territories with regard to such things as the organization and structure of their school systems, and even the promotion criteria and procedures that are adopted. All of these would have a bearing on the career patterns of teachers. In view of this, it was decided that the most suitable approach to adopt to achieve the set aims was for the study to concentrate on examining teachers in only one state education system.

Teachers' Career and Promotional Patterns

Teachers in the Tasmanian Education system were the ones chosen for study. Other important reasons, in addition to ease of access, as to why this state was chosen, are that:

- Tasmania has a relatively small school system which employs some 5000 full-time teachers. Such an education system was ideally suited to this study because it was large and complex enough to provide a diverse range of career and promotion patterns and to make for reliable data gathering, and yet small enough to apply appropriate sampling methods within the resources available for the study; and
- The Tasmanian system is a particularly interesting one to study for a topic of this type, because it contains a wider variety of school types, including matriculation colleges, district schools and district high schools, in addition to the usual primary and high schools, than does any other Australian state. These particular features of the Tasmanian system added a further dimension to the study for they increased the range of possible career patterns available to teachers in that state compared to other Australian states and territories.

Teachers in Promotion Positions
In addition to limiting the study to state school teachers in one state, it was also decided further to limit the study to examining those state school teachers who occupy promotion positions within the promotions hierarchy of the state education system being examined. These teachers were personnel engaged in supervisory, advisory and administrative duties, such as the Director-General of Education, the directors of sections within the Department, superintendents, supervisors, and education officers in the various service branches of the Department, as well as those occupying promotion positions in schools, such as principals, vice-principals, senior master/mistresses and senior teachers. This means that the study concentrates upon examining those teachers who have gained at least their first promotion within the Education Department and who have therefore been successful in terms of achieved vertical mobility within the promotions hierarchy. In all, 1157 or almost a quarter of the state's 4816 full time teachers, occupied promotion positions.

It was felt that teachers in promotion positions would prove to be the most interesting and fruitful group to study. In addition to the fact that they are generally the ones with the longest established, and most complex career patterns, they are also the ones who occupy the positions of greatest power within the state schooling system, for they have decision-making roles which enable them to have a considerable impact on the nature and functioning of the school system.

In addition, these teachers are the ones who can potentially have a

Teachers' Careers: Research Design and Procedures

considerable effect on the career patterns of other teachers in the system since they have, to varying degrees, a 'selection function' to perform. For example, teachers rely upon the principal of the school in which he or she works, as well as the superintendent for their particular school district, to provide the Promotions Committee with written reports about their competence as a teacher and their suitability for promotion. Teachers in promotion positions are also potentially influential as role models after whom those occupying lower positions in the promotion hierarchy model their own behaviour, partly in an attempt to enhance their promotion chances. This means that these teachers in promotion positions are not only of interest because of the promotion positions they have achieved, and the career patterns they have established, but also because their ideas and perceptions about the operation of the system are in varying degrees likely to have an important influence on the promotion and career patterns of others.

The Survey Population

A total of 5564 teachers were employed in the Education Department of Tasmania at the time data was collected. This consisted of 4816 full time and 748 part-time teachers, 87.6 per cent of whom were employed in school, 2.2 per cent in non-school, and 10.2 per cent in miscellaneous positions.[1]

It was decided to delimit the survey population by excluding part-time teachers, those who had not as yet gained their first promotion within the Education Department, and infant mistresses because they occupy a position within the promotions hierarchy that has not generally been open to both males and females. Part-time teachers were excluded because they are not typical of most teachers. They do not have a full range of career and promotion opportunities available to them, since they lack job tenure and are ineligible for promotion. Teachers who had not achieved their first promotion were also excluded from the survey population because the primary focus in this study was upon the career patterns of those teachers who had clearly committed themselves to a career, and had at least achieved some promotion in teaching, success in achieving their first promotion being used as a yardstick for judging this.

Table 5.1 shows the status, number and distribution of full time teachers in schools, and personnel engaged in supervisory, advisory or administrative duties, according to their sex.

In view of the boundaries drawn, that is full time teachers occupying promotion positions, except for infant mistresses, the *theoretical population* for the study consisted of 1079 teachers. This consisted of 984 teachers employed in various promotion positions in schools, and a further 95

Teachers' Career and Promotional Patterns

Table 5.1 Status of full time teachers and personnel engaged in supervisory, advisory or administrative duties[a]

	Male	%	Female	%	Total
1. School Positions					
Principals	224	90.0	25	10.0	249
Vice Principals	86	73.5	31	26.5	117
Senior Masters/Mistresses	315	74.3	109	25.7	424
Senior Teachers	62	32.0	132	68.0	194
Infant Mistresses	—	—	78	100.0	78
Teachers	1004	31.8	2154	68.2	3158
Total	1691	40.1	2529	59.9	4220
2. Service Positions					
Directors/Deputy Directors	12	92.3	1	7.7	13
Superintendents	15	75.0	5	25.0	20
Supervisors	14	87.5	2	12.5	16
Principal Education Officers	10	83.3	2	16.7	12
Senior Education Officers	16	64.0	9	36.0	25
Education Officers	3	30.0	7	70.0	10
Senior Guidance Officers	3	50.0	3	50.0	6
Regional Guidance Officers	2	66.7	1	33.3	3
Guidance Officers	1	100	—	—	1
Total	76	73.3	30	26.7	106
3. Miscellaneous[1]:	166	33.9	324	66.1	490
Grand Total	1933	40.2	2883	598.0	4816

(Source: Education Department of Tasmania Personnel Records)

teachers employed in supervisory, advisory or administrative duties out-of-schools.

Mainly due to the limited resources available for conducting the research, it was necessary to sample the theoretical population. It was decided to include all teachers employed in the theoretical population in non-school promotion positions, because their number was relatively small, while for those employed in schools it was decided to include all of those occupying the top promotion positions (principals and vice principals) and a one in two (50 per cent) randomised sample of senior masters/mistresses (SMs) and senior teachers (STs). Thus, the *survey population* consisted of 770 teachers in promotion positions, of whom 675 (87.7 per cent) were employed in school and 95 (12.3 per cent) in non-school promotion positions.

Procedures for Gathering Data and Nomenclature Used

Education Department Records on Teachers' Career Histories (see Appendix 2) Data on the career histories of members of the survey population (770) were obtained from Education Department Records, this being referred to as *Stage 1* data. A separate card on every teacher, which contained a record of the employment history of the teacher concerned, since they first joined the Department, is housed in the Personnel Section of the Department. Each entry showed: the date on which the teacher was appointed to a particular school or service branch position; the name of the school or section of the Education Department to which they were appointed; and their promotion position, salary and allowances at the time of each appointment. Any breaks in the teacher's employment were also recorded.

Questionnaire to Teachers (see Appendix 3)
The number of teachers who actually received questionnaires (*Stage 2* data) was 737. The difference of 33 between the number in the survey population, and those who actually received questionnaires, consisted of teachers who were unavailable to complete the questionnaire because they were on long service, study or extended leave without pay, and so not able to be contacted at the time of the survey. The characteristics and career histories of these 'unavailable' teachers were examined to discover whether they had any 'special features' that were likely to influence the data collected from the survey population. They were found to be typical of the 737 who received the questionnaire.

Of those in the survey population (770) who actually *received* questionnaires (737), 717 (or 93.1 per cent) returned them completed. These will be referred to as the *total respondents* or N. Not all respondents replied to every question, those who did reply to any particular questions being referred to as *the respondents* or n. Only the career histories of the total respondents are reported on in this book, in order that there is a match between Stage 1 and Stage 2 data. The overall response rate of 93.1 per cent, with no major differences occurring between respondents and non-respondents, was high for a postal survey of this type. Full details regarding how this high response rate was achieved are presented elsewhere in Maclean (1988).

Teacher Interviews (see Appendix 4)
Stage 3 of the study involved semi-structured interviews with individuals and groups of teachers. (These will be referred to as *the interviewees*) The reason why these interviews were semi-structured in format was to ensure that even though certain key areas were covered, that interviewees had the freedom to raise and discuss any other issues which they regarded as important. All interviews were tape recorded and then transcribed to facilitate analysis. The purpose of conducting teacher interviews was to obtain qualitative, more detailed information about areas which, as a result of the analysis of stage 1 and 2 data, were identified as being of special interest.

Individual interviews were conducted throughout the state with a trial of forty men and women teachers occupying various promotion positions, thirty in schools and ten in service positions.

A total of five group interviews were also held to discuss, with men and women teachers occupying various promotion positions, the range of views and ideas obtained through the individual interviews. Approximately eight teachers were invited to attend each group discussion session. One purpose of the group interview was to ascertain the extent to which views expressed by individuals were shared by a wider group of teachers.

All personnel employed by the Education Department under the Teaching Services Act of 1932 are called teachers. This is regardless of whether they actually work in schools, or are engaged in supervisory or administrative duties in the head or a regional office. In this study the term *teacher* is used to refer to all personnel employed on a full time basis in the Tasmanian Education Department, under the provisions of the Education Act of 1932, regardless of whether they are classroom teachers, school administrators, or work out-of-schools. When more specific reference is made to particular groups of teachers, this will occur in terms of their promotion positions such as that of principal, vice principal or superintendent. When reference is made to *classroom teachers* this will relate only to those in SM and ST positions in schools.

When personnel employed by the Education Department in supervisory, advisory or administrative duties out-of-schools are referred to *en masse* they will be called *service personnel*.

Conclusion

This chapter explains the research framework adopted for this study which centred on five clusters of concepts arising from the research literature on occupational careers in general, and the teaching career in particular, reviewed in Chapters 2 and 3 of this book. It also outlines the research design and procedures adopted in the study, including the characteristics of the theoretical and survey populations, the sampling process adopted, and the main ways in which the data was collected.

In writing up the results the choice was between undertaking a progressive, step-by-step analysis and discussion of the data presented or else mainly reporting on the data without discussion and interpretation, this being left until a later chapter. Because each results chapter is, in a sense, self contained since they report on data collected through different means (Education Department Records; a questionnaire; and interviews), and in order to facilitate the blending together of the quantitative and qualitative information gathered, it was decided to adopt the latter approach.

Note

1 'Miscellaneous' includes a wide variety of personnel who do not necessarily have a background in classroom teaching, such as media officers, social workers, speech pathologists, etc.

Chapter 6

Personal and Professional Characteristics of Promoted Teachers

The purpose of this chapter is to describe the personal and professional characteristics of the promoted teachers who comprise the survey population for this study. The material presented was mainly collected through administering a questionnaire (see Appendix 3) to promoted teachers in the Education Department of Tasmania, and (to a lesser extent) from personnel records held within the Department and other sources of information within the Education Department and Teachers Federation.

The chapter is divided into three main sections:

1 Personal background details;
2 Academic and professional qualifications; and,
3 Factors and views related to promotion in teaching.

The format to be followed in most cases is that the data relating to promoted teachers as a whole will be reported upon first, after which comparisons will be made between various groups of teachers, such as those occupying different promotion positions, males and females, and those employed in the various sectors of the Education Department.

It is important to note when interpreting the data presented in this chapter that not every member of the survey population answered each and every question in the questionnaire, and so the statistics presented here refer to the actual number of respondents to each question. When the *total respondents* answered a particular question they will be referred to as N, while when not all the respondents answered a question those who did reply will be referred to as *the respondents* or n.

Personal Background Details

Gender

Just over three quarters (75.7 per cent) of the total respondents were male, and 24.3 per cent female, this proportion being similar for teachers

Table 6.1 Distribution of respondents according to gender (N = 717)

Promotion Position	Males		Females		Total	
	No.	%	No.	%	No.	%
School Positions						
Principals	211	90.9	21	9.1	232	100.0
Vice Principals	92	78.6	25	21.4	117	100.0
Snr. Masters/Mistresses	152	77.2	45	22.8	197	100.0
Senior Teachers	27	29.3	65	70.7	92	100.0
Total	482	75.5	156	24.5	638	100.0
Service Positions						
Directors	8	100	—	—	8	100.0
Superintendents	10	71.4	4	28.6	14	100.0
Supervisors	13	86.7	2	13.3	15	100.0
Principal Education Officers	10	83.3	2	16.7	12	100.0
Senior Education Officers	16	72.7	6	27.3	22	100.0
Senior Guidance Officers Regional Guidance Officers	4	50.0	4	50.0	8	100.0
Total	61	77.2	18	22.8	79	100.0
Grand Total	543	75.7	174	24.3	717	100.0

employed in both school and service branch positions (table 6.1) This means that a disproportionately large number of promotion positions in the Education Department of Tasmania were occupied by males, since 40.2 per cent of full time teachers were male and 59.8 per cent female.

As table 6.1 shows, the general trend was that the higher a teacher's status within the promotion hierarchy the more likely it was that the person concerned would be a man rather than a woman: that is, men were more likely than women to occupy the 'top jobs' in the Education Department. This was true for both school and service personnel. For example, the vast majority of those who occupied advisory, supervisory and administrative positions were men: of seventy-nine such positions, sixty-one (77.2 per cent) were occupied by men and eighteen (22.8 per cent) by women. In schools, fewer than a tenth (9.1 per cent) of principals were women, while less than a quarter (21.4 per cent) of vice principals were women. In addition, when the gender of teachers occupying the same type of promotion position in the Education Department were examined one finds that the higher status, better paid positions were generally held by men. For example, all principals of secondary schools and colleges were men, the few women who were principals being concentrated in the relatively small primary schools which had fewer than 200 pupils (see Chapter 7).

While 69 per cent of all promoted teachers were in what could be called 'lower level' promotion positions, men only occupied 36.6 per cent of these positions. This meant that the majority of promoted men and a minority of promoted women occupied the top positions in the promotions hierarchy.

Table 6.2 Distribution of respondents according to age (N = 717)

Age in Years	Males & Females No.	%
60 – 64	21	2.9
55 – 59	75	10.4
50 – 54	91	12.6
45 – 49	106	14.8
40 – 44	140	19.6
35 – 39	142	19.8
30 – 34	116	16.2
25 – 29	26	3.7
Total	717	100.0

At the vice principal level, 21.4 per cent (25) of these positions were held by women, and of these all except one were employed at the secondary level. The under representation of women in principal and vice principal positions at the primary school level needs examining, given the fact that the majority (80 per cent) of teachers teaching at the primary school level were women, and the majority of senior teachers (70.7 per cent), from whom those in the higher promotion positions were selected, were women.

Age

As Table 6.2 shows, almost three quarters (74.1 per cent) of the promoted teachers surveyed were under the age of fifty years, with 34.3 per cent being in their forties. The mean age of promoted teachers was 41.8 years, the mode forty years and the median 41.8 years, it being encouraging that the mean, mode and median are so close together. As one would expect, the higher a promotion position within the status hierarchy, the higher was the average age of incumbents, there being (in general) a positive correlation between length of service and promotion position occupied (Table 6.3).

However, it is important to recognize that there was often considerable variation around the mean when it came to the age of teachers occupying different promotion positions. For example, although the average age of superintendents was 51.7 years, the range was from forty-two years to sixty-two years; while for principals in schools and colleges the average age was 44.3 years and the range was between twenty-seven years and sixty-three years. This wide range in the ages of promoted teachers is one of the things examined in greater detail in Chapter 8 since one aspect of this study was concerned with studying atypical as well as typical career patterns with particular reference to the characteristics of the most rapidly promoted teachers. As one would expect the oldest

Table 6.3 Age characteristics of respondents according to promotion position (N = 717)

Promotion Position	Mean	Mode	Median	Range
School Positions:				
Principals (N = 232)	44.3	37	43.3	27–63
Vice Principals (N = 117)	43.8	40	43.0	31–60
Snr. Masters/Mistresses (N = 197)	39.9	36	38.0	27–63
Senior Teachers (N = 92)	40.7	46	40.0	26–60
Service Positions:				
Directors (N = 8)	53.3	51	51.5	49–60
Superintendents (N = 14)	51.7	56	52.5	42–62
Supervisors (N = 15)	50.3	44	50.0	39–64
PEO's (N = 12)	48.5	40	49.5	34–60
SEO's (N = 22)	43.1	36	41.5	31–58
Guidance Officers (N = 8)	42.3	32	35.5	32–63

Table 6.4 Distribution of respondents according to marital status, by gender (N = 716)

Status	Males		Females		Males & Females	
	No.	%	No.	%	No.	%
Single	31	5.7	27	15.6	58	8.1
Married	495	91.1	116	67.1	611	85.3
Separated/divorced	15	2.8	17	9.8	32	4.5
Widowed	1	0.2	13	7.5	14	2.0
Other	1	0.2	–	–	1	0.1
Total	543	100.0	173	100.0	716	100.0

group of teachers in promotion positions were those in the top service branch positions: that is, directors (av. 53.3 years of age), superintendents (av. 51.7 yrs. of age) and supervisors (av. 50.3 yrs. of age).

It is interesting to note from Table 6.3 that the average age of teachers occupying middle level promotion positions in schools was slightly lower than it was for those occupying equivalent promotion positions in service branches: 39.9 years for SMs and 40.7 years for STs compared to 43.1 years for senior education officers. This was also true for vice principals compared to PEOs who are their service branch equivalent (43.8 years compared to 48.5 years).

Marital Status/Size of Family

The vast majority of teachers in promotion positions were married (85.3 per cent), with fewer than a tenth (8.1 per cent) never having been married (Table 6.4). In terms of fertility rates, 82.4 per cent of teachers had three or fewer offspring, while a third had two children (Table 6.5).

A greater percentage of women than men in promotion positions

Teachers' Career and Promotional Patterns

Table 6.5 Distribution of respondents according to number of children, by gender (N = 709)

Number of Children	Males		Females		Males & Females	
	No.	%	No.	%	No.	%
Nil	68	12.5	57	34.1	125	17.6
1	36	6.6	20	12.0	56	7.9
2	190	35.1	46	27.5	236	33.3
3	142	26.2	25	15.0	167	23.6
4	65	12.0	10	6.0	75	10.6
5	34	6.3	8	4.8	42	5.9
6	7	1.3	1	0.6	8	1.1
Total	542	100.0	167	100.0	709	100.0

Table 6.6 Distribution of respondents according to relatives who are, or have been, teachers, by gender (N = 717)

Rank Order M & F	Relative	Male (N = 543)		Female (N = 174)		Males & Females	
		No.	%	No.	%	No.	%
1	Own husband/wife	229	42.2	30	17.2	259	36.1
2	Cousin(s) on mother's side	124	22.8	60	34.5	184	25.7
3	Own sister(s)	131	24.1	46	26.4	177	24.7
4	Cousin(s) on father's side	119	21.9	55	31.6	174	24.3
5	Own brother(s)	89	16.4	21	12.1	110	15.3
6	Own mother	69	12.7	28	16.1	97	13.5
7	Own father	62	11.4	21	12.1	83	11.6
8*	Other relatives	363	66.9	164	94.3	527	73.5

N.B. This table indicates the relatives of teachers of whom more than 10 per cent were teachers.
* Other relatives, apart from those in this table, as listed in the questionnaire.

were single (15.6 per cent compared to 5.7 per cent),[2] while promoted women had smaller families than did men (Table 6.5).

Occupational Inheritance

Respondents were asked to indicate which of their relatives were, or had been, teachers. Table 6.6 shows that, for this survey population, teachers tended to occur within families: over a third (36.1 per cent) of respondents had a spouse who was a teacher; 40 per cent had either a sister or a brother who was a teacher; and, a quarter (25.1 per cent) had either a mother or father who were themselves teachers. This occupational inheritance factor appears to be stronger for teachers than it is for those in other roughly comparable occupations. For example, in her study of medical practitioners Fett (1975) found that 14.6 per cent had a parent who was a doctor.

When asked whether or not they would encourage a son or daughter

Table 6.7 Distribution of respondents according to whether or not they would encourage a son or daughter to become a teacher

Response	Son		Daughter	
	No.	%	No.	%
Strongly encourage	19	2.7	27	3.9
Encourage	103	14.6	151	21.5
Neither encourage or discourage	531	75.1	482	68.8
Discourage	39	5.5	25	3.6
Strongly discourage	15	2.1	16	2.3
Total	707	100.0	701	100.0

Table 6.8 Father's occupation of respondents at the time teachers completed secondary school (N = 717)

Occupational Category*	No.	%
1 Professional	120	16.7
2 Managerial	104	14.5
3 White collar	82	11.4
4 Skilled manual	81	11.3
5 Semi skilled manual	120	16.7
6 Unskilled manual	60	8.4
7 Farmers	94	13.1
8 Farm labourers	1	0.1
9 No occupation, as listed above	55	7.7
Total	717	100.0

* The occupational status classification adopted is that by Broom and Lancaster–Jones, 1976.

to become a teacher (Table 6.7) the vast majority of respondents indicated that they would neither encourage or discourage a son (75.1 per cent) or daughter (68.8 per cent) to enter this occupation. However, more would encourage or strongly encourage a daughter (25.4 per cent) than a son (17.3 per cent) to become a teacher, which implies that teaching was viewed as being a more suitable occupation for women than men.

Social Class Background

The social class background of promoted teachers, as indicated by fathers' and mothers' normal occupation at the time the respondents themselves completed their secondary schooling, was examined. An interesting pattern emerges (Tables 6.8 and 6.9).

With regard to fathers' occupation (Table 6.8), for promoted teachers as a whole the distribution was roughly comparable for four of the occupational status categories listed, these being professional, managerial, semi-skilled manual and farmers. The greatest proportion of promoted

Table 6.9 Mother's occupation of respondents at the time teachers completed secondary school (N = 717)

Occupational Category*	No.	%
1 Professional	43	6.0
2 Managerial	14	2.0
3 White collar	—	—
4 Skilled manual	26	3.6
5 Semi skilled manual	3	0.4
6 Unskilled manual	24	3.3
7 Farmers	18	2.5
8 Farm labourer	—	—
9 No occupation as listed above	589	82.1
Total	717	100.0

* The occupational status classification adopted is that by Broom and Lancaster – Jones, 1976.

teachers' fathers were either professionals (16.7 per cent) or semi-skilled manual workers (16.7 per cent). When some categories are collapsed into one another, we find that 42.6 per cent of promoted teachers had fathers who were professional/managerial/white-collar workers, 36.4 per cent were from the homes of manual workers, 13.2 per cent had fathers who were farmers or farm labourers, and 7.7 per cent were from homes where the father had no occupation.

With regard to mothers' occupation (Table 6.9), it appears that the vast majority of teachers had mothers who were not employed outside the home (82.1 per cent). Of those whose mothers were members of the labour force (128), approximately a third were in professional, 20.3 per cent in managerial and 14 per cent in skilled manual employment.

Academic and Professional Qualifications

Age Group Trained to Teach

As Table 6.10 shows, the vast majority of teachers (91.9 per cent) surveyed were trained in their course of teacher education to teach a specific age group of children, whether it be infant (4.9 per cent), primary (36.3 per cent), secondary (37.0 per cent), or both primary and secondary school (13.7 per cent). Only 6.4 per cent were not trained to teach any particular age group.

Length of Teacher Training

With regard to the length of the pre-service (or initial) teacher education course undertaken by respondents (Table 6.11), almost half (47.7 per

Table 6.10 Distribution of respondents according to age group of pupils trained to teach during initial teacher training (N = 716)

Age Group	No.	%
Infant	35	4.9
Primary	260	36.3
Secondary	265	37.0
Primary/Secondary	98	13.7
Not trained for specific age range	46	6.4
Other (not specified clearly)	12	1.7
Total	716	100.0

Table 6.11 Distribution of respondents according to years of preservice teacher training (N = 717)

Years of Training	No.	%
1 year trained	5	0.7
2 year trained	135	18.9
3 year trained	227	31.7
4 year trained	341	47.7
Untrained	2	0.3
Other (not specified clearly)	7	0.7
Total	717	100.0

cent) were four year trained teachers, approximately a third (31.7 per cent) three year trained, and almost a fifth (18.9 per cent) had trained for two years.

Further Study

The vast majority of teachers (81.6 per cent) were not studying for any further qualification relevant to their career; while of the 132 teachers who were undertaking further study, 41 per cent of these were studying for a Master's Degree, and the remainder (57 per cent) for a Bachelor's Degree (Table 6.12).

Graduate/Non-graduate Status

In this study a graduate is defined as being a teacher who has a degree from a university or college of advanced education, while a non-graduate is a person whose highest and only academic and/or professional qualification is a diploma or certificate from a university, college of advanced education or teacher's college.

Teachers' Career and Promotional Patterns

Table 6.12 Distribution of respondents according to whether they were studying for a qualification relevant to their career (N = 717)

Item	No.	%
Not studying for qualification	585	81.6
Bachelor's Degree	63	8.8
Master's Degree	45	6.3
Diploma/Certificate	8	1.1
Doctorate	2	0.3
Matriculation	1	0.1
Other qualification	13	1.8
Total	717	100.0

Table 6.13 Distribution of respondents according to graduate/non-graduate status, by gender (N = 717)

Status	Male		Female		Total	
	No.	%	No.	%	No.	%
Graduate	358	65.9	96	55.2	454	63.3
Non-Graduate	185	34.1	78	44.8	263	36.7
Total	543	100.0	174	100.0	717	100.0

Table 6.14 Distribution of respondents according to graduate/non-graduate status, by sector of employment (N = 717)

Sector	Graduate		Non-Graduate		Total	
	No.	%	No.	%	No.	%
Non-School Positions	75	94.9	4	5.1	79	100
Secondary Schools	228	80.3	56	19.7	284	100
District Schools	43	55.8	34	44.2	77	100
Primary Schools	110	39.7	167	60.3	277	100
Total	454	63.3	263	36.7	717	100

Over a half of the respondents (63.3 per cent) had a degree from a university or college of advanced education (Table 6.13).

As one would expect (Table 6.14), a greater proportion of promoted teachers in the secondary school sector (80.3 per cent) were graduates than were those in the primary sector (39.7 per cent). This is in keeping with the fact that most secondary school teachers were trained in universities while those employed in primary school were more likely to be trained in teacher's colleges, the latter not being degree awarding bodies.

Almost three quarters (74.9 per cent) of the principals of post primary schools surveyed had a degree, while 39.8 per cent of male primary school principals had degrees. A considerable variation occurred in the

Table 6.15 Distribution of respondents according to graduate/non-graduate status by promotion position (N = 717)

Promotion Position	Graduate No.	%	Non-Graduate No.	%	Total No.	%
School Positions						
Principals	123	53.0	109	47.0	232	100
Vice Principals	82	70.1	35	29.9	117	100
S.M.'s	144	73.1	53	26.9	197	100
S.T.'s	30	32.6	62	67.4	92	100
Total	379	59.4	259	40.6	638	100
Service Positions						
Directors	8	100.0	—	—	8	100
Superintendents	14	100.0	—	—	14	100
Supervisors	13	86.7	2	13.3	15	100
P.E.O.'s	12	100.0	—	—	12	100
S.E.O.'s	20	90.9	2	9.1	22	100
Guidance Officers	8	100.0	—	—	8	100
Total	75	94.9	4	5.1	79	100
Grand Total	454	63.3	263	36.7	717	100

qualifications held by principals in different types of post primary schools. While all the principals in matriculation colleges and high schools had a degree, less than half (47.1 per cent) of those in district schools had a degree. For the survey population, 75.5 per cent of vice principals in post primary schools had been awarded a degree, the proportion varying from 89.5 per cent in high schools and matriculation colleges to 27.3 per cent in district schools.

A smaller percentage of male (73.8 per cent) than female (85.7 per cent) VPs in post primary schools had a degree.

It is interesting to note that almost a third of vice principals in primary schools had a degree, which means that a higher proportion of VPs than principals in primary schools had been awarded this qualification.

As Table 6.15 shows, just over half (53 per cent) of the principals surveyed were graduates, while 70.1 per cent of vice principals had a degree. The explanation for this discrepancy between principals and vice principals is that 66 per cent of principals were in primary schools and so they were likely to have been trained in a non-degree awarding teachers college, while most (87 per cent) VPs were employed in secondary colleges, high schools and district schools and so were most likely university trained. This also helps explain why a larger proportion of senior masters/mistresses (73.1 per cent) than senior teachers (32.6 per cent) were graduates.

With the exception of a small proportion of supervisors and senior education officers, all teachers employed in service positions were graduates.

Table 6.16 Main subject specialisms of respondents with degree qualifications (N = 386)*

Main Subject	No.	%
History	159	41.2
Political Science	94	24.4
English	84	21.8
Geography	67	17.4
Psychology	57	14.8
Mathematics	54	14.0
Ancient Civilizations	38	9.8
French	37	9.6
Chemistry	36	9.3
Physics	35	9.1

* — Only subjects chosen by more than 9 per cent of teachers are included.
Some respondents had more than one subject specialism.

Table 6.17 Teaching method areas of respondents (n = 639)

Method Area	No.	%
1 Primary method	119	18.6
2 Mathematics	96	15.0
3 English	82	12.8
4 No specialist method	77	12.2
5 History	41	6.4
6 General secondary method	38	5.9
7 Physical education	35	5.5
8 Other method areas*	151	23.6
Total	639	100.0

* The other method areas were widely and thinly distributed between the other 48 categories listed in the questionnaire.

Subject Specialization

The subject specialisms of degree holders is shown in Table 6.16. What stands out from this table is the relatively large proportion of degree holders in promotion positions who had qualifications in the humanities/social science/language areas, with a minority being qualified in maths/science.

The survey population were also asked to indicate the teaching method areas in which they specialized during their course of pre-service teacher training, regardless of the length and type of training. Table 6.17 shows that the largest proportion of teachers (18.6 per cent) specialised in primary method, while the others undertook a variety of method areas such as maths (15.0 per cent), English (12.8 per cent), history (6.4 per cent) and physical education (5.5 per cent). Just over a tenth (12.2 per cent) of the survey population appeared to have no particular specialist subject in their course of teacher training, although there did seem to be

Table 6.18 Subjects taught by respondents employed in schools (N = 606)

Subject	No.	%
No specialist subject e.g. Prim/Infant; Sec. Gen. Studies	178	29.4
Non teaching position i.e. less than 20% of a F.T. teaching timetable	157	25.8
Mathematics	79	13.0
English	50	8.3
Science	35	5.8
Other subjects*	107	17.7
Total	606	100.0

* The other subjects taught were widely distributed between the various subject areas listed in the questionnaire.

some confusion regarding this question, as reflected by the relatively high non-response rate of 12.2 per cent. Given the material reported upon elsewhere in this chapter, it can be reasonably assumed that a substantial proportion of the 151 teachers who indicated 'other method areas' were trained to work in secondary schools.

Subjects Taught in Schools

Over a quarter (29.4 per cent) of promoted teachers in schools were teaching no specialist subject, which meant that they were either teaching primary age children or were teaching subjects such as general or vocational studies in a high or district/area school. A quarter (25.8 per cent) occupied a non-teaching position in schools, while the remainder taught one (or two) of a variety of subjects such as maths, English or science (Table 6.18).

Factors and Views Related to Promotion

Satisfactions Associated with Pursuit of a Career in Teaching

One facet of many people's lives is his or her work career which, in this research, was defined as being long term paid involvement in a particular profession or occupation. Respondents were asked to indicate how important to their overall personal satisfaction was the pursuit of a career (Table 6.19). The overwhelming majority (90.8 per cent) said that it was an important (47.0 per cent) or very important (43.8 per cent) facet of their lives, while 3.4 per cent said it was unimportant or very unimportant, and 5.9 per cent were uncertain of its importance.

Teachers' Career and Promotional Patterns

Table 6.19 Respondents' views regarding relative importance to overall personal satisfaction of pursuing a career (n = 715)

Important	Male		Female		Males & Females	
	No.	%	No.	%	No.	%
Very Important	232	42.9	81	46.6	313	43.7
Important	252	46.5	84	48.3	336	47.0
Uncertain of its importance	36	6.7	6	3.4	42	5.9
Unimportant	18	3.3	2	1.1	20	2.8
Very unimportant	3	0.6	1	0.6	4	0.6
Total	541	100.0	174	100.0	715	100.0

Table 6.20 Respondents' main satisfactions with teaching in schools (n = 712)

Rank Order	Item*	No.	%
1	Economic security	475	66.3
2	Staff-pupil relationships	394	55.0
3	Holidays	370	51.6
4	Opportunity to practice own ideas	305	42.5
5	Staffroom relationships	266	37.1
6	Working hours	192	26.8
7	Relationship with parents of pupils	160	22.3
8	Pastoral care given to individual pupils	159	22.2
9	Promotion prospects	139	19.4
10	Time to pursue personal interests	124	17.3
11	Consultation between principal and staff	118	16.5
12	Opportunity to meet parents of pupils	82	11.4

* Only items chosen by more than 10 per cent of respondents are listed.

Satisfactions and Dissatisfactions with Teaching in Schools

The questionnaire listed thirty-eight items relating to various aspects of teaching as an occupation (Appendix 3.2). Teachers were asked to select up to five items which they regarded to be the most satisfying, and up to five items which they considered to be the most unsatisfying features of teaching in schools. Tables 6.20 and 6.21 list in rank order the satisfactions and dissatisfactions with teaching that were selected by more than 10 per cent of the respondents.

Table 6.20 provides interesting insights into promoted teachers attitudes regarding the attraction of various facets of teaching as an occupation. Of particular interest is the fact that 'economic security' is the most chosen satisfaction with teaching. In fact, of the three factors that were selected by over 50 per cent of the teachers surveyed, two (economic security and holidays) relate to what may be called 'industrial' or working condition matters, while only one (staff-pupil relationships) refers to what may be called 'professional' matters.

Personal and Professional Characteristics of Promoted Teachers

Table 6.21 Respondents' main dissatisfactions with teaching in schools (N = 717)

Rank Order	Item*	No.	%
1	Size of classes: general	280	39.1
2	Pressure at work	278	38.8
3	Interruptions to lessons	246	34.3
4	Status of the profession in society	203	28.3
5	Extent of duties allocated e.g. playground supervision	190	26.5
6	School/classroom accommodation	187	26.1
7	Pupil discipline	127	17.7
8	Staffroom accommodation	114	15.9
9	Guidance offered by advisors/superintendents	109	15.2
10	Extent of extracurricula commitment required	102	14.2
11	Promotion prospects	97	13.5
12	Consultation between staff of different schools	83	11.6

* Only items chosen by more than 10 per cent of respondents are listed.

Table 6.22 Female respondents' main satisfactions with teaching in schools (n = 173)

Rank Order	Item*	No.	%
1	Staff-pupil relationships	126	72.6
2	Economic security	92	53.2
3	Opportunity to practice own ideas	74	42.8
= 4	Holidays	67	38.7
= 4	Staffroom relationships	67	38.7
6	Relationships with parents	49	28.3
7	Working hours	44	25.4
8	Pastoral care given to individual pupils	43	24.9
9	Opportunity to meet parents	37	21.4
10	Opportunity to pursue further qualifications	28	16.2
11	Time to pursue academic interests	21	12.1
12	Promotion prospects	20	11.6

* Only items chosen by more than 10 per cent of respondents are listed.

As Table 6.21 shows, there was less overall agreement about the dissatisfactions associated with teaching in schools, no item being selected by more than 40 per cent of those surveyed. It is interesting to note that the dissatisfactions with teaching in schools mainly refer to teaching related aspects of the work, such as size of classes, pressure of work, and the extent of extra duties (for instance, playground supervision), rather than to the more 'industrial' type matters such as level of remuneration or length of holidays.

There was some difference of opinion between men and women promoted teachers with regard to satisfactions and dissatisfactions associated with teaching in schools.

In terms of the satisfactions of teaching in schools, males (Table 6.23) rated economic security and holidays more highly than did women (Table 6.22), while women placed a greater emphasis on staff-pupil relationships; pastoral care given to individual pupils; and contact with

Table 6.23 Male respondents' main satisfactions with teaching in schools (n = 539)

Rank Order	Item*	No.	%
1	Economic security	383	71.1
2	Staff-pupil relationships	359	66.6
3	Holidays	303	56.2
4	Opportunity to practice own ideas	231	42.9
5	Staffroom relationships	199	36.9
6	Working hours	148	27.5
7	Promotion prospects	119	22.1
8	Relationship with parents	111	20.6
9	Time to pursue personal interests	109	20.2
10	Consultation between principal and staff	86	16.0

* Only items chosen by more than 10 per cent of respondents are listed.

Table 6.24 Female respondents' main dissatisfactions with teaching in schools (n = 170)

Rank Order	Item	No.	%
1	Size of classes: general	77	45.3
2	Pressure at work*	72	42.4
3	Interruptions to lessons	63	37.1
4	Extent of non-professional work required	61	35.9
5	Extent of duties allocated e.g. playground supervision	59	34.7
6	School/classroom accommodation	46	27.1
7	Status of the profession in society	40	25.9
= 8	Allocation of free periods	27	15.9
= 8	Consultation between staffs of different schools	27	15.9
10	Pupil discipline	24	14.1
11	Promotion prospects	23	13.5
12	Extent of extra curricula commitment	22	12.9
= 13	Time to pursue personal interests	21	12.4
= 13	Guidance offered by advising superintendents	21	12.4

* Only items chosen by more than 10 per cent of respondents are listed.

parents. There was little difference between men and women teachers regarding satisfactions associated with staffroom relationships, opportunity to practise own ideas and working hours. Promotion prospects were a greater source of satisfaction for men than women.

When the major satisfactions associated with the current promotion position occupied by those employed in non-school advisory. supervisory or administrative positions (Table 6.26) are examined one finds that the emphasis was less upon industrial matters, such as economic factors and holidays, and more upon those satisfactions that are closely linked to the specific nature of the work being undertaken, such as consultation with staff in different schools (90.0 per cent), opportunity to practise own ideas (81.8 per cent) and time to pursue academic interests (61.4 per cent). The satisfactions chosen stress autonomy, and the opportunity for professional development through the pursuit of personal interests, as well as

Table 6.25 Male respondents' main dissatisfactions with teaching in schools (n = 530)

Rank Order	Item*	No.	%
1	Pressure at work	206	38.9
2	Size of classes: general	203	38.3
3	Interruptions to lessons	186	35.1
4	Status of the profession in society	163	30.8
5	School/classroom accommodation	141	26.6
6	Extent of duties allocated e.g. playground supervision	131	24.7
7	Pupil discipline	103	19.4
8	Guidance offered by advisors/superintendents	88	16.6
9	Extent of non-professional work required	84	15.8
10	Staffroom accommodation	83	15.7
11	Extent of extra-curricula commitment	80	15.1
12	Promotion prospects	74	14.0
13	Influence of external exams	58	10.9

* Only items chosen by more than 10 per cent of respondents are listed.

Table 6.26 Satisfactions with current promotion position of respondents employed in non-school advisory, supervisory or administrative positions (n = 44)

Rank Order	Item*	No.	%
1	Consultation with variety of staff in different schools	40	90.9
2	Opportunity to practice own ideas	36	81.8
3	Time to pursue personal interests	30	68.2
4	Time to pursue academic interests	26	59.1
5	Pastoral care with regard to teachers in schools	16	36.4
6	Staffroom relationships	12	27.3
7	Relationships with parents of pupils	10	22.7
= 8	Working hours	6	13.6
= 8	Status of the profession in society	6	13.6

* Only those items chosen by more than 10 per cent of respondents are listed.

those associated with the chance to interact with a wide range of teachers and pupils in schools. There is also a greater element of agreement between those not employed in schools regarding the main satisfactions associated with their employment. However, this table needs to be interpreted with some caution because of the relatively low response rate (55.7 per cent) to the question.

Table 6.27 shows the main dissatisfactions with their current promotion position expressed by respondents employed in non-school promotion positions. As was the case with those working in schools, pressure at work and extra curricular commitments were ranked highly. Other dissatisfactions of service personnel, which were not of as great a concern to those employed in schools, included long working hours, lack of sufficient holidays, and insufficient time to pursue own interests. Due to the relatively low response rate (54 per cent) to this question, however, the results should be interpreted with some caution.

Table 6.27 Dissatisfactions with current promotion position of respondents employed in non-school advisory, supervisory or administrative positions (n = 44)

Rank Order	Item*	No.	%
1	Pressure at work	40	90.9
= 2	Extent of extra curricular commitment required	29	65.9
= 2	Long working hours	29	65.9
4	Limited promotion prospects	26	59.1
5	Relationships with those in some schools	11	25.0
= 6	Time and opportunity to pursue future qualifications	9	20.5
= 6	Lack of holidays	9	20.5
= 8	Relationship with parents	6	13.6
= 8	Extent of extra duties allocated	6	13.6
= 8	Extent of non-professional work required	6	13.6

* Only items chosen by more than 10 per cent of respondents are listed.

Table 6.28 Distribution of respondents according to whether they would feel (or have felt) loss or gain if they were to (or have) left the classroom for an administrative type promotion position (n = 716)

Item	Males		Females		Males & Females	
	No.	%	No.	%	No.	%
Much greater loss than gain	74	13.7	29	16.7	103	14.4
Greater loss than gain	69	12.7	24	13.8	93	13.0
Equal loss & gain	217	40.0	84	48.3	301	42.0
Greater gain than loss	138	25.5	26	14.9	164	22.9
Much greater gain than loss	44	8.1	11	6.3	55	7.7
Total	542	100.0	174	100.0	716	100.0

Benefit/Loss Associated with Leaving the Classroom for Promotion

Respondents were asked to indicate the extent to which they did (or believed that they would) feel gain or loss as a result of leaving the classroom for an administrative type post, either in or outside schools. Just over a quarter (27.4 per cent) indicated they did (or felt that they would) feel much greater or greater loss than gain through making such a career move, 30.6 per cent did or expected to feel much greater or greater gain than loss, and 42 per cent were ambivalent about the matter (Table 6.28).

Number of Times Moved Place of Residence

Promoted teachers were asked to specify the number of times they had moved their place of residence directly as a result of achieving promotion

Table 6.29 Number of times respondents moved place of residence as a result of gaining promotion, by gender (n = 716)

Number of Moves	Males No.	%	Females No.	%	Males & Females No.	%
No move/s	153	28.2	150	86.7	303	42.3
1 "	118	21.7	13	7.5	131	18.3
2 "	80	14.7	5	2.9	85	11.9
3 "	66	12.2	4	2.3	70	9.8
4 "	51	9.4	—	—	51	7.1
5 "	39	7.2	1	0.6	40	5.6
6 "	28	5.2	—	—	28	3.9
7 "	6	1.0	—	—	6	0.8
8 "	—	—	—	—	—	—
9 "	2	0.4	—	—	2	0.3
Total	543	100.0	173	100.0	716	100.0

(Table 6.29). A substantial proportion of teachers (42.3 per cent) had never moved their place of residence as a result of gaining promotion, while a further 30.2 per cent had moved once or twice. The vast majority (86.7 per cent) of women had never moved their place of residence as a result of gaining promotion, with the men teachers surveyed being much more mobile in this regard than were the women.

As Table 6.30 shows, the trend appears to be that the higher a teacher's position in the promotions hierarchy within schools the greater the number of times they had moved their place of residence as a result of achieving promotion. Frequency of move was also positively correlated with level achieved in the promotions hierarchy. The position was less straight forward for service personnel, where a clear trend did not emerge regarding number of moves of place of residence and an individual's position in the promotion hierarchy.

Likelihood of Achieving Further Promotion

Forty two percent of teachers rated their chances of gaining further promotion with the Education Department of Tasmania (Table 6.31) as being either good (30.9 per cent) or excellent (11.0 per cent), while a third rated their chances as being fair. Of the remaining teachers, 25 per cent rated their chances as being either poor (14.0 per cent) or non-existent (11.0 per cent), the majority (55 per cent) of these being teachers within five years of retirement who were unlikely, because of their age, to have many promotion opportunities available to them. A greater proportion of men (46.2 per cent) than women (28.7 per cent) rated their chances as either excellent or good, whereas a greater proportion of women (31.0

Teachers' Career and Promotional Patterns

Table 6.30 Number of times respondents moved place of residence as a result of gaining promotion, by promotion position occupied (n = 716)

Promotion Position		Nil	1	2	3	4	5	6	7	8	9	Total
School Positions												
Principals	No.	40	26	34	37	35	33	19	6	—	2	232
	%	17.3	11.3	14.8	15.9	15.1	14.2	8.2	2.3	—	0.9	100%
V. Principals	No.	46	23	15	18	9	4	2	—	—	—	117
	%	39.3	19.7	12.8	15.4	7.7	3.4	1.7	—	—	—	100%
S.M.'s	No.	111	61	19	3	—	1	1	—	—	—	196
	%	56.5	31.3	9.7	1.5	—	0.5	0.5	—	—	—	100%
S.T.'s	No.	69	11	8	3	1	—	—	—	—	—	92
	%	75.0	12.0	8.6	3.3	1.1	—	—	—	—	—	100%
Service Positions												
Dir.'s	No.	1	—	1	2	—	—	4	—	—	—	8
	%	12.5	—	12.5	25.0	—	—	50.0	—	—	—	100%
Supt.'s	No.	4	1	2	4	1	—	2	—	—	—	14
	%	28.6	7.1	14.3	28.6	7.1	—	14.3	—	—	—	100%
Supvrs.	No.	7	3	3	1	—	1	—	—	—	—	15
	%	46.6	20.0	20.0	6.7	—	6.7	—	—	—	—	100%
P.E.O.'s	No.	4	1	1	1	4	1	—	—	—	—	12
	%	33.4	8.3	8.3	8.3	33.4	8.3	—	—	—	—	100%
S.E.O.'s	No.	15	4	1	1	1	—	—	—	—	—	22
	%	68.3	18.2	4.5	4.5	4.5	—	—	—	—	—	100%
Guidance Officers	No.	6	1	1	—	—	—	—	—	—	—	8
	%	75.0	12.5	12.5	—	—	—	—	—	—	—	100%
TOTAL	No.	303	131	85	70	51	40	28	6	—	2	716
	%	42.3	18.3	11.9	9.8	7.1	5.6	3.9	0.8	—	0.3	100%

Table 6.31 Respondents' estimated chances of gaining further promotion, by gender (n = 706)

Chances	Males		Females		Males & Females	
	No.	%	No.	%	No.	%
Excellent	71	13.3	7	4.1	78	11.0
Good	176	32.9	42	24.6	218	30.9
Fair	164	30.7	69	40.4	233	33.1
Poor	71	13.3	28	16.4	99	14.0
No chance	53	9.8	25	14.6	78	11.0
Total	535	100.0	171	100.0	706	100.0

per cent) than men (23.1 per cent) rated their chances as poor, or as having no chance at all.

It is interesting to note that of those people working in schools, the higher a teacher's position in the promotions hierarchy the better they rated their chances of gaining further promotion; and that senior teachers rated their chances of gaining promotion higher than did senior masters (Table 6.32).

Table 6.32 Respondents' estimated chances of gaining further promotion, according to promoting position occupied (N = 717)

Chances	Princ. (N=232) %	V.P. (N=117) %	S.M. (N=197) %	S.T. (N=92) %	Dir. (N=8) %	Supt. (N=14) %	Supvrs. (N=15) %	PEO (N=12) %	SEO (N=22) %	Guidance (N=8) %
Excellent	12.7	14.2	8.2	6.7	—	7.1	13.3	16.7	22.8	12.5
Good	38.6	35.4	21.4	34.4	37.5	71.6	13.3	25.0	31.8	12.5
Fair	23.7	34.5	41.8	41.1	—	21.3	26.7	25.0	22.8	50.0
Poor	10.5	8.8	18.9	13.3	37.5	—	—	25.0	18.1	—
No chance	14.5	7.1	9.7	4.4	25.0	—	46.7	8.3	4.5	25.0

Promotion Inside or Outside Schools

More than half the respondents (59.2 per cent) indicated that when they considered their career and promotion in the Education Department, they mainly thought in terms of the range of positions available in schools. Almost a tenth (9.6 per cent) mainly considered their career and promotion in terms of outside schools, and just under a third (31.2 per cent) in terms of both school and service positions. There was little difference between males and females in their outlook regarding this matter (Table 6.34).

Considerable differences occurred in the outlook of teachers regarding this matter depending upon their current promotion position in the Education Department (Table 6.33). The majority of individuals in non-school promotion positions (directors, supervisors, superintendents and PEOs) mainly viewed their future careers in the Education Department in terms of non-school positions. Thus it does appear that once a teacher obtains an advisory, supervisory or administrative position away from schools, they are unlikely to seriously consider the possibility of returning to work in schools. For instance, only 4.5 per cent of senior education officers mainly considered their future career in terms of positions in schools, while for senior masters/mistresses and senior teachers (who occupy an equivalent position in the promotions hierarchy) the majority (70 per cent) mainly thought of their future career in terms of school positions.

Attitudes regarding Desirable Characteristics of Schools in which Teachers are Employed

In order to ascertain teachers' views about the characteristics of a desirable work location, with regard to a school's size, geographical location and the socio-economic status of pupils attending the school, teachers were asked to respond to several statements regarding these matters.

City versus Country Location:
The vast majority (80.8 per cent) of teachers either agreed (59.3 per cent) or strongly agreed (21.5 per cent) with the statement that most teachers prefer to work in city rather than country schools. However, when asked to indicate their own personal preference regarding this matter, there was much less agreement: 36.4 per cent indicated that they would prefer to work in city rather than country schools, while just over half (51.6 per cent) expressed a preference for working in country areas (Table 6.35).

Large versus Small Schools:
When asked for their opinion as to whether or not most teachers prefer to work in large rather than small schools, just over a quarter (26.8 per cent)

Table 6.33 Respondents' view regarding pursuit of a career in the Education Department in or outside schools, according to promotion position occupied

Work Location	Princ. (N = 232) %	V.P. (N = 117) %	S.M. (N = 197) %	S.T. (N = 92) %	Dir. Supt.* Supvrs. (N = 37) %	PEO (N = 12) %	SEO (N = 22) %	Guidance (N = 8) %
In Schools	67.7	65.0	57.4	81.8	5.4	—	4.5	—
Outside Schools	5.6	1.7	3.6	2.2	56.8	58.3	45.5	87.5
In and outside Schools	26.7	33.3	39.1	16.3	37.8	41.7	50.0	12.5

* These service personnel have been bunched together because they are all in non-school positions and share very similar views regarding this matter.

Teachers' Career and Promotional Patterns

Table 6.34 Respondents' views regarding pursuit of a career in the Education Department in or outside schools, according to gender (N = 717)

Work Location	Males		Females		Males & Females	
	No.	%	No.	%	No.	%
In Schools	318	58.5	106	60.9	424	59.2
Outside Schools	53	9.8	16	9.2	69	9.6
In & Outside Schools	172	31.7	52	29.9	224	31.2
Total	543	100.0	174	100.0	717	100.0

Table 6.35 Distribution of respondents according to preference of teachers to work in city rather than country schools (N = 717)

Response	Most Teachers		Self	
	No.	%	No.	%
Strongly agree	154	21.5	85	11.9
Agree	425	59.2	176	24.5
Uncertain	86	12.0	86	12.0
Disagree	50	7.0	264	36.8
Strongly Disagree	2	0.3	106	14.8
Total	717	100.0	717	100.0

of respondents believed that most would prefer to work in large schools, 40.3 per cent felt that most would prefer small schools, and a third were uncertain. With regard to their own personal preference, the vast majority (60.4 per cent) indicated a preference for small schools, 29.1 per cent favoured large schools, and 10.5 per cent were uncertain about this matter (Table 6.36).

Social-economic Status of Schools:
In order to test the opinions of teachers regarding the socio-economic status of their desired work location, respondents were asked to indicate the extent to which they agreed or disagreed with the following statement: 'most teachers prefer to work in schools in middle class rather than working class areas.'

Well over two thirds of respondents (71.8 per cent) believed that this statement was true for most teachers, 8.7 per cent disagreed and a fifth (19.6 per cent) were uncertain. Teachers were in less agreement regarding their own personal preference about this matter. While almost half the respondents (46.0 per cent) said they would prefer to work in schools in middle class rather than working class areas, 38.4 per cent indicated a preference for teaching in lower socio-economic schools and 15.6 per cent were undecided (Table 6.37).

Table 6.36 Distribution of respondents according to preference of teachers to work in large rather than small schools (N = 717)

Response	Most Teachers		Self	
	No.	%	No.	%
Strongly agree	15	2.1	37	5.2
Agree	177	24.7	171	23.8
Uncertain	236	32.9	75	10.5
Disagree	247	34.4	299	41.7
Strongly Disagree	42	5.9	135	18.8
Total	717	100.0	717	100.0

Table 6.37 Distribution of respondents according to preference of teachers to work in schools in 'middle class' rather than 'working class' areas (N = 717)

Response	Most Teachers		Self	
	No.	%	No.	%
Strongly agree	134	18.7	65	59.1
Agree	381	53.1	265	37.0
Uncertain	140	19.5	112	15.6
Disagree	60	8.4	239	33.3
Strongly Disagree	2	0.3	36	5.0
Total	717	100.0	717	100.0

Factors that Do, and Those That Ought to, Influence Promotion

Teachers were asked to indicate the five main factors which (in their view) generally favoured promotion *at present*, and the five main factors which they believed *ought* generally to favour promotion. In both cases they were asked to make their selection from a list of forty possible factors that could influence promotion. Table 6.38 presents respondents' views regarding factors which currently favoured promotion within the Education Department of Tasmania, with only items selected by more than 10 per cent of respondents being included.

It is interesting to note that few items which related to various aspects of being a good classroom teacher, such as ability to control pupils, familiarity with new ideas in education, or flexibility in teaching methods, appeared towards the top of the list. Instead, three of the first six items related to various aspects of getting along well with those who may be regarded to be the 'power brokers' in the promotion stakes: superintendents, principals, advisors and others whose opinion can have an important influence on an individual's promotion prospects. Seniority (41.9 per cent) and administrative ability (37.2 per cent) also rated highly.

Table 6.38 Respondents' views regarding factors that currently favour promotion (n = 709)

Rank Order	Factor*	No.	%
1	Length of teaching service	300	41.8
2	Conformity with views of advisors and/or superintendent	267	37.7
3	Administrative ability	259	36.5
4	Willingness to move to other areas	220	30.7
5	Personal/social contacts with people who can influence promotion	218	30.7
6	Good relationship with principal	211	29.8
7	Participation in innovative practices	192	26.8
8	Having expertise in a particular subject/method	189	26.7
9	Being a graduate	182	25.7
10	Membership Tas. Teachers Federation	151	21.3
11	Higher degree qualifications in education	134	18.9
12	Ability to control pupils	122	17.2
13	Familiarity with new ideas in education	117	16.5
14	Experience in a variety of schools	115	16.2
15	Qualification in subject in which there is a teacher shortage	112	15.8
16	Flexibility in teaching methods	84	11.8
17	Having a strong personality	82	11.6
18	Good relationship with other staff	77	10.9
19	Service in isolated schools	73	10.3

* Only factors that were chosen by at least 10 per cent of respondents are included.

It is also helpful to identify those factors which only a small proportion of teachers chose as being ones which favoured promotion. Some of the lowest rated items were: concern for the welfare of individual pupils (8.4 per cent); being a man (6.2 per cent); service in country schools (4.7 per cent); long-service in a particular school (4.2 per cent); and, attendance at in-service courses (2.5 per cent).

There was substantial agreement between male and female teachers regarding the factors that currently favoured promotion (Tables 6.39, 6.40), although women stressed seniority, willingness to work in other areas, and having a strong personality more than did men, while men stressed conformity with the views of advisors and/or superintendents, being a graduate, and ability to control pupils, more than did women.

In Table 6.41 those factors which at least 10 per cent of respondents believed *ought to* favour promotion are presented in rank order. It is interesting to note that the most important single factor identified by the teachers surveyed was administrative ability (62.9 per cent). This may help explain the popularity of Educational Administration courses in the 1970s and 1980s. Apart from this item, none of the other top five items chosen as being ones that ought to influence promotion coincide with the five main items which respondents believed actually do influence promotion.

Items which relate to being an effective classroom teacher, such as a concern for the welfare of individual pupils (45.7 per cent), flexibility in teaching methods (43.5 per cent), and familiarity with new teaching

Personal and Professional Characteristics of Promoted Teachers

Table 6.39 Female respondents' views regarding factors that currently favour promotion (n = 170)

Rank Order	Factor*	No.	%
1	Length of teaching experience	73	42.9
= 2	Administrative ability	57	33.5
= 2	Conformity with views of advisors and/or supts.	57	33.5
4	Willingness to work in other areas	52	30.2
5	Having expertise in a particular subject or method	51	30.0
6	Good relationship with principal	50	29.4
7	Personal/social contact with people who can influence promotion	49	28.8
8	Having a strong personality	46	27.1
9	Higher degree qualifications in education	41	24.1
= 10	Membership, Tas. Teachers Federation	39	22.9
= 10	Participation in innovative practices	39	22.9
12	Being a graduate	37	21.8
13	Qualification in subject for which there is a teacher shortage	36	21.2
14	Experience in a variety of schools	33	19.4
15	Being a man	29	17.1
16	Familiarity with new ideas in education	27	15.9
17	Ability to control pupils	20	11.8
18	Flexibility in teaching methods	19	11.2

* Only factors chosen by at least 10 per cent of respondents are included.

Table 6.40 Male respondents' views regarding factors that currently favour promotion (n = 539)

Rank Order	Factor*	No.	%
1	Conformity with views of advisors and/or superintendent	210	39.0
2	Length of teaching experience	209	38.8
3	Administrative ability	202	37.5
4	Being a graduate	145	28.6
5	Participation in innovative practices	153	28.4
6	Having expertise in a particular subject or method	138	25.6
7	Ability to control pupils	102	18.9
8	Higher degree qualifications in education	93	17.3
9	Familiarity with new ideas in education	90	16.7
10	Experience in a variety of schools	82	15.2
11	Qualification in subject for which there is a teacher shortage	76	14.1
12	Flexibility in teaching methods	68	12.1
13	Service in isolated schools	56	10.4

* Only factors chosen by at least 10 per cent of respondents are included.

methods (43.5 per cent), plus having a good relationship with other staff (44.9 per cent), were stressed as being the ones which ought to favour promotion. Apart from some minor differences in emphasis there was substantial agreement between men and women teachers regarding the factors that ought to influence promotion (Tables 6.42, 6.43).

The items least selected by the survey population as being ones which ought to favour promotions were: service in country schools (5.9

Teachers' Career and Promotional Patterns

Table 6.41 Respondents' views regarding factors that ought to favour promotion (n = 707)

Rank Order	Factor*	No.	%
1	Administrative ability	451	63.8
2	Concern for welfare of individual pupils	328	46.4
3	Good relationship with other staff	322	45.5
4	Flexibility in teaching methods	312	44.1
5	Familiarity with new ideas in education	290	41.0
6	Experience in a variety of schools	261	36.9
7	Length of teaching experience	211	29.8
8	Ability to control pupils	207	28.3
9	Having expertise in a particular subject/method	188	26.6
10	Willingness to move to other areas	107	15.1
=11	Having a strong personality	76	10.7
=11	Higher degree qualifications in education	76	10.7
13	Participation in innovative practices	74	10.5

* Only factors that were chosen by at least 10 per cent of respondents are included.

Table 6.42 Male respondents' views regarding factors that ought to favour promotion (n = 538)

Rank Order	Factor*	No.	%
1	Administrative ability	312	58.0
2	Concern for welfare of individual pupils	217	40.3
3	Flexibility in teaching methods	193	35.9
4	Experience in a variety of schools	182	33.8
5	Good relationship with other staff	172	32.0
6	Familiarity with new ideas in education	160	29.7
7	Ability to control pupils	144	26.8
8	Having expertise in a particular subject or method	121	22.5

* Only factors chosen by at least 10 per cent of respondents are included.

Table 6.43 Female respondents' views regarding factors that ought to favour promotion (n = 169)

Rank Order	Factor*	No.	%
1	Administrative ability	89	52.7
2	Concern for welfare of individual pupils	75	44.4
3	Familiarity with new ideas in education	70	41.4
4	Flexibility in teaching methods	69	40.1
5	Having expertise in a particular subject or method	59	34.9
6	Experience in a variety of schools	56	33.1
7	Good relationship with other staff	49	29.0
8	Length of teaching experience	48	28.4
9	Ability to control pupils	36	21.3
10	Higher degree qualification in education	22	13.0

* Only factors chosen by at least 10 per cent of respondents are included.

Table 6.44 Principals' views regarding factors that affect promotion (N = 232)

Rank Order	Factor*	No.	%
1	Conformity with views of advisors and/or superintendents	108	46.6
2	Administrative ability	105	45.3
3	Length of teaching service	79	34.1
4	Participation in innovative practices	73	31.5
5	Willingness to move to other areas	69	29.7
6	Personal/social contact with people who can influence promotion	65	28.0
7	Familiarity with new ideas in education	60	25.9
8	Being a graduate	58	25.0
9	Having expertise in a particular subject or method	57	24.6
10	Ability to control pupils	44	19.0
=11	Membership Tas. Teachers Federation	43	18.5
=12	Expertise in a variety of schools	41	17.7
=12	Good relationship with principal	41	17.7
14	Flexibility in teaching methods	40	17.3
15	Higher degree qualifications in education	39	16.8
16	Having a strong personality	28	12.1

* Only factors chosen by at least 10 per cent of respondents are included.

per cent); having a good relationship with one's principal* (2.2 per cent); attendance at in-service courses (1.4 per cent); long service in a particular school (1.4 per cent); conformity with views of advisors and/or superintendent* (0.7 per cent); successful experience with examination candidates (0.7 per cent); and, personal/social contact with people who can influence promotion* (0.3 per cent). It is interesting to note that three of the least chosen factors (see those marked * above) were the same as those which were chosen most frequently by teachers as being the ones which currently did influence promotion in the Education Department.

It was decided to examine the views of principals and superintendents regarding those factors that did, and those that ought to, influence promotion. The reason is that principals and superintendents are very influential in determining who gets promoted in schools, because they are the ones who write the teacher reports upon which the Promotions Committee base their judgments.

Tables 6.44 and 6.45 present the views of principals and superintendents regarding the factors that currently influenced promotion in the Education Department of Tasmania. There was a strong element of agreement between their views and those of the other teachers surveyed (Table 6.38) with factors such as conformity with views of advisors and/or superintendent, length of service and administrative ability rating particularly highly. However, principals rated administrative ability more highly than did superintendents, while the latter gave greater weight to teachers having a good relationship with their principal.

There was also substantial agreement between principals, superintendents and other promoted teachers regarding those factors that ought to influence promotion (Tables 6.46, 6.47). Administrative ability was rated

Teachers' Career and Promotional Patterns

Table 6.45 Superintendents' views regarding factors that affect promotion (N = 14)

Rank Order	Factor*	No.	%
1	Length of teaching experience	9	64.3
=2	Conformity with views of advisors and/or superintendent	6	42.9
=2	Good relationship with principal	6	42.9
=4	Higher degree qualifications in education	5	35.7
=4	Administrative ability	5	35.7
=4	Personal/social contacts with people who can influence promotion	5	35.7
=4	Willingness to move to other areas	5	35.7
=8	Being a graduate	4	28.6
=8	Having expertise in a particular subject or method	4	28.6
=8	Qualification in subject for which there is a teacher shortage	4	28.6
=11	Experience in a variety of schools	3	21.4
=11	Ability to control pupils	3	21.4
=13	Participation in extra-curricula activities	2	14.3
=13	Participation in innovative practices	2	14.3

* Only factors that were chosen by at least 10 per cent of respondents are included.

Table 6.46 Principals' views regarding factors that ought to affect promotion (N = 232)

Rank Order	Factor*	No.	%
1	Administrative ability	153	65.9
2	Concern for welfare of individual pupils	112	48.3
3	Flexibility in teaching methods	108	46.6
4	Good relationship with other staff	104	44.8
5	Familiarity with new ideas in education	99	42.7
6	Experience in a variety of schools	88	39.9
7	Length of teaching experience	63	27.2
8	Ability to control pupils	59	25.4
= 9	Willingness to move to other areas	40	17.3
= 9	Having expertise in a particular subject or method	40	17.3
11	Successful experience with examination candidates	35	15.1
12	Service in country schools	28	12.1

* Only factors chosen by at least 10 per cent of respondents are included.

highly by all groups of teachers, as were having a good relationship with other staff and flexibility of teaching methods. Length of teaching experience was emphasised more by superintendents than principals, while the latter placed greater stress on a concern for the welfare of individual pupils.

Conclusion

The purpose of this chapter has been to describe the questionnaire data collected on the background details and teacher views that are relevant to

Table 6.47 Superintendents' views regarding factors that ought to affect promotion (N = 14)

Rank Order	Factor*	No.	%
=1	Administrative ability	8	57.1
=1	Good relationship with other staff	8	57.1
3	Length of teaching experience	7	50.0
=4	Having expertise in a particular subject or method	6	42.9
=4	Flexibility in teaching methods	6	42.9
=4	Having a strong personality	6	42.9
7	Familiarity with new ideas in education	5	35.7
=8	Experience in a variety of schools	4	28.6
=8	Concern for welfare of individual pupils	4	28.6
=10	Being a graduate	3	21.4
=10	Higher degree qualification in education	3	21.4
=10	Experience in education apart from teaching	3	21.4
13	Ability to control pupils	2	14.3

* Only factors chosen by at least 10 per cent of respondents are included.

studying promotion and careers in teaching. These findings will be discussed and related to the other data collected in this study on the careers of state school teachers in Tasmania in Chapter 9.

Notes

1 What is meant by 'lower level promotion positions' are those towards the bottom end of the promotions hierarchy: that is, first promotion positions such as senior masters/mistresses, senior teachers, and senior education officers.
2 In her study of medical practitioners, Fett (1975) found that 22.3 per cent of women and 6.9 per cent of men were never married.
3 In terms of fertility rates, 82.4 per cent of teachers had three or fewer offspring, while a third had two children (Table 6.5).

Chapter 7

Career Patterns of Teachers

This chapter describes the actual career behaviour of the group of teachers who comprise the survey population for this study. What is documented are the career and promotion histories of the teachers involved, this information being obtained from the records of the Education Department of Tasmania. In Chapter 9 the data presented in this, and the other two results chapters, will be analysed and discussed, with special reference to the extent to which there is a match between teacher perceptions about a career in teaching, and their actual career histories.

Methodology for Analysing Teacher Career Patterns

Several difficulties were encountered when constructing teacher career profiles. As was indicated in Chapter 4, a major problem was that over the time span being examined the school system and opportunity structure within which individuals pursued their careers was dynamic rather than static. There were major changes in the structure of the school system, with, for example, the move from a selective to a comprehensive system, and the establishment of matriculation colleges. The school system also expanded considerably over the period in terms of student enrolments, with the resultant increase in the demand for teachers, and in the range of promotion opportunities. The characteristics of the teaching force itself changed over time with (for instance) a greater proportion of teachers being four year trained graduates of a university or college of advanced education. There were changes in the hierarchy of promotion positions in teaching, in the nomenclature of promotion positions, and in the procedures and criteria used to determine who was promoted.

It is important that the career profiles and promotion patterns described in this chapter are considered with this changing context in mind, this being described in some detail in Chapter 3 'Opportunity Structure of Tasmanian Teachers'.

When identifying and analysing teacher career patterns and profiles it was the school or section of the Education Department the teacher was working in at the time the study was conducted, and the promotion position they occupied at that time, that was used for the purposes of analysis. This was despite the fact that some teachers had moved between school types during their career: for example, from primary to district schools, or from high schools to matriculation colleges. However, an examination of the career history information available indicated that most teachers (approximately 95 per cent) had remained in the same type of school over the length of their career, and so this was not regarded as being a major distorting influence when interpreting teacher career profiles. Other teachers had moved between subject specialisms, such as from teaching social science to computer studies.

A further consideration was that some teachers did not have 'normal' careers in the sense that they were willing to take (and even seek) a demotion down the promotions ladder in order to achieve a move to what they regarded as being a more desirable work location. This was particularly the case for those working in isolated or country regions of the state who wanted a move to one of the larger cities. Thus a teacher's career cannot be necessarily viewed in upward 'developmental terms', or as necessarily representing a logical sequence of increasing status. Promotion is not the main motivation for all teachers, and what is regarded as progress up the promotions ladder is not always clear. For example, when the principal of a small school became the senior teacher in a large primary school, should this have been viewed as a move up or down the promotions ladder? In all cases, salary level was the main criteria used to decide this matter.

It was decided to construct career profiles for those occupying various promotion positions (for instance, principals, senior teachers) in different types of schools, (for example, secondary colleges, primary schools), as well as for those employed in non-teaching promotion positions (for example, directors, superintendents) in the head or regional offices of the Education Department. An analysis was not undertaken for those employed in special schools, or in the guidance branch, because it was felt that the numbers of teachers involved were insufficient to enable meaningful calculations to be undertaken. In addition, theirs was a highly specialised area of employment that was not open to many teachers.

For each category of teachers, calculations were made to determine the number of years of experience the person had within the Education Department at the time they were awarded their current promotion position. While the mean number of years it took teachers to achieve their promotion position was important in giving a measure of the average time it took teachers to reach their particular status position within the Education Department, the actual length of time involved often varied considerably between teachers. For this reason, the 25th and 75th percentiles, between which lie the middle half of the promoted teachers, were also calculated. These teachers were regarded as being 'typical' or 'normal'.

Later in the chapter, attention is given to the career pathways developed or adopted by secondary school principals, primary school principals and directors in the Education Department. These were the people who occupied the top positions in schools and the services section of the Department.

In this section of the chapter the main interest is with finding out how long it took particular groups of teachers to achieve various positions in the promotions hierarchy, and in identifying the career contingency factors which appeared to influence the extent and rate of their progress. Are there differences in the rate at which teachers employed in different types of schools achieved promotion; what effect did a teacher's gender and academic/professional qualifications have upon their probability of achieving, and rate of, promotion; and, were there changes in these things over time? In addition, what is the degree of teacher horizontal mobility between schools, and the extent to which these moves are directed at achieving a 'more desirable' work location rather than vertical mobility?

The career profiles of teachers are presented here in graph form (Figures 7.1–7.14) with the more detailed information upon which the graphs are based being contained in Appendix 5. In the graphs, for each particular promotion position: the mean is shown to indicate the *average* time it took teachers to achieve elevation to the particular status level in the promotions hierarchy; and, the 25th and 75th percentiles are plotted to show how the length of time varied among teachers who could be regarded as having typical rather than exceptional career patterns. In Appendix 5 the most frequent level of experience (the mode), and the full range of the distribution amongst the teachers studied, are also shown.

When the career information about teachers is presented in diagram form in this chapter it is done so in a way which may imply that each status level is of equal value. This is an oversimplification of the actual situation which must be borne in mind when these career profiles are being interpreted.

The career profiles of teachers are examined in two main ways: first, comparisons are made between those occupying various status positions in the promotions hierarchy within the same sector of the school system (for example, those in primary schools) in terms of such variables as their gender and qualifications; and, second, comparisons are then made between particular groups of teachers occupying equivalent promotion positions in different sectors of the school system (for example, principals in secondary schools are compared with senior teachers in primary schools). In addition, the career profiles of teachers in non-teaching advisory, supervisory and administrative positions are also presented.

In some cases, the sample contained so few teachers in a particular promotion position that it was not possible to calculate a reliable mean, mode, or 25th and 75th percentile. For example, there were very few women occupying higher level promotion positions, and so a meaningful breakdown and analysis of these promotion positions by gender was not possible.

Where appropriate, promotion positions are shown according to the size[1] of the school in which the person concerned was working, since this can have an important effect upon the relative status of the position within the promotions hierarchy. For example, principals were classified according to whether they were employed in a large, medium or small school. In cases where the numbers in each category to be analysed were too small to enable a meaningful comparison to be made, cells were collapsed (e.g. large, medium/small) to overcome this problem.

Teachers in Primary Schools

Overall Situation

Figure 7.1 (Table 5.1 Appendix 5) shows the average number of years of teaching experience when promoted teachers in primary schools were awarded their current promotion position.

One quarter of primary teachers who had achieved their first promotion obtained this after between three and six years of teaching experience, a half after between seven and fourteen years of experience, and the remainder between fifteen and twenty-five years. The average level of experience was eleven years. Vice principals took an average of 14.3 years to achieve this elevation, although a quarter achieved this after between five and eight years of teaching experience.

The average number of years of teaching experience when primary principals achieved their current position was 22.5 years for those employed in large schools (that is, those with pupil enrolments of more than 351), 17.3 years in medium sized schools (151–350 pupils), and 9.8 years for those employed in small schools (8–150 pupils). When the number of years it took the middle half (25th and 75th percentiles) of teachers to achieve promotion to principal of a primary school is examined, the trend as presented in Figure 7.1 is for there to be a positive correlation between number of years of teaching experience and whether the teacher is the principal of a large, medium or small primary school.

In terms of the middle 50 per cent of teachers, there was a substantial range in the years of experience when the promotion position was achieved: from 17–28 years for the principals of large schools, to 13–17 years for the principals of medium schools.

The career profiles of vice principals and senior teachers are not presented according to school size because vice principals only occur in

Teachers' Career and Promotional Patterns

Figure 7.1 Promoted teachers in primary schools

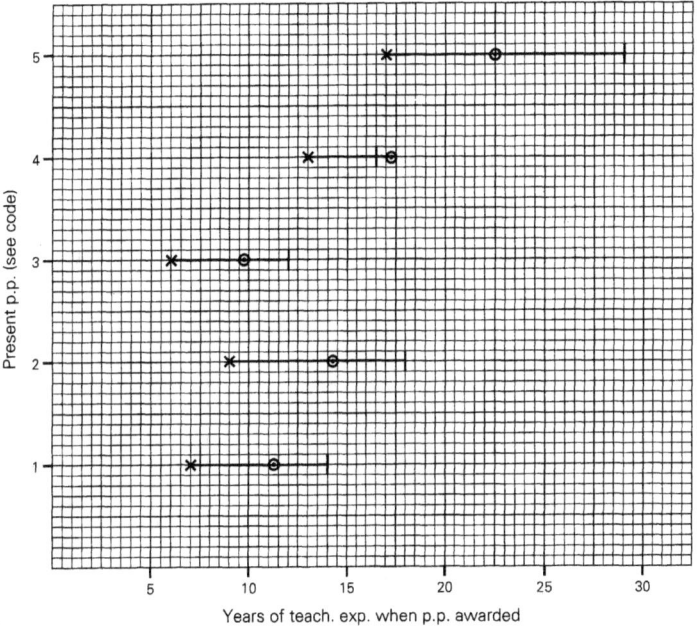

Code

5. Principals: lge. schls.
4. Principals: med. schls.
3. Principals: sml. schls.
2. Vice principals
1. Senior teachers

✗ 25th Centile
I 75th Centile
⊙ Mean

large schools; while if the salary paid to senior teachers is used as the criteria, there is no difference in their relative status according to the size of the school in which they are employed. As a result, any attempt at analysis of the career profiles of teachers in these promotion positions in terms of the size of school in which an individual worked would not be helpful.

It is interesting to note that on average it took vice principals (14.3 years) and senior teachers (11.0 years) a greater number of years to achieve their promotion position than it did the principals of small primary schools. There was also a wide range in the number of years taken by promoted teachers to achieve the various status positions in primary schools.

Figure 7.2 Promoted teachers in primary schools, by gender

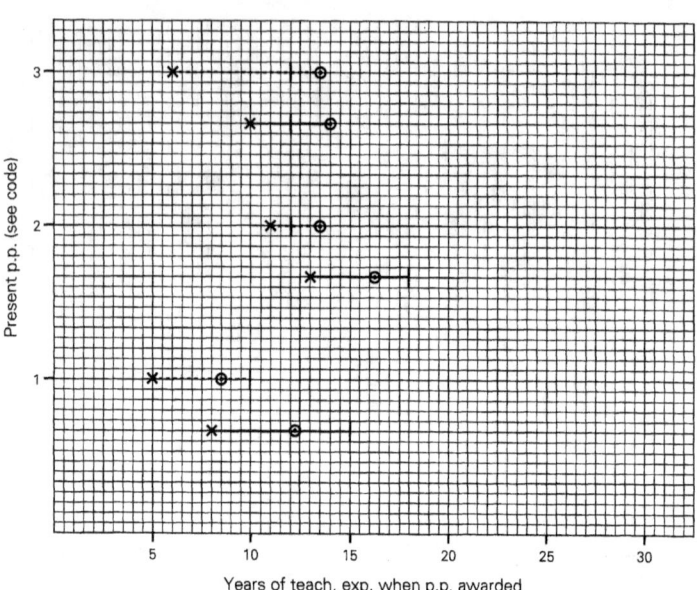

Code
3. Principals: med./sml. schls.
2. Vice principals
1. Senior teachers

✗ 25th Centile
| 75th Centile
⊙ Mean

Gender

Male: ················

Female: ─────

Gender

When the career profiles of women and men occupying the same promotion positions in primary schools are compared, we find that (on average) men gained promotion more quickly than did women (Figure 7.2; Table 5.2, Appendix 5). For senior teachers the average length of teaching experience was 11.9 years for women compared to 9 years for men; for vice principals it was 16.1 years for women and 13.7 years for men; and, in the case of the principals of medium/small schools it was 13.2 years for women compared to 9.5 years for men.

When the teaching experience of the middle 50 per cent of men and women teachers in each of the promotion positions in primary schools is compared, we find that women (on average) had a greater number of years of teaching experience before achieving their current promotion position than did men, although the range was similar for both groups of teachers.

With regard to principals in large primary schools, it was not possible to undertake an analysis on the basis of gender because there was only one woman occupying this particular promotion position; while the categories for primary medium and small schools were collapsed together because there was only one woman principal of a medium sized primary school and so separate analysis was not helpful.

Qualifications

When the teaching experience of graduates is compared to that of non-graduate VPs and STs in primary schools (Figure 7.3; Table 5.3, Appendix 5), graduates were promoted faster than were non-graduates. However, in the case of principals, it was the non-graduates who were promoted earlier than the graduates. A possible explanation for this is that principals, especially those in the large and medium sized schools, were amongst the oldest members of the teaching force, undertaking their teacher training at a time when it was virtually unknown for a primary school teacher to be a graduate. By comparison, senior teachers were building their careers at a time when an increasing proportion of teachers were graduates, and so it is to be expected that over time a greater proportion of primary school principals would be graduates.

Teachers in Secondary Schools

Overall Situation

The career profiles of principals, vice principals, and senior masters/mistresses in secondary schools are presented in Figure 7.4 (Table 5.4, Appendix 5). For the purposes of the analysis undertaken secondary colleges and high schools were bunched together because of the relatively small number (six) of secondary colleges in the school system being examined. In addition, when examining the career profiles of teachers with regard to the size of the school in which they were currently employed, only two classifications were considered: large and medium. The reason is that there are no small secondary schools: that is, schools with an enrolment of fewer than 350 students.

As was the case with teachers in primary schools, there was a difference in the average number of years of teaching experience of pro-

Career Patterns of Teachers

Figure 7.3 Promoted teachers in primary schools by graduate/non-graduate status

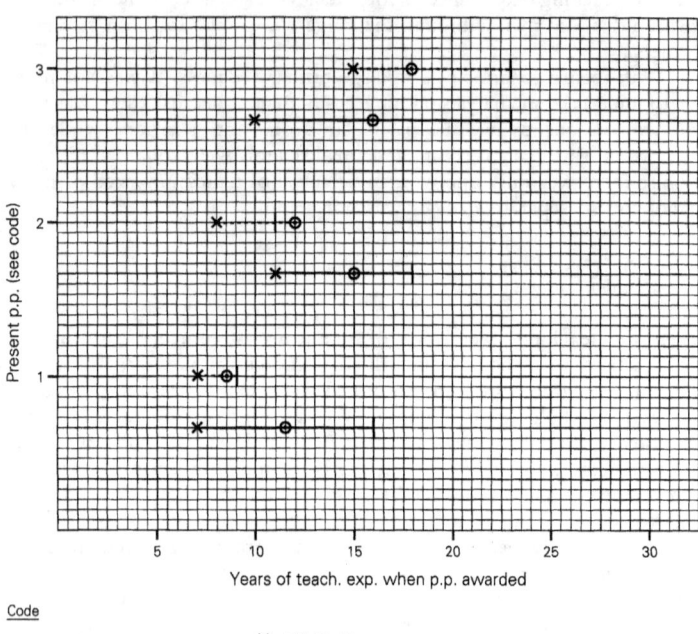

Code

3. Principals
2. Vice principals
1. Senior teachers

X 25th Centile
I 75th Centile
◉ Mean

Qualifications

Graduate: ----------------

Non-Graduate: ⎯⎯⎯

moted teachers in different promotion positions in secondary schools. Principals had an average level of experience of 21.4 years (in large schools) and 21.8 years (medium schools); vice principals had 17.1 years (large schools) and 15.2 years (medium schools); and senior masters/ mistresses had an average of 9.2 years teaching experience when they achieved this promotion position.

In the case of vice principals there was a considerable difference in the average length of experience when the promotion position was first awarded, according to the size of the school: 17.1 years for those in large schools compared to 15.2 years for those in medium sized schools. This was not the case for principals.

Teachers' Career and Promotional Patterns

Figure 7.4 Promoted teachers in secondary schools

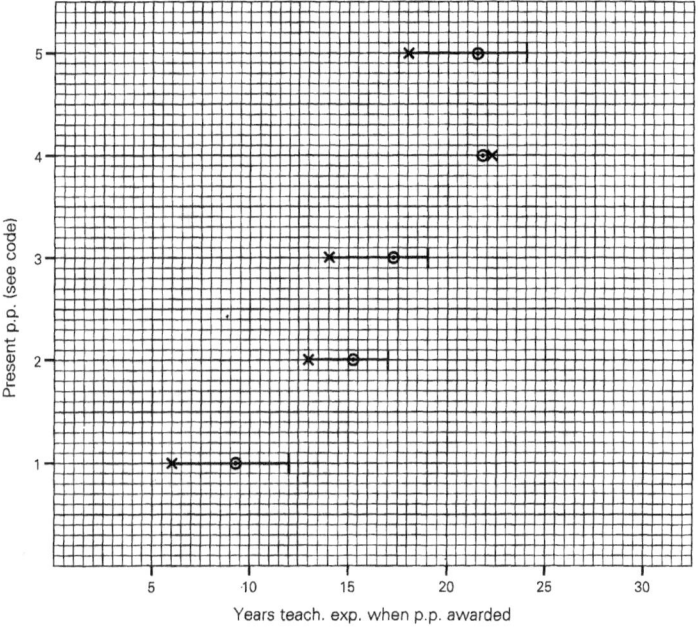

Code

5. Principals: Lge. schls.
4. Principals: Med. schls.
3. Vice Principals: Lge. schls.
2. Vice Principals: Med. schls.
1. Senior Masters/Mistresses

X 25th Centile
| 75th Centile
◉ Mean

Gender

When women and men teachers in secondary schools were compared, some interesting facts become immediately apparent (Figure 7.5; Table 5.5, Appendix 5). It is not possible to compare the career profiles of men and women principals because there were no women principals of either secondary colleges or high schools. With regard to vice principals employed in large schools, women take longer to achieve this position than do men, the average number of years of experience being 18.7 years for women and 16.5 years for men. In addition, the middle 50 per cent of male teachers achieved this status earlier than did the comparable group of women. This pattern is also true for senior masters and mistresses,

Figure 7.5 Promoted teachers in secondary schools, by gender

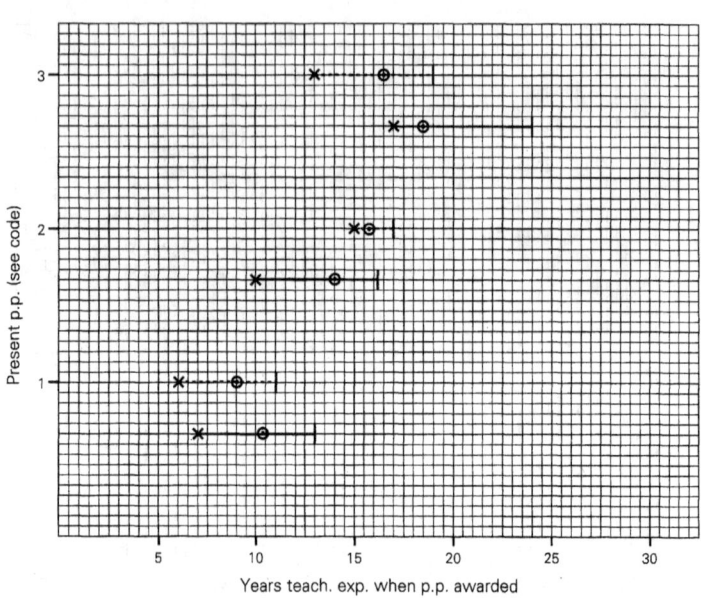

Code
3. Vice principals: lge. schls.
2. Vice principals: med. schls.
1. Senior masters/mistresses

X 25th Centile
I 75th Centile
⊙ Mean

Gender

Male: --------------

Female: ⎯⎯⎯⎯

where the average level of experience was 8.9 years for men compared to 10.1 years for women.

The significance of this situation is even more apparent if it is remembered that the focus here is upon those women who have actually *achieved* these promotion positions, and that there is a substantial under-representation of women in the promotion positions being examined.

When the situation applying to vice principals employed in medium sized schools is examined, we find that women were promoted earlier than men in that they had a lower average level of experience than did men when this promotion was won (14.2 years compared to 15.9 years). One explanation could be that this was the highest promotion position in secondary schools to which many women aspired and for which they

Teachers' Career and Promotional Patterns

Figure 7.6 Promoted teachers in secondary schools by graduate/non-graduate status

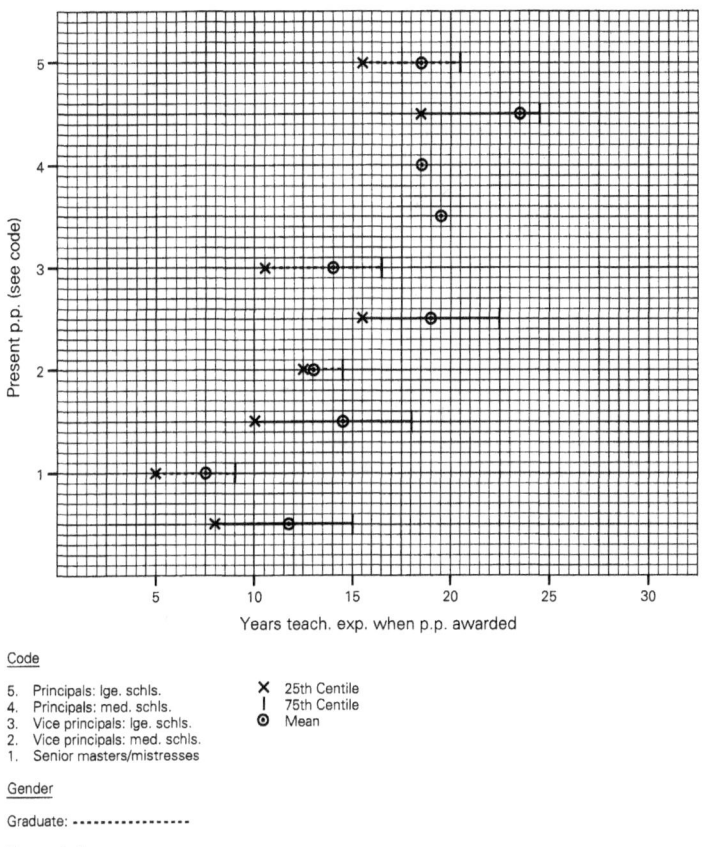

Code
5. Principals: lge. schls.
4. Principals: med. schls.
3. Vice principals: lge. schls.
2. Vice principals: med. schls.
1. Senior masters/mistresses

✗ 25th Centile
| 75th Centile
⊙ Mean

Gender

Graduate: ·················

Non-graduate: ─────

competed, whereas in terms of their career pathways men sought this promotion position in the larger schools.

Qualifications

Figure 7.6 (Table 5.6, Appendix 5) compares the career profiles of promoted teachers in secondary schools according to whether they were University/C.A.E. graduates or non-graduates. For principals in both

Career Patterns of Teachers

large and medium sized schools, graduates achieved promotion, on average, earlier than did non-graduates. However, the advantage enjoyed by graduates was more pronounced for those employed in the larger schools. This benefit also occurred for graduates who were vice principals in large secondary schools, and by senior masters/mistresses who were graduates.

It should be noted that graduate vice principals in medium sized secondary schools actually took longer than non-graduates to achieve this status, the average teaching experience of graduates being 15.5 years compared to 14.8 years for non-graduates. In addition, the middle 50 per cent of graduates achieved this promotion position after between fifteen and seventeen years of teaching experience, while in the case of non-graduates it took between ten and eighteen years. If one interprets these findings alongside those in Figure 7.5 it could be speculated that the explanation for this is that women took less time, on average, than men to achieve this particular promotion position, considering the fact that women were more likely than men to be non-graduates.

Figure 7.7 (Table 5.7, Appendix 5) presents the career profiles of teachers according to whether they were employed in a high school or secondary college. Principals are examined as one group because all secondary colleges were classified as large and thirty two of the thirty six high schools were classified as large. For principals there was no substantial difference in their average level of experience at the time they were promoted: 21.5 years for those in high schools compared to 21.3 years for those in secondary colleges. However, there were differences in other promotion positions, with vice principals and senior master/mistresses employed in the secondary college sector being promoted earlier than those employed in high schools.

Teachers in District Schools

Overall Situation

District schools warrant being examined separately because these schools employ both primary and secondary teachers since they are involved with teaching children in the K to grade 10 age range.

In Figure 7.8 (Table 5.8, Appendix 5), which shows the career profiles of promoted teachers in district schools, principals have been classified according to whether they worked in a large, medium or small school. Vice principals are not divided up in this way because they were only employed in large schools. Since district schools employ both primary and secondary teachers, the promotion positions of both senior teachers and senior master/mistresses occur within them.

A clear age grade system appeared to exist for promoted teachers employed in district schools, the average number of years of experience at

Figure 7.7 Promoted teachers in different types of secondary schools

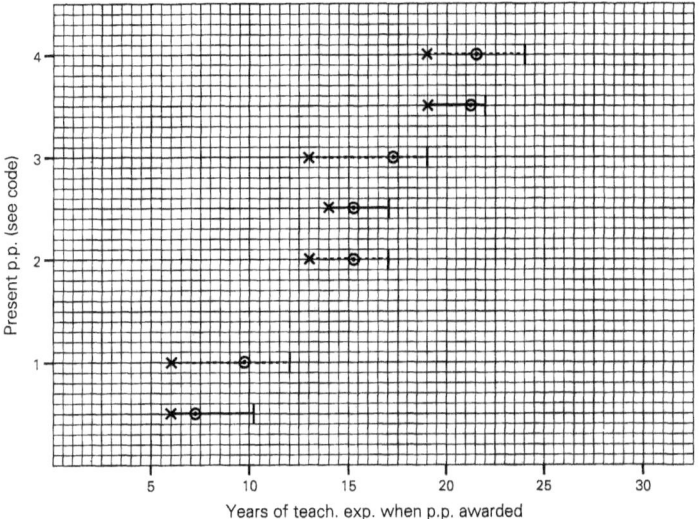

Code
4. Principals
3. Vice principals: lge. schls.
2. Vice principals: med. schls.
1. Senior masters/mistresses

X 25th Centile
I 75th Centile
◉ Mean

School type

High school: ······················

Secondary College: ―――――

the time an individual was awarded their current promotion position being positively correlated with their relative position in the promotions hierarchy. The average length of teaching experience was: for principals (large schools, 24.3 years; medium, 20.4 years; small, 11.4 years); vice principals (15.4 years); senior teachers (10.1 years); and senior masters/mistresses (9.4 years).

Gender
The career profile information regarding teachers in district schools was not classified according to the gender of the teacher because so few teachers in these positions were women. For example, there were no women principals or vice principals; and only five (or 0.8 per cent) of senior masters/mistresses in the survey population were women.

Figure 7.8 Promoted teachers in district schools

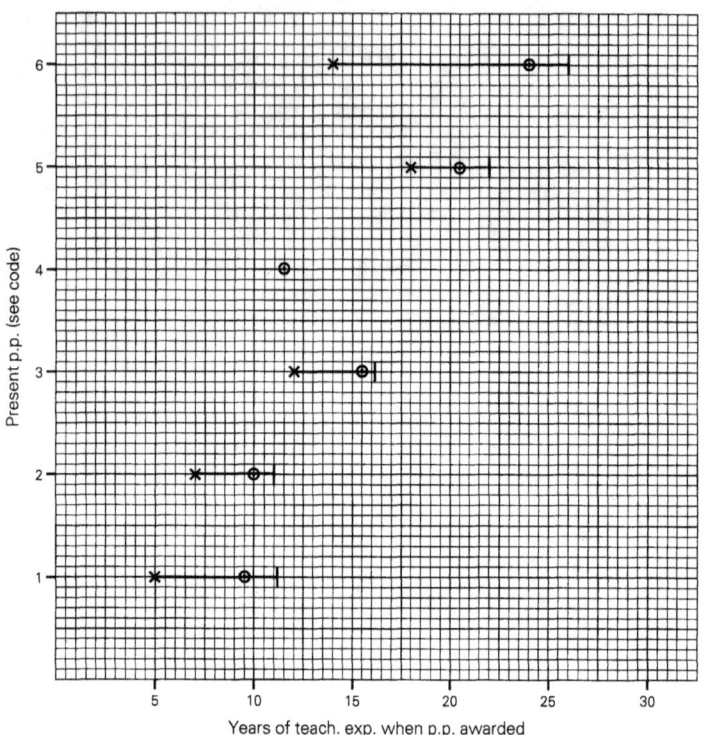

Code
6. Principals: lge. schls.
5. Principals: med. schls.
4. Principals: schl. schls.
3. Vice Principals
2. Senior teachers
1. Senior Masters/Mistresses

X 25th Centile
I 75th Centile
⊙ Mean

Qualifications
Figure 7.9 (Table 5.9, Appendix 5) compares teachers in district schools according to whether or not they were graduates. Principals are examined as one group rather than according to school size because of the small number of graduates in some schools. It is interesting to note that for principals and vice principals, graduates actually took longer than non-graduates, on average, to achieve these positions. This was not the case

131

Teachers' Career and Promotional Patterns

Figure 7.9 Promoted teachers in district schools by graduate/non-graduate status

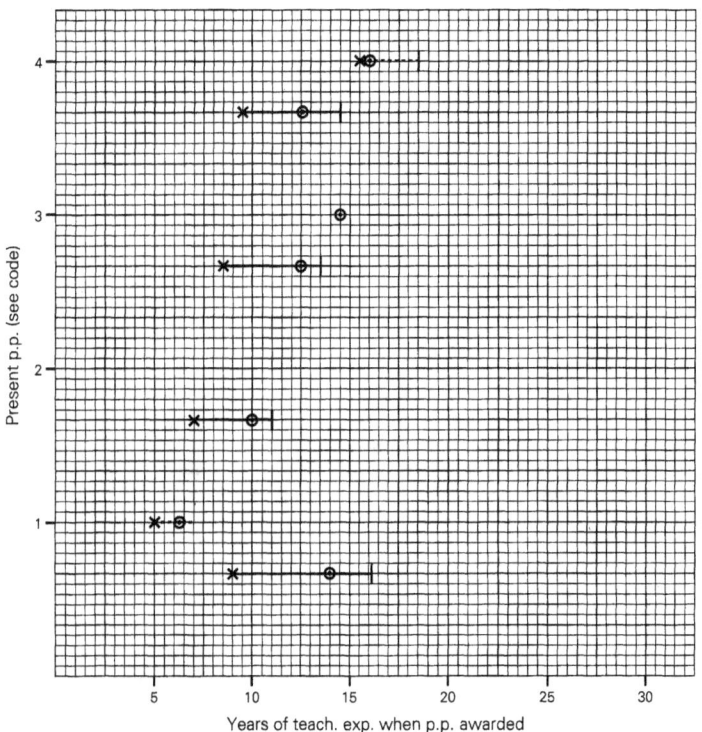

Code

4. Principals
3. Vice principals
2. Senior teachers
1. Senior masters/mistresses

X 25th Centile
I 75th Centile
◉ Mean

Qualifications

Graduate: ------------------
Non-Graduate: _____

for senior masters/mistresses since, on average, graduates were awarded this position after 6.3 years, while for non-graduates it took 14.0 years. However, the level of experience was similar for the middle 50 per cent of graduates and non-graduates, being five to seven years for the former and five to six years for the latter.

Teachers in Non-school Advisory, Supervisory and Administrative Positions

This chapter has so far examined promoted teachers employed in schools. Attention will now be directed to those employed in the services and administrative branches of the Education Department. It was decided not to document the careers of teachers employed in the guidance branch because their small numbers (there were only three regional guidance officers and six senior guidance officers), and the fact that their positions are highly specialized ones which are not open to many teachers, meant it was not helpful to compare them to teachers in equivalent positions in other sections of the Education Department.

Figure 7.10 (Table 5.10, Appendix 5) demonstrates that there was a positive correlation between a teacher's relative status in the non-school promotions hierarchy and the average number of years teaching experience they had at the time they achieved the promotion position in question. The average length of experience for directors, who are the most senior members of the Education Department, was 28.4 years; for superintendents it was 23.2 years; and for supervisors, 20.2 years. It is of interest to note that there was a considerable difference in the range of time it took those in different non-school promotion positions to achieve their current position: from a low range of 27–30 years for directors, to a high of 15–29 years for superintendents.

The average level of experience for principal education officers (20.7 years) was very similar to that for supervisors. This is not surprising since, if salary is taken as the yardstick, they have an equivalent status within the promotions hierarchy.

Because of the extremely small number of women in non-school positions (see Table 5.1, Chapter 5), and the fact that almost all the teachers filling these positions were graduates, these promotion positions have not been classified according to an individual's gender or qualifications.

Mobility Between Work Locations

The career profiles of promoted teachers were analysed to ascertain the number of schools, and/or sections of the Education Department, they

Teachers' Career and Promotional Patterns

Figure 7.10 Promoted teachers in non-school positions

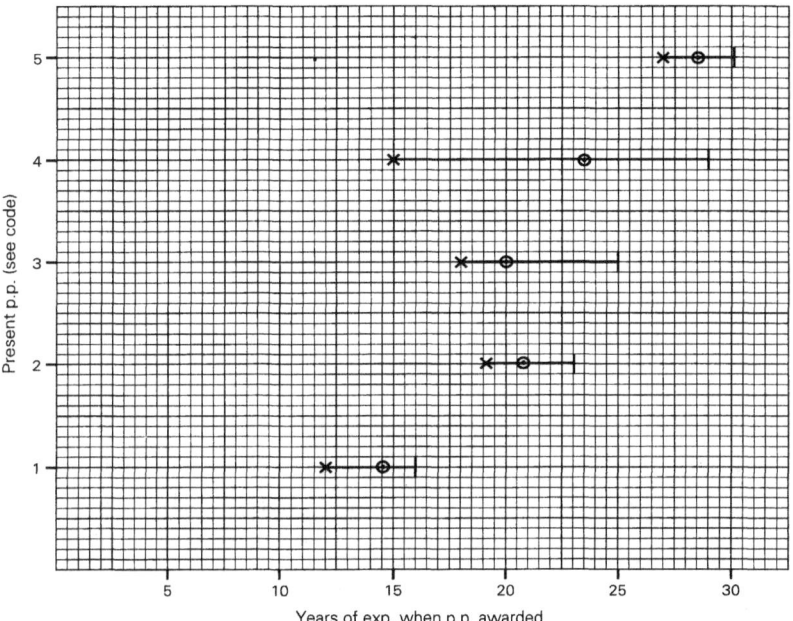

Code

5. Directors
4. Superintendents
3. Supervisors
2. P.E.O.'s
1. S.E.O.'s

X 25th Centile
I   75th Centile
⊙ Mean

had worked in up to the time they gained their current promotion position. The purpose of undertaking this analysis was to see if the most promoted teachers had moved more frequently between work locations than had the others.

Figure 7.11 (Table 5.11, Appendix 5) shows the number of times principals moved between schools or other work locations over their teaching career, this information being classified according to the type and size of school in which the individuals were employed. As was the case with the career information presented earlier, the average for the group in question, and the 25th and 75th percentiles, are both presented. A point to note is that this figure shows all job moves including those when a teacher moved between schools for perhaps only two to three months, in a relieving capacity.

Figure 7.11 Number of principals' moves between school/work locations

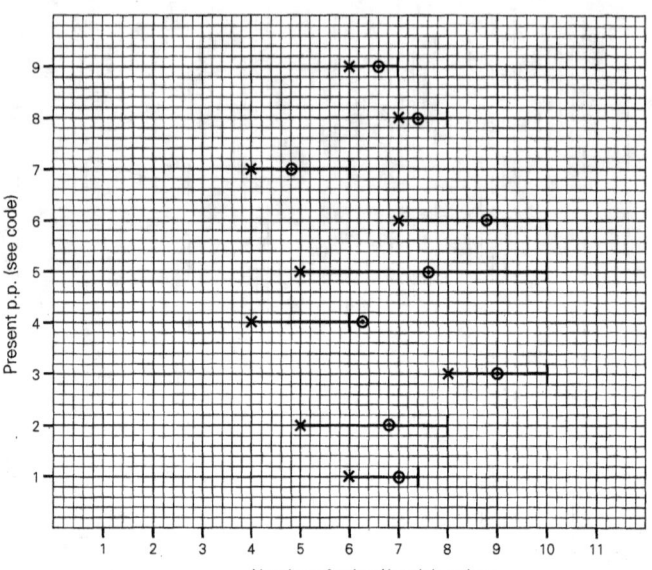

Code

9. Secondary College
8. High schls. lge.
7. High schls. med.
6. Primary schls. lge.
5. Primary schls. med.
4. Primary schls. sml.
3. District schl. lge.
2. District schl. med.
1. District schl. sml.

X 25th Centile
I 75th Centile
⊙ Mean

Primary principals in large (8.7 moves) and medium (7.6 moves) sized schools moved their job location more frequently than any other group of promoted teachers. They were followed by those in large high schools (7.3 moves) and secondary colleges (6.6 moves). It is interesting that with the exception of the principals of medium sized primary schools the middle 50 per cent of teachers in these promotion positions are closely bunched.

From the information presented, it appears that there was no close positive correlation between the number of times a principal moved school, and the extent of their promotion within the status hierarchy, although this is a proposition that needs to be tested elsewhere in this book. However, promotion appeared to come earlier for those who moved their job location more frequently than the average.

If the information presented in Chapter 6 on the number of times teachers moved their place of residence due to promotion is linked to that presented here, a pattern emerges. It is that although promoted teachers moved more frequently than did other teachers between job locations, they did so within a restricted geographical area. As a result they were able to move between schools without needing to move their place of residence. In addition, many of these moves were between a restricted number of schools so that, for example, although a teacher may have moved (say) eight times, this may only have been between two or three schools, the individual working in the same school on several different occasions.

We now turn our attention to examining the number of job moves of those in other promotion positions, namely senior teachers, senior masters/mistresses and those in service positions. In the case of SMs and STs a comparison will also be made between men and women.

Table 7.1 shows the number of times senior masters/mistresses and senior teachers had moved between school/work locations during their teaching career. STs had moved more times, on average, that had SMs with the most mobile group being male STs (5.1 moves on average). In all cases there was a wide range in the number of times teachers had moved their work location, from one to ten times for SMs to three to eight times for male STs.

In the case of those employed in non-school positions, the higher an individual's promotion position the greater the number of times they had moved their school/work location (Table 7.2).

Horizontal Versus Vertical Mobility

An analysis was undertaken to determine the proportion of promoted teachers moves between schools and/or sections of the Education Department that resulted in horizontal mobility, compared to the proportion that were associated with vertical mobility. Table 7.3 presents this for principals according to the type of school in which they were employed.

This table concentrates on moves between different work locations, and takes no account of vertical mobility that occurred without there being any change of job locations, within the same school or section of the department.

With the exception of the principals of small primary schools (35.7 per cent), an average of between 46 per cent–61 per cent of moves were associated with vertical rather than horizontal mobility. Almost half (46 per cent) the moves of principals in secondary colleges and high schools

Table 7.1 Number of times senior masters/mistresses and senior teachers had moved between schools/work locations during teaching career, by gender (N = 289)

	Senior Masters/Mistresses		Senior Teachers	
	Males (N = 152)	Females (N = 45)	Males (N = 27)	Females (N = 65)
Mean No. of moves	3.5	3.6	5.1	4.3
25th Centile	2	2	4	3
75th Centile	4	5	6	5
Range	1–10	1–10	3–8	1–8
Mode	3	4	5	3

Table 7.2 Number of times promoted teachers in non-school positions moved between school/work locations (N = 71)

	Directors (N = 8)	Superintendents (N = 14)	Supervisors (N = 15)	PEO's (N = 12)	SEO's (N = 22)
Mean No. of moves	7.25	7.0	6.8	6.8	5.2
25th Centile	7	6	5	5	3
75th Centile	8	8	8	8	7
Range	5–9	3–11	5–11	4–11	1–12
Mode	8	6	6	5	6

between different work locations coincided with them gaining promotion. In view of this it can be reasonably assumed that the purpose of the move was to achieve vertical mobility. In the case of principals employed in large and medium sized primary schools just over half (51–53 per cent) the moves co-incided with vertical mobility, while for principals in small primary schools over a third (36 per cent) of moves between schools were linked to vertical mobility. With the exception of principals employed in medium sized primary schools, the mode was 50 per cent in terms of the proportion of moves between schools that were associated with vertical mobility.

Table 7.4 shows that, on average, a greater proportion of the moves of male than female SMs and STs between work locations were for promotion rather than horizontal mobility reasons. About a fifth of male job moves were for vertical mobility reasons, compared to 12 per cent — 15 per cent for females.

In the case of those employed in non-school positions, the higher a teacher's promotion position, the greater the proportion of job moves, on average, that were for promotion rather than horizontal mobility reasons, the proportion ranging from 68 per cent for directors (47 per cent for superintendents, 39 per cent for supervisors, 34 per cent for PEOs) to 19 per cent for SEOs.

Table 7.3 Proportion of principals' moves between schools/work locations over teaching career associated with vertical, rather than horizontal mobility (n = 219)

	*Sec. Coll. (N = 6) %	High Schools Large (N = 32) %	High Schools Medium (N = 4) %	Primary Schools Large (N = 49) %	Primary Schools Medium (N = 47) %	Primary Schools Small (N = 50) %	District High Schools Large (N = 3) %	District High Schools Medium (N = 14) %	District High Schools Small (N = 14) %
Mean Prop.	46	46	46	51	53	36	52	61	48
25th Centile	43	40	33	44	43	33	53	57	43
75th Centile	50	50	50	57	71	50	56	75	55
Range	22–71	23–67	33–50	33–76	23–100	17–75	50–57	33–83	29–75
Mode	50	50	50	50	66	45	50	50	50

* All secondary colleges were classed as large schools.

Table 7.4 Proportion* (%) of senior masters'/mistresses' and senior teachers' moves between schools/work locaitons over teaching career associated with vertical rather than horizontal mobility (N = 289)

	Senior Masters/Mistresses		Senior Teachers	
	Males (N = 152)	Females (N = 45)	Males (N = 27)	Females (N = 65)
Mean Prop.	22	12	18	15
25th Centile	0	0	14	0
75th Centile	33	25	25	25
Range	0–100	0–33	0–33	0–50
Mode	0	0	17	0

* Rounded to nearest whole number.

Table 7.5 Proportion* (%) of moves by non-school promoted teachers between school/work locations and teaching career associated with vertical rather than horizontal mobility (N = 71)

	Directors (N = 8)	Superintendents (N = 14)	Supervisors (N = 15)	PEO's (N = 12)	SEO's (N = 22)
Mean Prop.	68	47	39	34	19
25th Centile	67	38	33	29	13
75th Centile	75	50	42.9	40	25
Range	44–80	25–100	22.2–60.0	18–50	0–50
Mode	75	50	33	40	17

* Rounded to nearest whole number.

Teachers in Different Sectors of the Education Department

We have so far analysed the career profiles of promoted teachers according to the particular type of school or sector of the Education Department in which they were employed. But other important questions arise which warrant investigation: for instance, were there significant differences between those in comparable promotion positions, according to the sector of the school system in which they were employed; were the career profiles of senior teachers in district schools different to STs employed in primary schools; and, what were the similarities and differences between the career profiles of teachers occupying comparable (but different) promotion positions in different sections of the education system.

Figure 7.12 (Table 5.12, Appendix 5) provides information on the number of years of teaching experience which principals in different types of schools had at the time they achieved their current promotion position. Principals were also classified according to whether they were in charge of a large, medium or small school.

There was little difference between the average level of teaching experience of principals in different types of large schools, with the variation being from 20.8 years for those in district schools, to 22.0 years

Figure 7.12   Principals in different types of schools by size of school

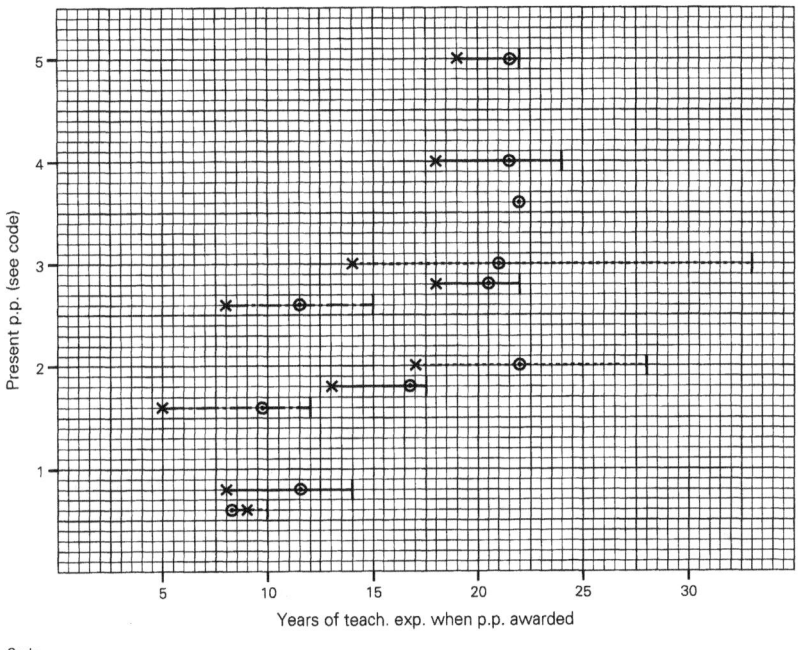

Code
5. Secondary Colleges
4. High Schools
3. District Schools
2. Primary Schools
1. Special Schools

✗ 25th Centile
| 75th Centile
☉ Mean

School Size

Large ----------------
Medium ————
Small —·—·—·—

for the principals of large primary schools. The mode (17–18 years) was also much the same for each group of principals.

There was quite a difference in the time taken by the middle 50 per cent of principals surveyed. The greatest variation occurred in the case of district schools (14–33 years) and the least for those in secondary colleges (19–22 years).

For principals employed in medium sized schools there was considerable variation in the average level of experience: from 11.6 years for those

Career Patterns of Teachers

in special schools to 21.8 years for those in high schools. For small schools the range was between 8.2 years for special schools to 11.4 years for district schools, with the mode for those in small primary schools being four years.

Figure 7.13 illustrates the situation for vice principals in different types of schools, plus PEOs who occupy an equivalent promotion position in the services area. VPs in the large schools did, in terms of average years of experience, take longer to achieve this promotion position than did those in medium sized schools; while those in secondary schools reached this position, on average, earlier than did those in other types of schools. PEOs had more years of experience when this status was awarded than did VPs.

Figure 7.14 shows that SMs had, on average, more teaching experience when this promotion position was awarded than did senior teachers; and that SEOs took longer, on average, to reach this promotion position than did either SMs or STs.

Distribution of, and Competition for, Promotion Positions

Was it easier or more difficult for teachers in the Education Department of Tasmania to gain promotion at the time of the survey, compared to earlier periods; and, were there differences in the opportunities available to those employed in different sectors of the Education Department? Were most of the opportunities in country or city schools, and has this situation changed over time?

In order to help answer these types of questions information was gathered on the distribution of, and competition for, advertised promotion positions within the Education Department in two particular years: 1970 and 1980. Due to the paucity of information available, it was not possible to provide comparable information for earlier times.

Between 1970 and 1980 there was almost a three fold reduction (from 241 to 84) in the number of promotion positions advertised increasing to 108 in 1988. This is an example of how the number and range of opportunities available to teachers can change over time. There was also a change in the distribution of available promotion positions between different sectors of the school system. For instance, if the situation in 1970 is compared with that in 1980 in order to illustrate the point, a reduction occurred in the proportion of positions advertised in senior secondary (13.3 per cent to NIL) and high schools (36.1 per cent to 25.9 per cent). Despite a reduction in the overall number of positions advertised there was an increase in the proportion of these positions available in primary (34.0 per cent to 42.4 per cent), district (13.3 per cent to 28.2 per cent) and special (2.0 per cent to 3.5 per cent) schools. In the administrative and services areas, three positions were advertised in 1970 and none in 1980.

Teachers' Career and Promotional Patterns

Figure 7.13 Vice principals and principal education officers in the different sectors of the Education Department

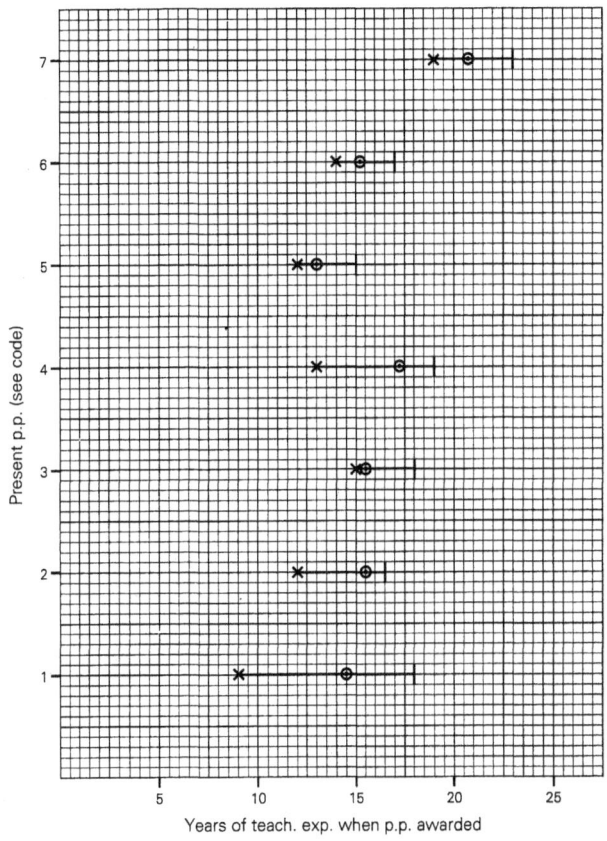

Code

7. P.E.O.'s
6. V.P.'s – Sec. Colleges: Large
5. V.P.'s – Sec. Colleges: Medium
4. V.P.'s – High Schools: Large
3. V.P.'s – High Schools: Medium
2. V.P.'s – District Schools
1. V.P.'s – Primary Schools

X 25th Percentile
| 75th Percentile
☉ Mean

Figure 7.14 Senior masters/mistresses, senior teachers and senior education officers in different sectors of the Education Department

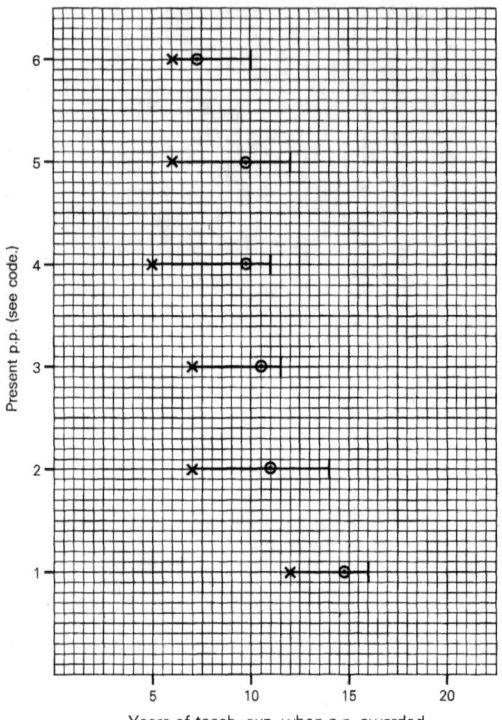

Code
6. S.M.'s – Secondary Colleges
5. S.M.'s – High Schools
4. S.M.'s – District Schools
3. S.T.'s – District Schools
2. S.T.'s – Primary Schools
1. S.E.O.'s

✕ 25th Percentile
| 75th Percentile
⊙ Mean

Over the same ten year period examined there was a shift in the distribution of promotion positions between country and city schools. An increase occurred in the proportion of promotion positions advertised in isolated (10 per cent to 18.8 per cent) and country (26.1 per cent to 35.3 per cent) regions of the state, while at the same time there was a reduction in the proportion of positions in urban (63.9 per cent to 45.9 per cent) areas.

It is clear from this information that if, for instance, the situation in

Table 7.6 Promotion positions advertised, according to school/branch type

School/Branch Type	1970		1980	
	Number	Percentage of total promotion positions	Number	Percentage of total promotion positions
Senior Secondary Schools	32	13.3		No Promotion positions advertised
Secondary High Schools	87	36.1	22	25.9
District High/Area Schls.	32	13.3	24	28.2
Primary Schools	82	34.0	36	42.4
Special Schools	5	2.0	3	3.5
Services/Admin. Branches	3	1.3		No Promotion positions advertised
Total	241	100	85	100

(Source: Tasmanian Education Department Records)

Table 7.7 Promotion positions advertised, according to urban, country or isolated location

Location *	Number	Percentage of total Promotion Positions	Number	Percentage of total Promotion Positions
Urban	154	63.9	39	45.9
Country	63	26.1	30	35.3
Isolated	24	10.1	16	18.8
Total	241	100%	85	100%

(Source: Tasmanian Education Department Records)
* Urban = Hobart, Launceston, Burnie and Devonport
  Country = West and North/West Coast of Tasmania
  Isolated = All other areas apart from Urban and country as described above.

1970 is compared with that in 1980 there was an overall reduction in the promotion opportunities available to teachers so that it was likely to be more difficult to gain promotion. In addition, the extent to which particular groups of teachers were affected depended upon the sector of the department in which they were employed, and the geographical area of the state in which they wished to work.

Table 7.8 shows the average number of applicants per promotion position advertised, according to the sex of the applicants. This shows that over the 1970–1988 period referred to in the table, there was also a substantial reduction in the amount of competition for all promotion positions advertised.

If the average number of applicants per promotion position advertised is taken as the yardstick, competition amongst men for promotion was greater in both 1970 and 1980 (and also in 1988) than it was for women, although the competition amongst women remained largely unchanged over the period. While for men there was a more than fifty per cent reduction in the average number of applicants per position, from twenty-five in 1970 to eleven in 1980 and 1988, there was also a change in the relative demand for different positions, the greatest reduction occurring in the demand to become a principal or senior teacher.

The decline in the average number of applicants per promotion position advertised occurred in all sectors of the school system (Table 7.9) with the greatest reduction occurring for positions advertised in primary and district high schools.

The reduction in the average number of applicants for promotion occurred for positions advertised in all geographical regions of the state, with the greatest reduction occurring for those advertised in isolated geographical regions (Table 7.10).

Rate at which Promotion Occurs

We noted above that the promotion opportunities available for teachers in the Tasmanian Education Department declined over the last twenty years. There was also a shift in the distribution of promotion positions between different sectors of the school system and geographical regions of the state.

But a further question arises with regard to the actual time it took teachers to gain promotion to various promotion positions: has there been a change in this situation? In order to help answer this question, a comparison was made between principals in the survey population to see how long it took them to gain their first promotion, depending upon the year in which they commenced work in the Education Department. The results, which are presented in Table 7.11, must be treated with some

Table 7.8 Average number* of applicants for promotion positions advertised according to gender of applicant

Promotion Position	1970			1980			1988		
	Male	Female	Total	Male	Female	Total	Male	Female	Total
Principal	36	1	37	11	1	12	12	3	15
Vice Principal	37	3	40	21	3	24	15	4	19
Senior Master/Mistresses	20	5	25	14	2	16	Nil	Nil	Nil
Senior Teacher	25	4	29	7	8	15	5	6	11
Superintendent	9	1	10	Nil	Nil	Nil	Nil	Nil	Nil
All Positions	25	3	28	11	3	13	11	4	15

(*Source*: Tasmanian Education Department Records)
* Figures rounded to nearest whole number.

Table 7.9 Average number* of applicants per post for promotion positions advertised in different types of schools

School/Branch Type	1970	1980
Senior Secondary	17	No P.P. advertised
Secondary	27	24
District High/Area	36	11
Primary	51	10
Special	9	7
Services/Admin Branches	30	No P.P. advertised
Total	28	13

(*Source*: Tasmanian Education Department Records)
* Figures rounded to nearest whole number.

Table 7.10 Average number of applicants per post for promotion positions advertised in urban, country and isolated locations

Location	1970	1980
Urban	18	16
Country	35	15
Isolated	30	7
All locations	28	13

caution because of the small numbers that occur in some of the time span categories.

For primary principals, those who joined the department in 1940–44 or 1970–74 gained their first promotion fastest (4.8 years on average, and 4.1 years on average, respectively). The slowest promoted were those who commenced work in 1950–54 (6.4 years on average).

Secondary principals who commenced work in the Education Department between 1955–64 gained their first promotion most rapidly (5.7 years on average), while those employed 1945–49 were the slowest to be promoted (8.2 years on average).

In the case of those employed in district schools, the fastest to gain their first promotion were those employed between 1965–69 (2.4 years on average), 1970–74 (4.5 years on average) and 1945–49 (4.8 years on average). Those employed between 1960–64 were the slowest to gain their first promotion (8.0 years on average).

One explanation for these differences are the changes that occurred in the school system, and opportunity structure, over the past half century, which were referred to in Chapter 4.

Table 7.11 Principals in different types of schools: years of teaching experience when first promotion awarded, in five year time spans 1940–74

Primary Schools (N = 127)	1940–44 (N = 5)	1945–49 (N = 18)	1950–54 (N = 13)	1955–59 (N = 17)	1960–64 (N = 31)	1965–69 (N = 29)	1970–74 (N = 14)
Mean Exp.	4.8	6.1	6.4	5.2	5.5	5.9	4.1
25th Centile	—	5	4	4	4	4	3
75th Centile	—	9	7	7	6	7	4
Range	3–8	2–10	2–12	3–10	2–14	2–12	2–7
Mode	3	9	4	4	5	6	4
Median	4	6	6	4	5	6	4

Secondary Schools (N = 38)	(N = 2)	(N = 6)	(N = 16)	(N = 11)	(N = 3)		
Mean Exp.	7.0	8.2	7.5	5.7	5.7	—	—
25th Centile	—	—	6	5	—	—	—
75th Centile	—	—	9	6	—	—	—
Range	2–12	7–11	4–12	3–8	5–6	—	—
Mode	—	8	8	6	6	—	—
Median	—	8.5	7.5	6	5.5	—	—

District Schools (N = 27)		(N = 5)	(N = 3)	(N = 7)	(N = 5)	(N = 5)	(N = 2)
Mean		4.8	6.7	7.3	8.0	2.4	4.5
25th Centile		—	—	7	—	—	—
75th Centile		—	—	8	—	—	—
Range		2–13	4–8	6–9	5–10	2–3	4–5
Mode		2	8	7	—	2	—
Median		2	8	8	8	2	—

Career Pathways of Directors and School Principals

In pursuing their work careers teachers have to operate within the existing opportunity structure: they discover, and in some cases make, pathways in their pursuit of promotion. These career pathways are to a large extent dictated by the opportunity structure existing at the particular time, in terms of the characteristics of the school system and promotions hierarchy.

Within these structures, individuals can adopt various courses of action since there are likely to be several, rather than just one or two, career pathways in existence. This is apparent from the data on the career pathways adopted by various groups of Tasmanian teachers presented in Figures 7.15, 7.16 and 7.17.

Figures 7.15, 7.16 and 7.17 imply that teacher career pathways occur in a strictly developmental or hierarchical form. However, this was not actually the case, because, in building their careers, teachers sometimes occupied promotion positions at various levels, both up and down the promotions hierarchy. For example, a primary teacher may become the principal of a small school, then a senior teacher in a large school, an acting vice principal in a medium size school, a senior teacher again, and then finally the principal of a large primary school (see Figure 7.15).

For the eight directors surveyed, there is little variation between individuals in the career pathways adopted. All, at some stage in their career, were superintendents; all were school principals; senior masters/mistresses or senior teachers; and, before that, classroom teachers. A small minority (two) were also: an acting director (one); acting superintendent (two); acting principal (one); and/or teachers college lecturer (two).

Figure 7.16 illustrates the career pathways adopted by secondary principals. At first sight there may appear to be a greater diversity of pathways adopted by secondary principals compared to directors. However, if the situation is examined more closely, this first impression is not accurate. Almost half (46 per cent) the principals had been acting principals, at some time in their career, and virtually all of them (95 per cent) had been either vice principals or acting vice principals. All of them had been a senior master/mistress, and a minority (27 per cent) had also acted in this capacity. All had commenced their careers as classroom teachers. All but one secondary school principal had spent their whole career in schools.

Figure 7.17 illustrates the career pathways adopted by primary principals. There was a greater variety of pathways for primary principals than for the other teachers examined, but this may be a function of the fact that there were so many more primary principals than there were secondary principals or directors.

Almost half (41 per cent) the primary principals had been acting

Teachers' Career and Promotional Patterns

Figure 7.15 Pathways in the promotion of directors

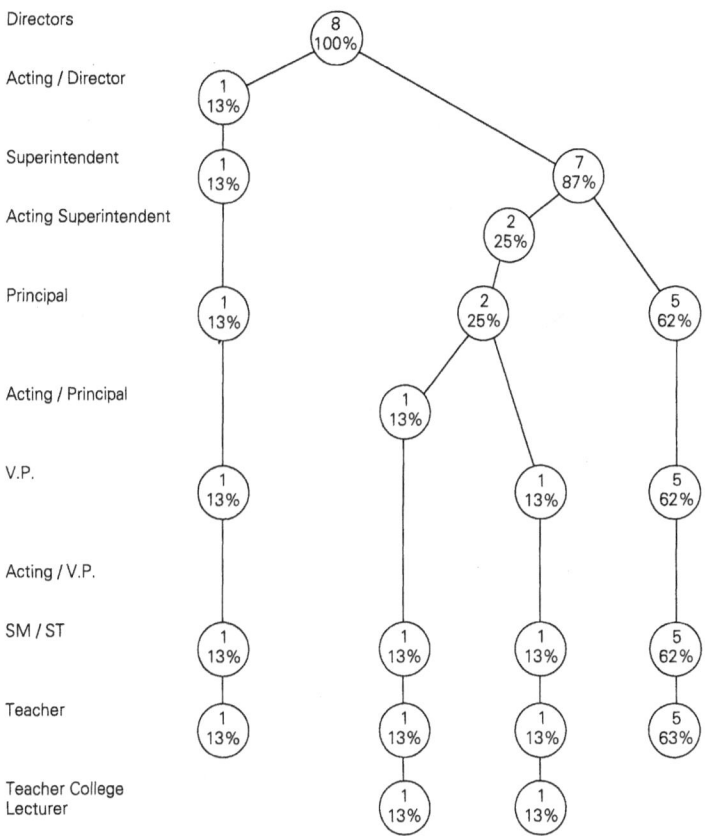

principals at some time in their teaching career; 27 per cent had been vice principals; and 6 per cent acting vice principals. The majority had been senior teachers (49.6 per cent) and/or acting senior teachers (10.2 per cent) during their career and all had been classroom teachers. Over a quarter (28 per cent) had moved straight from being a classroom teacher to become the principal of a small primary school. As was the case with secondary school principals, very few (2.2 per cent) had ever occupied a position out-of-schools.

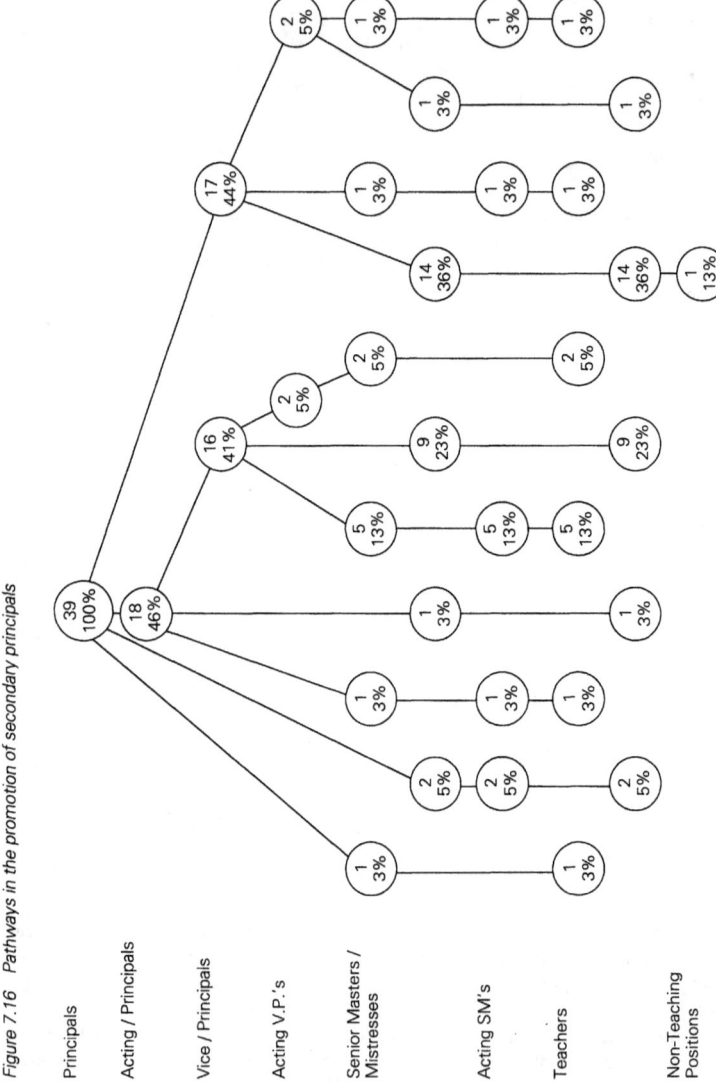

Figure 7.16 Pathways in the promotion of secondary principals

Teachers' Career and Promotional Patterns

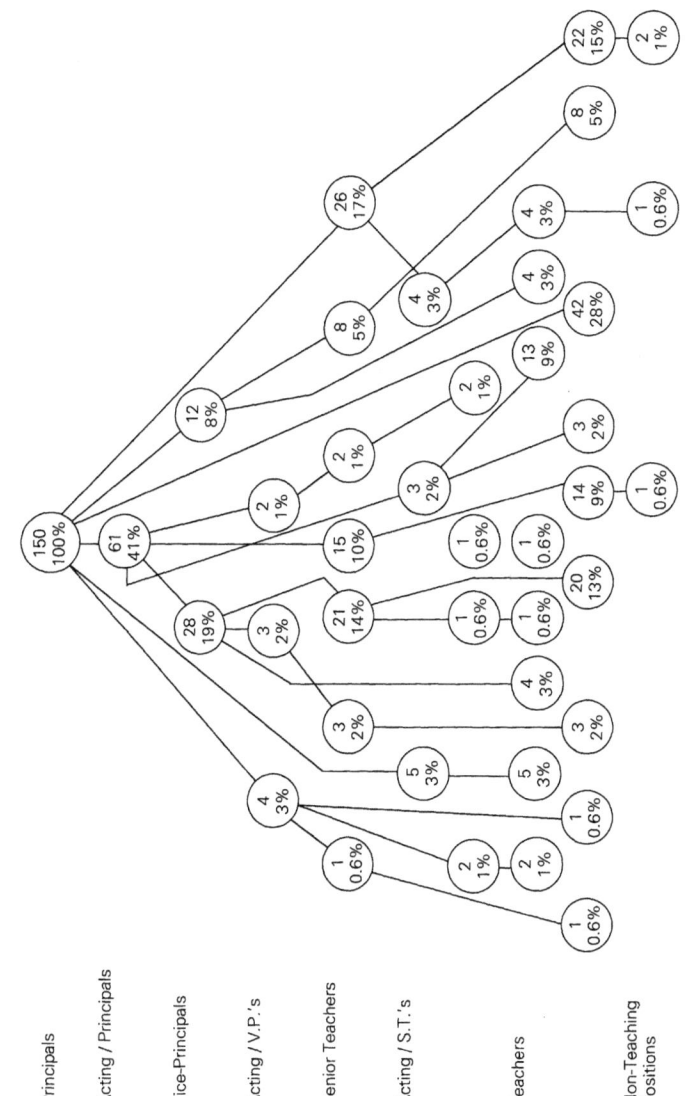

Figure 7.17   Pathways in the promotion of primary principals

Conclusion

This chapter has described the career and promotion patterns of teachers employed in the Education Department of Tasmania. The career histories of promoted teachers have been analysed according to the sector of the department in which they are employed and the type of promotion position occupied. Comparisons were made between male and female teachers and between graduates and non-graduates. Mobility between work locations, the relationship between horizontal and vertical mobility in the careers of teachers, the distribution of and competition for promotion positions, and changes over time in the rate at which promotion occurs, were also examined.

Whereas this chapter has been concerned with the actual career behaviour of teachers, the next chapter will present teacher perceptions regarding these matters.

Note

1 School size was determined, according to the number of student enrolments, as follows:
   — large school: 351 + students.
   — medium school: 151–350 students.
   — small school: 8–150 students.

Chapter 8

Teacher Perceptions of the Teaching Career

The research material contained in this chapter deals with the phenomenological dimension of this study: that is, it is concerned with presenting teacher views about the teaching career, in order to put 'empirical flesh' on the 'structural bones' built up in Chapters 6 and 7. However, these results should not be viewed in isolation, for there is a close interrelationship between the data presented in the three results chapters.

The information presented in this chapter was largely obtained from two sources: first, from forty semi-structured interviews conducted with teachers occupying a variety of promotion positions in different sectors of the school system; and, second, from five group interviews (each of which involved eight teachers) conducted throughout the state. It was hoped that these interviews would present illustrative material of a type that would provide an insight into the likely career perceptions of the survey population as a whole, although the possible shortcomings of such generalization must be borne in mind. The interview procedures were explained in detail in Chapter 5: Research Design and Procedures; while copies of the interview schedules used are in Appendix 4.

For the sake of convenience the material presented here has been organized under several headings, but it should be remembered that this is an artificial division, for there is a close interrelationship, and in some cases overlap, between information contained in various sections of this chapter.

Teaching as a Career

Occupational and Organizational Careers

The majority of interviewees regarded schoolteaching to be an occupation that offered recruits the possibility of pursuing a career. This was illustrated by the fact that they perceived there to be a clearly delineated promotions hierarchy and career structure in the Education Department through which individuals could progress in a logical and orderly way. As one senior teacher expressed it:

> As a teacher you have a sense of development and change in your employment over time in terms of the work available to you. You move up a promotions ladder and take on extra responsibilities. I suppose this partly occurs because the Department is bureaucratically organized.

A distinction is drawn in the literature between occupational careers and organizational careers. Most interviewees saw their careers first and foremost in terms of the organization in which they were employed. They saw themselves as, and spoke about themselves as being, 'Education Department teachers', rather than as members of the teaching profession. For most of those interviewed there was no clear distinction between their occupational and their organizational careers.

In addition, the more promotions minded a teacher the greater the extent to which they stressed their career in organizational rather than occupational terms. The trend was that men placed greater emphasis than did women on mainly viewing their career in organizational terms; and those teachers who were trying to maximise their upward mobility through the promotions structure, particularly during the early years of their career, also stressed defining their career in organizational rather than occupational terms.

Career Patterns

Although the teachers interviewed did not use the term 'career pattern' to describe their work-related movements, it was clear from their comments that all of them were conscious of the fact that they moved in patterned and generally planned (rather than random) ways between various job locations and/or promotion positions. For example, some spoke about the need to work in country or isolated schools as part of an overall career strategy if they were to maximize their chances and rate of promotion; while others indicated an intention to organize their career in such a way that they would be able to move to city areas when their own children were of secondary school age.

Vocation and Profession

In addition to offering a career, many believed that teaching was more than just work: it was also a vocation in the sense that it was expected that those who became teachers would have a genuine concern for the individual welfare of their pupils, and a strong commitment to improving the educational performance levels of those in their charge.

The vast majority of interviewees said their work as teachers was a very important source of satisfaction in their lives. As one senior master put it:

> It is much more than just a way of earning a living: it's also important and worthwhile work. I can't think of any equivalent occupation in terms of job satisfaction apart from perhaps medicine or social work. But the job is becoming more and more difficult and anxiety creating because of the increasing incidence of bad behaviour among students in schools.

Teachers indicated that 'at the feeling level' they regarded themselves as being members of a profession. At the same time they did not believe that the occupation had a true professional standing within the wider community, because the ascribed status of the teacher in society had declined over the past decade or so due to such things as increased teacher militancy and industrial action, and the general demystification of the professions in society.

Different Types of Careers

The type of mobility and career pathway a teacher establishes, or seeks to establish, within an Education Department depends upon a wide variety of factors, the most important ones probably being: their motives for becoming a teacher; the type of training undertaken; their level of ambition regarding promotion; and, the level of success achieved in establishing a career within the Department.

Several interviewees in their mid forties and older, who occupied middle and higher level promotion positions, expressed the view that the Education Department offered a variety, rather than simply one type, of career for teachers. Some, for example, had chosen a career pathway which kept them directly involved in the classroom, while others established a career which lead to an administrative-type, non-teaching job at the school level. Still others sought non-school promotion positions, in an advisory, supervisory or administrative capacity, in a head or regional office of the Department. The one thing that was common to them all, regardless of which type of career pathway they chose (or had thrust upon them), was that virtually all of them had commenced their careers as classroom teachers.

The particular type of career chosen depended very much on the values of the teacher concerned, and his or her motives for becoming a

Perceptions of the Teaching Career

teacher. This influenced, for example, whether he wanted to stay in the classroom, or whether he sought an administrative or non-school type position early in his career. Consider, for example, the likely career pattern implications of the following comments by interviewees regarding why they decided to become teachers:

> I was never all that interested in spending my working days with kids. Almost from the beginning I wanted to establish a career in the Department in either educational research or curriculum development.
>
> (Superintendent)

> Most of all, I enjoy being with children.
>
> (Senior Teacher)

> I come from a working class background and so the question of job security has always been important to me.
>
> (Vice Principal)

> I love history and wanted to be able to communicate this love of subject to others.
>
> (Senior Mistress)

> I didn't think that I could cope with the rat race out there in industry.
>
> (Senior Teacher)

> I get a great deal of satisfaction by organizing the school in a way that facilitates the work and success of my classroom teachers.
>
> (Primary School Principal)

These comments by teachers have been included to make it clear that, in view of the range of opinions presented, there is likely to be considerable value differentiation (and even a clash of values) over what individuals believe constitutes a worthwhile career in the Education

Department. Thus one needs to think in terms of the possible *range of careers* rather than *a single career* in teaching.

Virtually all the younger teachers interviewed, who were in their 20s and 30s, had not as yet come to view the Department as offering a variety, rather than just one type, of career. It seems that this realisation only comes to a minority of teachers, generally in mid career. This would influence the career pathways they follow, and may explain why a relatively small proportion of teachers seem interested in entering the non-school advisory, supervisory and administrative services areas.

Occupational Inheritance

It was partly due to what they regarded to be the declining status of school teaching as an occupation in society, and the increasingly difficult nature of the job, that the majority of interviewees said they would not actively encourage a son or daughter to enter this occupation. For many, teaching had become a 'dead end' occupation for the young, as evidenced by a paucity of employment and promotion opportunities. However, they did say that they would be more likely to encourage a daughter rather than a son to become a teacher because of the relatively short working hours involved, and the long holidays. A typical comment was:

> School teaching is particularly well suited to a woman's responsibilities as a housewife and mother. There's no other job I know of that fits in so well with a woman's role in society, and I haven't been reluctant to point this out to my teenage daughter.
> (Senior Teacher)

A further reason why most interviewees would not recommend that a son become a teacher was that the employment, promotion and career opportunities available in teaching had declined in recent years, and they did not believe that this situation would improve in the foreseeable future. Those few interviewees who said they would recommend the occupation to a son did so because of the potential security it offered at a time of economic instability and upheaval in society.

Many men from working class backgrounds had been encouraged by their own parents to enter the Education Department as a way of financing post secondary studies at a teacher's college or university. As one principal expressed it:

> If I hadn't been able to get a teaching bursary to pay for my education I wouldn't have gone to University when I did. My father wanted me to join the railways as a trainee fireman until

he realized that I could support myself at University through a teaching studentship: it's as simple as that.

Several male interviewees from middle class backgrounds had entered teaching for a very different reason. For them it was a second or third choice occupation, entered into after their preferred choices were unavailable to them.

The majority of women interviewees had been encouraged by their parents to become teachers for much the same types of reasons that they themselves would encourage their own daughters to become teachers: that is, it was seen as an occupation that suited 'a woman's maternal temperament' (Senior Teacher), and combined well with home duties.

Stages in the Teaching Career

Interviewees were asked to indicate the extent to which, and the ways in which, the school teaching career could be conceived of as consisting of a number of different stages. There was widespread agreement that the teaching career was in fact made up of seven distinct stages, these being:

1 The decision to become a teacher, and the undertaking of a pre-service course of teacher education;
2 Induction into the Occupation: The second stage consisted of the first four to five years of a person's teaching career during which time it was believed that the transition from being a teacher education student, to becoming a fully-fledged, and competent classroom teacher, was achieved for most individuals.
3 Employment as a Classroom Teacher: The third stage occurred from the time when the neophyte was inducted into the occupation (after four–five years) until they achieved their first promotion. During this stage the teacher had to decide how important promotion was to them, develop career goals, and decide upon the ways to achieve these goals.
4 Achieving Promotion: The view was expressed that a teacher enters stage four of the teaching career when they achieve their first promotion. There can, however, be several 'promotion stages' in an individual's teaching career depending upon the number of times they achieve substantial elevation in the promotions hierarchy. For the ambitious, the type of career planning that occurs in Stage 3, in terms of career goals, strategies and timetables, continues in this stage.
5 Employment in Non-School Positions: All interviewees drew a sharp distinction between employment in schools, and employment in non-school positions. This distinction was particularly

sharply drawn by those currently employed in non-school promotion positions. Since the vast majority of teachers were employed in schools, this 'stage' only actually occurred for a small minority of teachers, when they were employed in the services area on a permanent or seconded basis.
6 Achieving an Optimum Work Location: Men in particular spoke about their career strategy in terms of moving between different work locations and geographical regions early in their career in search of promotion, after which they wanted to settle in one geographical region, find a 'good school', establish a permanent home, and put down roots. At this stage in their career they were no longer willing to move about as freely in search of promotion. Instead, stability of family and work life, attendance of their own children at a suitable secondary school, and the importance of finding a 'satisfying' work location, were regarded as more important than simply seeking further promotion.

For women interviewees this stage generally occurred considerably earlier in their teaching career than was the case for men, and often replaced stage four, that of achieving promotion.
7 Temporary exit from the occupation — that is, 'leave without pay': The majority of women, and almost a quarter of the male interviewees, regarded 'leave without pay' as an important and separate stage in the type of teaching career currently available to individuals. This was particularly true for younger teachers in their twenties and thirties.

For women, this stage occurred if they left the occupation for several years to travel and/or raise a family; while for men it represented a planned, although temporary, break in their teaching career, usually for the purposes of overseas travel, work experience or further study.

The interviewees identifying this stage saw it as being 'time out' from mainstream career considerations, and as a period for rejuvenation, there being no intention to leave the occupation on a permanent basis. It was viewed as being a particularly important stage in the teaching career at a time of reduced promotion opportunities and mobility.
8 Permanent Exit from the Occupation: This stage, which was only mentioned by interviewees who were close to retirement age, was seen as being the final stage in the teaching career.

Why Do Teachers Seek Promotion?

It is clear from the interviews conducted that the wish to gain promotion did not explain the career behaviour of all teachers. The reason was that teachers defined success and failure in their employment in a variety of ways, and were motivated for different reasons. Some, for example, sought unlimited promotion, while others were more modest in their expectations. However, it is also clear that most of those interviewed were interested in achieving some promotion, no matter how modest, at some time during their career. The major difference between teachers when it came to promotion related to how avidly they sought promotion, and the length of time over which they sustained this interest. There were many reasons as to why this variation occured between individuals. These arose partly due to the employment situation in the Education Department, and also due to family and wider social circumstances.

The following main reasons, which do not appear in any order of relative importance, were given by interviewees regarding why they sought promotion:

1 For some teachers promotion was the logical step to take if they were to achieve the types of goals they set themselves at the time they decided to become a teacher.

> I became a teacher in order to help children develop their abilities to the full and because I like them as people. The more promotion I achieve the more power I will have to influence the nature of children's schooling experiences in a positive way.
>
> (Senior Teacher)

2 For some, the motivation for seeking promotion came from the accumulation of experience which gave the teacher confidence that they could do a good job at a higher level on the promotion ladder.

> Having been an acting SM for a few months I felt that I could do the job well, and so I decided to try for promotion.

3 The wish to earn more money was a motivation for some.

> I have a young family to support and my wife doesn't work now. We're trying to do things like buy a house so the extra money from further promotion would come in very, very handy.
>
> (Senior Master)

4 Some teachers, as a result of observing their colleagues, came to the conclusion that they could do a better job than those who had already achieved promotion.

> After being a vice principal in this school for some time I came to realize that I would be a better, more humane and effective principal than the fellow who is in charge

here now. The frustrating thing is to see someone who is less competent above you. That gave me confidence to apply for promotion.

5   Some sought to establish new professional challenges due to a feeling of boredom in their current post.

After you've been an ST for ten years or so you get sick of the same old routine. I pretty well know what's going to happen each day before it actually does happen. I'm in a rut at the moment: things are running too smoothly. You also want a change in the type of job you do, and one way to get it is to be promoted further up the ladder. When I've been an acting VP there's been something different and unpredictable each day: I thrive on that sort of thing.

6   Some teachers sought promotion as a matter of pride or because they felt that if they didn't seek promotion it was a public admission of incompetence.

I hate being overtaken by younger men because it somehow adversely reflects upon me and my professional capabilities.
(Principal Education Officer)

7   Some individuals applied for promotion after receiving encouragement from colleagues who said such things as 'you can do it' or 'we think you would make a good senior teacher'.

8   Some wanted the public, systems level recognition of competence which promotion implied.

It's nice to get a pat on the back in the form of promotion: we all thrive pretty well on that type of thing. Getting promoted is a way of proving myself to myself, my colleagues, friends and family.
(Vice Principal)

9   Some people wanted promotion more for the influence than the money.

I want to have a positive affect on the system, to put into effect at the school level what has worked for me in my own classroom and so influence the overall philosophy of the school.
(Principal)

It is not being suggested here that these reasons as to why teachers seek promotion are necessarily complete. Rather, they simply reflect the views of the relatively small number of teachers interviewed for this study regarding this matter.

With regard to the relative importance of the reasons given by interviewees for seeking promotion, it must be said that the motives of teachers appeared to vary enormously. However, it is possible to make some observations about this matter. For the majority of interviewees the main aim which guided their career behaviour appeared to be the maximisation of job satisfaction. This was mainly seen as being achieved by the teacher doing the very best they could to make a useful contribution, through their work, to assist in furthering the education of children. They sought to achieve this by maximizing their sphere of influence within the particular school or section of the Education Department in which they were employed. Given the current career structure and pathways within the department, and the means available to exert influence, for many this goal became operationalized in terms of them climbing the promotions ladder.

From the interviews conducted, it would appear that the most important reasons for teachers seeking promotion were:

1. A wish to maximise their influence and power within their school (and/or the education system) with a view to improving that school (and/or system);
2. A wish to have more freedom in their work; and,
3. A need to establish new challenges in order to relieve or reduce the threat of boredom.

According to many, the additional money associated with promotion was not regarded as being very important.

Career Contingency Factors

The teachers interviewed were asked for their views regarding the factors that have an important influence on a person's promotion prospects within the Education Department, in terms of both the level and rate of promotion achieved. The main characteristics identified (which are not presented in any order of relative importance, because it was not possible to adequately judge this from interviews) were:

Gender

Being male, was regarded as being a distinct advantage.

> Most who have gained promotion are men, but I'm not sure whether that's because women don't apply for advancement,

because they aren't as well qualified, or because the system discriminates against them in some way.

(Senior Mistress)

Qualifications

Having a degree, preferably from a University, was believed to give a teacher an advantage when seeking promotion, because it was believed that academic qualifications were favoured by those who determine who gets promoted.

> The teacher who is a university graduate has a big start on the others entered in the race for promotion. The advantage of being a graduate is greatest in the primary area where such a small proportion of teachers have degrees.
>
> (Superintendent)

Movement between Schools

Many interviewees believed that promotion comes as a result of moving between schools, the view being expressed that a teacher is unlikely to gain promotion within the one school. This means that promoted teachers (and especially those who gained rapid promotion) were seen as being those who were willing to move frequently between schools to further their career. An important aspect of being willing to move between schools, often at short notice, was that a teacher could take full advantage of career possibilities as they arose. In addition, it was felt that a teacher's willingness to move was seen by potential sponsors as an indication of their enthusiasm, energy and commitment to a successful career.

At the same time it was pointed out that a teacher could move too often between schools, so that they never stayed in one school long enough to build up contacts with advisors or sponsors who could benefit their quest for promotion. In addition, they could come to be seen as professionally irresponsible and opportunist in approach. Thus an important part of a successful career strategy was to work out the optimum time to stay in each school.

Geographical Mobility

Some teachers were only willing to move between schools in a restricted geographical region that were within commuting distance of their place of residence. Others were more geographically mobile, in that they were more-or-less willing to move to any job location that captured their interest in any part of the state: that is, they were 'cosmopolitans' rather than 'locals'. Due to perhaps a lack of regional ties, and a willingness to move their place of residence, these teachers were especially flexible in their career moves. However, such a high degree of flexibility was generally only offered by some teachers early in their careers. As one male principal put it:

> It's O.K. to be geographically mobile early in your career, when you're hungry for promotion and adventure and want to achieve Rome in a day. But after a while you tend to become tied to one region of the state for family reasons, or just because you're sick of the personal and professional disruption associated with moving all over the place. At that stage you drop the anchor, and become more careful about what you're willing to chase after or accept in terms of your career.

Short Time in any Particular School

A widely held belief was that if a teacher is to maximise promotion opportunities, they should spend no more than five years in the same school. This was particularly true during the early years of a person's career, when promotion possibilities, and the ability of a teacher to take advantage of these, were likely to be greatest.

> Promotion doesn't really, when it comes right down to it, depend upon length of teaching service or length of service in a particular school. The ones who gain promotion are those who jump from job to job, and from place to place.
>
> (Principal)

Further Study

Many believed that a willingness to undertake further study at the in-service or the post-graduate level increased a teacher's competitiveness in achieving promotion. It was a mark of their keenness and professional responsibility, and also helped to set them apart from the majority of teachers.

> I took on a part-time M.Ed. at the University mainly for career reasons, although I also enjoyed quite a few of the subjects. I saw it as a way of putting myself ahead of other people in the Depart-

ment, and so increasing my promotion prospects. It's a ladder out of my groove. It's also one way of proving my commitment to a career in teaching, and helps bring me to the attention of the right people.

(Vice Principal)

Many believed that undertaking courses in Educational Administration was particularly worthwhile in that many promotion positions expected a teacher to have some skills in this area.

Extra Curricula Involvement

It was believed that a heavy involvement in extra-curricular activities in the school, and sometimes the local community, which were often undertaken with the specific objective of improving promotion prospects was important. Many felt that an important expectation on the part of those who influence promotion was that an individual should do considerably more than just be a good classroom teacher.

You have two roles in a school: one is as a classroom teacher and the other is as a staff member. When it comes to the second role, extra curricula activities have a very favourable effect on promotion prospects because they show a readiness to give yourself to the school outside the minimum limits. Also, conspicuous activity of the right type brings you to the attention of those who influence promotion such as those in the Head and Regional Offices. It implies that you're interested in and committed to your work. At the school level it's a standing joke that whoever is the announcer on sports day will be the next teacher to get promoted.

(Supervisor)

Systems Level Involvement

To gain advancement to the highest promotion positions, many interviewees believed that there was a need to make a useful and valued contribution not only at the school level but also at the systems level.

It doesn't seem an unreasonable expectation that those who are promoted to head or regional office type positions should first show that they can make a contribution at the macro level. This may take the form of being an office bearer in their particular subject association, or being on an Education Department Committee. There is also no doubt that the person who is known more widely than the school situation is generally advantaged in the promotions system.

(Vice Principal)

A Career Plan and Strategy

It was believed that a set of career *goals* and a career *strategy* clearly indicated where and how a teacher hoped to accomplish their career expectations.

> In my second year of teaching I decided that my aim was to become the principal of a reasonably large school as soon as possible (which I estimated would take me about fifteen years) and then a Superintendent. So I set out to read the promotions game in much the same way as you read a game of chess. I'm not sure whether it was luck or not, but I was able to achieve my goals without many setbacks along the way.
>
> (Superintendent)

Interviewees felt that the career map and strategy developed by any particular teacher depended upon such matters as their age and level of experience, qualifications, sector of the system in which they were employed, gender, marital status, whether they had a 'limited success' or 'unlimited success' career outlook, and the opportunity structure in the Education Department at any given time.

A Career Timetable

A strong sense of a time perspective, when it comes to achieving various promotion goals that the person has set for themselves, was seen as important.

> I've always had some sort of time-line in mind when it comes to promotion. For example, I always planned to apply for my first promotion after five years of teaching. Also I know you have to make sure you're a Vice Principal in a high school by the age of thirty-five otherwise you've missed the boat.
>
> (Senior Master)

Fast First Promotion

Some stressed the ability to obtain at least their first promotion in the minimum time, which for teachers in the top jobs (e.g. Principals, Superintendents, Directors) was usually after approximately five years of employment.

'Good Luck'

Some referred to luck as playing some part in their success in building a career, due to the opportunity structure expanding or developing in ways which favoured their particular career plans and aspirations.

> I was fortunate in my career in that I always seemed to be at the right place at the right time. Also, I was a beginning teacher when the whole education system in this State was expanding and being restructured, so in a sense I was swept along by it all.
> (Principal Education Officer)

Having a Sponsor

Some noted that one of the ways in which a teacher who is ambitious to gain promotion can improve their chances of achieving their aim is to develop a career strategy which includes the attraction and maintenance of a sponsor. It was said that one way to achieve this was to draw themselves to the attention of powerful people in the Education Department who influence who gets promoted. That is, one seeks a sponsor or patron.

> Perhaps it is because this is such a small education system, where everyone seems to know everyone else, that it is almost essential that if a teacher wants to be very successful they must gain the support and 'nod' from those in what is called 'the golden circle'.... that is, the fifteen or so people in the Department who wield most of the power and influence.

> It is important to get to know what goes on in the inner sanctum. I suppose that early in your career you also need to make sure that you don't get your principal off side because they are the ones who write the reports on teachers seeking promotion. Patronage is important and natural because, in any organization,

those at the top are going to pick out the ones who are 'the goers', and reward them.

(Director)

Interviewees said that for those employed in schools the most valuable sponsors were superintendents and principals (in that order), while for those employed in non-school positions it was the Director General of Education and Regional Directors. They adopted a number of different strategies to attract a sponsor, many of which will be outlined shortly in greater detail. These included: extra-curricular involvement at the school level to attract the attention of the principal, who was likely to identify the teacher as being energetic, enthusiastic and more than just a classroom teacher; various types of involvement at the systems level, in order to attract the attention of those who were powerful in determining who gets promoted, such as superintendents; and, various other ways of developing a high visibility in the school system which helped the teacher become well known.

Non-Threatening to Superiors

Leading on from the previous point, some felt that in order to successfully gain a sponsor a teacher generally had to conform to the views of their principal and supervisors: to put it in a nutshell, to be seen as someone who did not 'rock the boat'.

> The principals' and superintendents' reports are vitally important, so you can't afford to get off side with them. If you want to go against them and their wishes you have to consider whether they will still write you a good report and give you a highly recommended one. On the other hand, I know some of my colleagues who feel that as long as you are polite and can justify your views soundly and logically there will not be any backlash due to non-conformity.

(Senior Teacher)

Experience in Unpopular Work Locations

A willingness to work in undesirable and unpopular work locations was regarded by some interviewees to be important.

> If you want rapid promotion you go to an isolated or unpopular area where the competition is less. You go onto the islands, down the west coast, or into a housing commission type area.

(Senior Mistress)

Administrative Experience

Some teachers stressed the importance of gaining some administrative type experience.

> Most promotion positions require you to take on administrative tasks so if you want to have a chance you need to show that you are a capable administrator. This is particularly hard to achieve for the ordinary classroom teacher who has yet to achieve their first promotion.
> (Senior Teacher)

Being a Competent Classroom Teacher

To be seen as being a competent classroom teacher was mentioned by many interviewees, this being particularly important to gaining the first promotion.

> To become a senior teacher you must show above average ability in the classroom — to manage kids, to be well organised, committed to what you're doing, and to have an interesting and fulfilling curriculum.
> (Senior Teacher)

Length of Service

Interviewees believed that an age-grade system (or length-of-experience-grade system) existed within the promotions hierarchy, although they also pointed to cases where individuals had been promoted unusually quickly, given the norms that had developed over time.

Having presented teacher perceptions regarding the characteristics of the most successful teachers in the promotion race it is important to note that not all of these factors were identified by the same teachers, or by all the teachers. Indeed, interesting insights are gained if we identify those characteristics chosen by different groups of teachers, such as the rapidly promoted. However, it is only possible to point to trends since it was not possible to, in any statistically rigorous way, quantify the interview material collected.

Almost all of those interviewed identified certain factors, such as being a graduate, as important; while some items, such as the importance of sponsorship, was mainly identified by the successful and those who had sought further promotion but had not been successful in achieving this. However, while the less successful freely offered comments regarding the importance of sponsorship, often as an explanation as to why, despite what they saw as being their excellent qualities, they were not promoted (the 'its not what you know but who you know' factor), the most promoted teachers spoke less freely and openly about sponsorship. Perhaps this was because to do so would be to devalue the importance of their own professional capabilities and other personal characteristics which they believed had secured their promotion. Many teachers also identified sponsorship as being in some significant sense an unfair advantage, and so they did not want to talk about this when it came to their own career, perhaps because it may have served to tarnish or devalue their own accomplishments. These teachers were much happier and relaxed when talking about the role of sponsorship in gaining promotion for others, rather than themselves.

Some characteristics, such as the importance of having a career timetable, strategy and career map were mainly identified, as one would logically expect, by those who were the most successful in terms of the rate and/or level of promotion achieved.

Career Anchorage Perspectives

The majority of interviewees adopted a 'limited success' career perspective in that rather than measuring their progress in the promotions hierarchy against the full range of promotion positions available, they stressed how much promotion they had already accomplished and often felt quite satisfied with the amount of success achieved, particularly at a time of reduced promotion opportunities. However, teachers career anchorage perspectives did change over time and depended (at any particular time) upon such variables as their age, level of experience, gender, marital status, and current promotion position.

The younger, male teachers mostly adopted a 'limited success' career perspective up until the time they married, after which many of them changed to an 'unlimited success' career perspective, in that they stressed vertical rather than horizontal mobility. However, as they gained experience and wanted to 'put down roots' in one region of the state, many changed back to a 'limited success' perspective. Thus the career anchorage perspectives of men were not fixed, but re-assessed and re-adjusted by the individual at various times during their career, particularly as personal (and especially family) circumstances changed.

Those employed in non-school advisory, supervisory and administrative duties were more likely than those employed in schools to have an 'unlimited success' career anchorage perspective over the length of their career.

All the women interviewed had adopted a 'limited success' career perspective from the very beginning of their career and this had not changed to any great extent over time, regardless of their marital status, level of experience, or current promotion position.

In developing a career outlook most teachers did not think in terms of the full range of promotion positions available in both the school and non-school sectors of the department. Instead, those employed in schools who adopted an 'unlimited success' career anchorage perspective thought of the top position to which they could aspire as being the principal of a large school, while those employed in non-school promotion positions adopted a career perspective which almost exclusively thought in terms of the promotion opportunities available out of schools.

Many other sections of this chapter, such as those dealing with teachers' motivations for seeking promotion, and the place of horizontal mobility in the teaching career, also relate to this issue of teacher career anchorage perspectives.

The Promoted Teacher: A Composite Picture

It is useful to summarise the views of interviewees regarding the characteristics of promoted teachers by presenting a composite picture of what the most promoted and rapidly promoted teachers in the Tasmanian Education Department was likely to be like. In Chapter 9, we will seek to match this composite picture, which is based on teacher perceptions, against the actual, more objectively assessed career histories and characteristics of promoted teachers.

Interviewees believed that the most successful teacher in gaining promotion in the Education Department of Tasmania was likely to be male and university educated. He would have been geographically mobile throughout his career, but most especially during the first ten or so years of teaching. During that time he displayed a willingness to work in what many of his colleagues would have regarded as being undesirable, unpopular work locations, such as schools in isolated areas of the state or in lower socio-economic status communities.

As the member of a school's staff he demonstrated his competence as a classroom teacher, but also as an administrator. In addition to his usual duties as a teacher, he had a substantial involvement in extra curricula activities at the school level in areas such as coaching sporting teams, organizing the school fete, and editing the school magazine. He was also seen as being an innovator within the schools in which he worked, this leading to him being seconded for two years to the curriculum branch to develop curriculum materials for use in schools. In addition, he was actively involved with his profession at the state level, being an office bearer in his subject association, the member of an important committee established by the Education Department, and on the Executive of the Teachers Federation. One of the reasons he actually involved himself in these extra curricula activities was to draw himself to the attention of those at the upper levels of the Education Department who were influential in determining who achieved promotion, although he also found these activities interesting for their own sake.

Throughout his career his views on education-related matters had generally conformed to those of his principal, superintendent and advisors. However, when he has held divergent views he has not been unwilling to express them, but has been careful to ensure that they have been presented in a well argued, polite and non-threatening way, which has not been regarded as disloyal or undermining of his superiors.

From the very beginning of his teaching career within the Education Department he was committed to gaining promotion. In doing this he had a time perspective in mind, based upon what he felt were the main career norms within the occupation. He knew, for example, where he wanted to be at the age of thirty years, forty years and so on, and developed a career strategy to assist him in achieving his goals. He was successful in gaining promotion from the very beginning of his career, having achieved his first promotion in, or close to, the minimum time. Luck played some part in his career success in the sense that he was seeking promotion at a time when the education system was expanding; and, he also benefited in terms of career outcomes when the system was restructured at various times.

In view of the points made above, based upon the interview data gathered for this study, a clear pattern seems to emerge regarding the characteristics of those who have been successful in the Education Department, in terms of the degree and speed at which promotion has been gained. Generally speaking, those teachers who have been hierarchically successful had a realistic career plan regarding the promotion positions they wanted to achieve, a strategy to help them achieve their goals, and a time line (or career timetable) with regard to when they hoped to achieve particular goals.

When considering the information given above on various facets of promotion, as this applies to teachers, it must be borne in mind that the ideas raised refer to 'teacher perceptions' about promotion within the Education Department: to what they believe to be the case rather than what may in fact have been the case. The actual career patterns of promoted teachers were presented in Chapter 7.

Teachers Who do not Seek Promotion

It needs to be pointed out that not all teachers are avidly seeking promotion. There were many reasons why a teacher did not seek further promotion. For instance, some believed that promotion mainly went to those who were willing to move between schools in various parts of the state, and they were not keen to commit themselves to the instability in overall lifestyle that this was likely to bring with it.

> Regarding geographic mobility and the wish to follow the promotions ladder, my priority lies in maintaining the stability of my family and home situation and so quite early on in my career I decided that I was not prepared to cart my family around the state just to gain promotion.

It seems that others did not want to progress further up the promotions ladder if it meant taking on a more or less administrative type post. Yet it is important that the system recognizes that these teachers may still need and want promotion and/or some systems level recognition for their talents as classroom teachers.

One senior teacher commented:

> Nobody in their right mind would want to get involved with the administrative side of things. Although the power thing may be psychologically satisfying for some, from my point of view there is little of value. The principal is nothing more than a waste paper basket; he's the dumping ground for complaints — he's there to be shot at.

This move on the part of some teachers to emphasise rewards, apart from promotion, is examined in greater detail later in this chapter when we probe horizontal mobility.

Operation of the Promotion System

Teachers were asked to indicate how satisfied they were with the way in which the promotions system operated. After analysing the responses of interviewees two things became very clear:

1. Some did not fully understand, except in the very broadest sense, how the promotions system operated. As a result some of the criticisms made occurred due to misconceptions or ignorance regarding how the promotions system functioned. This general lack of knowledge about something which most teachers regarded as important, and which had a direct influence over their professional lives and careers, was somewhat surprising. A typical type of comment was:

   > I guess that it would be true to say that I don't really know much about how the system operates. What I do know is that I have to put in an application and have a

good report on my work from my principal and local superintendent and that if I'm not successful I have the right to appeal. The rest is out of my hands so I don't bother myself about it.

(Senior Mistress)

However, one principal commented:

> Those who are really interested in getting promoted find out how the system operates: those who don't bother aren't all that interested.

2 Notwithstanding the point made above, there was substantial criticism of some central promotion procedures, in particular those which reflected upon whether or not the system was seen to be operating fairly and in the best interests of all concerned. For example, many felt that the system of appeals did not work well, and that the form in which applications for promotion were made should be improved. A typical comment about the operation of the appeals system was:

> The appeals system as it currently operates is crazy because almost everyone who isn't successful appeals. It turns out that you end up with two promotions committees rather than one. Too many teachers treat the promotions committee as merely a stepping stone on the way to the Appeals Committee.

(Principal)

Others were more concerned about a system of sponsorship operating which they claimed had an important influence on determining who gained promotion. Most of these comments took the form of the cliche 'it's not what you know but who you know'.

However, others felt that any promotion system inevitably had to be partly based upon subjective judgments regarding the personal qualities which should carry weight.

The main suggestion made to improve the operation of the promotions system was the introduction of a system of open interviewing, which would make appointments far more understandable, and remove the 'faceless area' of the current promotions system. Many felt that a short list of candidates should be drawn up for each promotion position to be filled, and that these teachers should then be interviewed in order to help select the successful candidate. There was some disagreement about whether the interviewing panel should consist of the currently constituted Promotions Committee, or whether the Principal, staff and parent representatives from the school in which the position is to be filled should also be on the selection panel. Some felt it would be a good thing if representatives of the school were present at the interview because this would increase the likelihood that the person selected would fit into the school concerned.

Currently the Director General of Education makes his own appointments when filling the top advisory, supervisory and administrative positions within the Education Department. Interviewees expressed mixed feelings about this practice, with the majority favouring a more open system of selection when determining who wins such highly prized positions.

While the majority of interviewees stressed changes to the promotion system that would benefit teachers, a small minority argued that when considering changes the focus should be upon 'what is best for schools and the children in them, not the individual teacher'.

Horizontal Mobility

Interviewees were asked about the relative importance of vertical and horizontal mobility in their own careers. It is clear from the comments made that teachers were particularly willing to move between schools and geographical regions of the state early in their career in search of promotion. Promotion was seen as being easiest to gain in schools that were not generally favoured as a desirable work location, these schools being in isolated or country areas of the state, and in socially disadvantaged areas.

The career strategy identified by interviewees was that younger teachers were willing to work in such schools in order to maximise promotion opportunities. Having achieved promotion, a teacher's aim was then to gain horizontal mobility to a school in a more 'desirable' work location. These schools were identified as being those within the main population centres, and, in particular, those serving middle-class type communities. In these schools the potential problems associated with a teachers' work were most likely to be kept within manageable limits.

Women expressed a different view. Although all the women interviewed had achieved some promotion within the Education Department, with the exception of two unmarried women, all women stressed that obtaining a desirable work location was the most important factor influencing their career moves. In addition, married women were less geographically mobile than married men, and their key aim was to obtain a school in a middle class area close to home. The only women who expressed a different point of view were the two unmarried women interviewees who regarded themselves as being geographically mobile. To these women promotion was more important than was horizontal mobility.

With the reduction in promotion opportunities and teacher mobility that has occurred in recent years, due to a contraction in the school system, the career strategies and behaviour of teachers are likely to have been affected. Many teachers said they were concerned that if they moved to an isolated or country region in order to gain promotion, they may find themselves trapped in that position for many years, due to reduced opportunities for horizontal mobility. In view of this, many would rather forego the opportunity to gain promotion to an isolated region, and instead seek horizontal mobility to a preferred work location.

There was a belief amongst some interviewees that because many teachers were increasingly unwilling to be posted anywhere in the state, and with a reduction in the number of bonded students entering the occupation who could be forced to work in unpopular schools, the Education Department was likely to find it increasingly difficult to staff some schools. In order to encourage teachers to accept and even seek a posting to some of the 'less desirable' work locations it was suggested that the Department should provide those who accepted appointments to such schools with the promise of future reward: a type of 'deferred gratification' factor for teachers.

A senior teacher in a city school interested in seeking promotion to a VP position said:

> If you go wherever they send you or to an unpleasant work location in one of those 'social welfare' institutions then the Department should promise you a good post a few years later to make up for it; to reward you. For example, I would only be willing to apply for promotion to VP in a West Coast school if I knew that I'd be guaranteed a school in a better area after about five years.

One thing which the individual and group interviews sought to establish was the extent to which teachers were prepared to make (and sought) horizontal moves, why these moves were made, and what the teachers hoped to gain as a result. This was seen as an important area of teacher behaviour to examine since lateral moves are likely to become increasingly important during a period of contracting promotion opportunities, while for some teachers the securing of a desirable work location without promotion may be more important than obtaining promotion to an undesirable work location.

In terms of the responses obtained from interviewees, the following were the most common reasons given for a teacher seeking horizontal mobility between posts:

1   Some, who believed they were in 'dead end' positions where there would be few promotion opportunities available to them in the future, sought to make a horizontal move in the hope of opening up career opportunities. For example, a person in a

Service Branch which was contracting sought to move to another branch where this was not a problem;
2 A teacher who felt that there were no further promotion opportunities available to him had sought to move to a more pleasant part of the State in order to develop his hobbies and plans for retirement;
3 Family reasons were important for some, such as a wish to live nearer to parents;
4 Some saw moving to a new school as a way of revitalizing their interest in teaching. 'A change was like a breath of fresh air', was a frequent comment; and
5 A particular work location may have become an unpleasant one due to, for example, the fact that some staff don't get along with other staff, such as a new principal. Teachers who found themselves in an undesirable work location were likely to seek to move to another school.

In terms of the interviews conducted for this study, three things became clear. First, many teachers were coming to place greater emphasis on the importance of securing a desirable work location rather than achieving a higher status within the promotions hierarchy: 'I would rather be an SM in Hobart than a VP on the West Coast'. Second, although some interviewees defined a desirable work location in terms of the characteristics of the school in which they taught ('What I want is a small school with "normal" kids: not a housing commission area or anything like that'), many teachers were coming to define a 'desirable work location' in terms of out-of-school and geographic location factors rather than the actual characteristics of the school in which they worked. Third, several teachers expressed their willingness and intention to drop back in status within the promotions system in order to achieve a more desirable work location. This was a frequently expressed viewpoint amongst teachers who had worked in schools in isolated or lower socioeconomic areas for several years.

These outlooks are ones which could have a considerable and important influence on the career patterns and mobility of teachers. It is an area which warrants further investigation in order to ascertain how widespread is this outlook, and to explore the implications for both the teaching profession and the overall operation of the school system.

Teachers Who do not Seek Mobility

The emphasis so far has been upon teachers who sought various forms of mobility within teaching, whether it be of the horizontal or vertical kind. However, it should not be assumed that a willingness to move between schools was shared equally by all teachers. Some did display loyalty and ties to specific institutions, and rejected 'career moves' as being unethical and contrary to their view of what being a good teacher was all about. There were others who had long established commitments which held them to a particular area or community, and who were therefore reluctant to move. Some views regarding this matter were:

> You have to balance career prospects against overall satisfactions in life. I wouldn't take a job with higher pay if it meant that I had to leave this place where I'm living — I like the locality and have invested too much in my house to think of selling it.
>
> (Senior Master)

> I like it in this part of the State and would put up with lots of intolerable things at school to stay here because I have a very pleasant out-of-school life.
>
> (Vice Principal)

In the case of married women teachers, many put their husband's career ahead of their own, and so in terms of pursuing their own career they were more or less immobile.

One factor which reduced the mobility of most teachers at some stage in their career was a dependent family, and in particular children of school age.

> I wouldn't dream of moving house for at least four to five years. My eldest child has just started school and I wouldn't want to introduce instability into his schooling at this stage. I'm not geographically mobile at present because the welfare of my family is my top consideration.
>
> (Senior Teacher)

It was also clear that a willingness to move house was far less common than was a willingness to move school, mainly because of the expense and overall disruption involved. This often meant that teachers preferred to transfer to another school in the same locality rather than move to a different part of the state.

The situation discussed here regarding teacher mobility raises a paradoxical situation regarding the geographical mobility of those who occupy the most senior promotion positions who have often shown the greatest commitment to obtaining promotion. From the interviews conducted it appears that those who are most promoted in the Education Department are likely to be the ones who have an attitude of mind which allows them to move freely about the state in order to maximise the horizontal and/or vertical mobility advantages available to them, while those who are tied to a particular community by dependents, friends, relatives and a whole range of community-based loyalties are, it seems, less likely to achieve promotion to the most senior posts.

One needs to ask: does this, in fact, mean that there is an imbalance in the types of persons recruited to the more senior promotion positions in schools, in that they are likely to be less committed to a particular community than are those who are less likely to gain promotion? The answer to this question is particularly important at a time when Tasmanian Education authorities are expecting senior staff to take on an important role in the establishment of school councils and in increasing community involvement in schools.

Changing Opportunity Structure in Teaching

Interviewees were keenly aware that an 'opportunity structure' existed in the Education Department in which they were employed, although they did not use this particular term themselves. They referred to the hierarchy of promotion positions and opportunities that existed in teaching. They were also conscious of the structure of the school system itself, and how changes in this impinged upon the career and promotion opportunities available to them. Teachers in their 50s and 60s spoke at length about the types of changes that had occurred over the past three to four decades in the organization and structure of the Tasmanian school system: the periods of expansion and contraction in school enrolments, and the impact these changes had on the opportunity structure and career pathways available to them and their colleagues within teaching.

Many of these teachers said they had built their careers between the early 1950s and the mid 1970s, at a time when the education system was expanding, so that any competent teacher who sought promotion could expect to achieve this in time. In addition, the rate of teacher mobility between schools was sufficiently high to ensure that any teacher who wanted to teach in a particular area of the state would not have this denied them for long. Referring to this period of expansion, one principal said:

> I started my career at a time when the school population was expanding and there was a shortage of teachers. As a graduate I was sitting pretty. Anyone who was reasonably good at their job was swept along by it all and could easily gain rapid promotion. One problem is that some of those who were promoted at that time were really pretty hopeless: they were simply seeking promotion at a time when it was hard to find enough talented people

to fill all the vacancies. That wouldn't happen today because the competition is so great.

They noted that with a contraction in the school system since the mid 1970s there had been a substantial reduction in and restriction of promotion opportunities available for teachers. As a result, individuals had to change their expectations and career timetables to take account of these changed circumstances; to look for different types of success and sources of satisfaction within their careers, and to re-adjust their high expectations regarding what were fulfillable goals. A young senior master in his early thirties said:

> If I dwelt on the current situation too much I'd get really resentful but that wouldn't really help matters. So it's a matter of adjusting my expectations to accept the fact that promotion doesn't come easily these days. You have to look more to the enjoyment you can get from the kids for your satisfactions and feelings of worth, and accept that not getting further promotion doesn't mean that you are a poor teacher.

Several of the older teachers interviewed commented that what teachers had to realize was that the period between 1960 and the 1970s, when promotion and career opportunities in teaching had mushroomed due to an expanding education system, was atypical, and that all that was happening now was a return to the more typical pre-1950s situation.

Interviewees commented on the fact that with a contraction in the school system in recent years, and reduced opportunities for promotion and mobility within the teaching service, it had become necessary for teachers to take stock of their careers and their priorities: to formulate new career timetables and maps; look for different types of success and sources of satisfaction within their careers; and, to adjust their high expectations regarding what were fulfillable goals. A teacher who had gained his first promotion, but who was now keen on achieving a more administrative position in a school's promotion hierarchy, commented:

> The trouble is that the jobs just aren't there to apply for, and that can be awfully frustrating if you feel that you are good at your job and deserve promotion. At the same time, if there aren't the jobs to apply for then a person doesn't feel unsuccessful if they don't gain further promotion.

It became clear that the teachers most likely to suffer in the changed promotion climate, at a time when there was a contraction in the opportunity structure, were those who were unable to realistically adjust career expectations that had developed during a period of expansion.

Chances of Gaining Further Promotion

When teachers were asked to estimate their chances of gaining further promotion within the Education Department most of those who had at least gained their first promotion felt their chances were reasonably good. In fact, the higher a teacher's current promotion position the greater they rated their chances of gaining further promotion.

Many of those interviewed felt that the first promotion was the most difficult one for a teacher to achieve, because the individual was required to compete with such a large number of other teachers for promotion to the position of senior master/mistress or senior teacher. At the time this study was conducted there were some 3158 full-time teachers who had yet to gain their first promotion and only 424 SM and 194 ST positions and so there was a great deal of potential competition for the relatively small number of available 'lower management' promotion positions.

Many felt the first promotion was the most important one for a teacher to achieve because it represented the first major form of public, conspicuous recognition of a teacher's talents by Education Department authorities. It constituted recognition at the 'systems' level whereas before the first promotion was achieved this was only available at the 'local' or school level. A further reason for the importance of the initial promotion was that it represented the first step on the promotions ladder, the achievement of which opened up the way to other higher status, more powerful and better paid promotion positions. A senior teacher said: 'Until you get your first promotion you are never sure that you are appreciated as a teacher'; while a senior mistress commented: 'In career terms you are stagnant until you get that first promotion. Once you get the first promotion you feel that in a sense anything is possible'.

Many expressed the view that the problem of reduced promotion opportunities was not as great for those who had gained their first promotion within the promotions hierarchy because the pool of people with whom they had to compete gets smaller. For example, there were only 424 SM's and 194 STs to compete for the 117 VP and 249 principal positions. Others disagreed, and said that the move from a senior master/mistress or senior teacher position to that of VP or principal was the most difficult promotion to achieve. As a secondary school SM said regarding this matter:

> The first promotion (to SM) is the easiest to get because you're judged on what you've been trained for: that is, being an effective classroom teacher. Also, you're only competing against subject peers, that is, those who work in the same subject area. But the next promotion is made difficult by the fact that you have no training to be an administrator and it is difficult to accurately judge a person's ability in this area until they have actually been

promoted. Also you are competing with all SMs not just those in the same subject area. The higher you go the tighter it becomes.

A senior master pointed to the special problems faced by those in particular subject areas:

> The problem is that no matter how good you are, if you happen to be a subject specialist in the wrong area then your promotion opportunities are screwed. If you're in Music or Modern Languages for instance you have Buckley's chance of getting ahead even though you may be better than a Maths or Social Science teacher who does get promoted. This feature of the promotions system causes lots of upsets for many teachers.

This comment points to the problem that as the middle level of the career structure which rewards subject specialists (at least at the secondary school level) comes into conflict with the changed need at the school level to employ and deploy generalists, in order to maintain viable curricula in a contracting school system, some major re-adjustment of the existing promotions and reward system will need to be made.

In view of what was said by the teachers interviewed, it is clear that reduced promotion opportunities are regarded by most to be one of the major problems currently confronting those employed in the occupation of teaching. It was widely felt that changes need to be made to the career structure to ensure that when a teacher undertakes good work, that this is acknowledged in a formal sense.

Reduced Promotion Opportunities, Teacher Behaviour and Morale

Several quite different viewpoints were expressed about this particular matter. The majority of those interviewed felt that reduced promotion opportunities in the teaching service would have a very detrimental influence upon teacher morale. It was felt that this would occur because able and conscientious teachers, who would in earlier times have gained promotion in recognition of their talents and commitment, would no longer have such promotion as readily available to them. A school principal said:

> With reduced promotion opportunities we are going to have a morale problem. In the past we have said that if you are a good teacher you will get promoted, and there weren't that many good teachers in the past who were not able to get recognition in the

form of promotion. Now the talented person isn't assured of promotion so you have the problem of reduced morale.

Many interviewees felt that poor employment prospects outside teaching meant that many teachers who were disgruntled about reduced promotion prospects, and who would in the past have sought employment outside teaching, would now feel trapped in teaching and so their morale would suffer as a result. A counter viewpoint was that in view of employment prospects in society in general being currently so restricted, those who had a job but limited promotion prospects would count themselves as lucky and approach their work in a suitably positive way.

> When it comes to promotion it is important to remember that it is very difficult for a teacher to move out of the Education Department. You have got certain skills and talents that are useful in schools but not elsewhere in places like business. If you leave teaching what can you do? There are not many other places where a teacher's talent can be applied.
>
> (Senior Teacher)

Many felt that the problem of reduced morale would be exacerbated by the quite widespread feeling in some quarters that some of those who gained promotion in the past, when the education system was expanding and many more opportunities for promotion existed, were not as well qualified as were many of the teachers who had yet to achieve promotion. This had the potential to result in considerable stress and strain in staff room relations where able but unpromoted teachers felt that they were answerable to less able but already promoted colleagues who happened to be (to use that awful cliche) 'at the right place at the right time'. As one vice principal put it:

> If we pride ourselves on having a promotion system which is meant to reward the most able members of the service, then we should also accept that mistakes sometimes do happen and that some people, once promoted, 'die on the job' so to speak. There are so many talented young people around these days so it is essential that we devise some mechanism to get rid of the dead wood.

Another teacher noted that the Teachers Federation would need to play an important part in helping to devise and monitor the operation of a suitable mechanism whereby the demotion, as well as the promotion, of a teacher was possible. He said:

The Teacher's Federation should not make it so difficult for the Department to demote or even fire the incompetent teacher. After all, it is in the interests of kids and teachers as a whole that the lazy or incompetent principal or teacher is not allowed to continue in his position.

(Principal)

Several expressed the view that the way in which the Education Department currently seemed to cope with the problem of the incompetent or lazy teacher was to 'pass them around the school system so that they don't get to do too much damage in any one school', or to post them to a Service Branch position where they wouldn't have direct contact with children.

Although there was widespread agreement about the likelihood of tensions, frustrations and resentment building up over time (due to the situation outlined above) there was less agreement about the likely effect of this on teacher behaviour. Some felt that reduced promotion opportunities would result in teachers competing more fiercely and aggressively for the fewer positions available. Others believed teaching was an occupation that attracted people who would do the job to the best of their ability regardless of reduced promotion opportunities. It was argued that if teachers were 'true professionals', reduced promotion opportunities should not worry them and that over time they would come to accept the reality of the changed situation, and adjust their expectations regarding promotion accordingly. Those who held the latter viewpoint differed in their opinions regarding the affect of such acceptance on teacher behaviour. In the opinion of some the teachers involved would continue to invest a considerable amount of time and effort in undertaking their work in classrooms, while others felt they would probably cut back on the time they devoted to their work as teachers to develop other interests outside work in areas such as hobbies, which would occupy an increased importance in the life of the individuals involved. Typical comments regarding this matter were:

The situation is now so tight that I know that if I want promotion (which I do) I can't relax for a moment. I have to totally dedicate myself to playing the promotions game well if I'm to have a chance of success, which means partly pulling out all the stops.

(Vice Principal)

I accept that promotion just isn't on for most people these days, and get on with my aim to become the best senior master possible, and to do the very best I can for the kids in my charge.

(Senior Master)

I've bought a small farm and what I plan to do is look to getting more of my satisfactions from out-of-school and leisure type activities.

(Senior Teacher)

It became clear that for the vast majority of those interviewed the main motive for seeking promotion was not the extra remuneration, but rather a wish to be challenged professionally and to have more influence over how their school or department was run, in the interests of providing a better education for children. A recently promoted teacher said:

Lets face it, there isn't much in it money-wise, being at the top of the four year trained scale compared to being a senior teacher. Given all the extra responsibility involved, no one would surely take on this promotion just for the money. I wanted promotion as a way of being better able to implement more of my ideas to make this school a better place for the kids who attend it.

Not all, however, agreed with this altruistic view.

Regardless of what they say, most teachers want promotion mainly because of the extra money involved. That's particularly so if they have a wife and a young family to support.

(Director)

Overall, it was clear that the majority of those spoken to felt that new ways urgently needed to be found to provide the more talented and energetic teachers with some form of conspicuous, systems-level recognition of their abilities and capabilities. Otherwise, morale will suffer.

Conclusion

The purpose of this chapter has been to report on teacher perceptions regarding main aspects of existing career, promotion and mobility patterns within the Education Department of Tasmania, and to examine the likely influence of reduced career opportunities and mobility upon the behaviour and morale of the teaching service.

Chapter 9

Teachers' Careers: Summary, Discussion of Results and Conclusions Drawn

This chapter draws together the various results reported in the last three chapters into a coherent and unified whole. In so doing, it will blend together the structural and phenomenological perspectives on promotion and careers in teaching adopted in this research. The discussion of the results will be organised using the research framework outlined in Chapter 5; and comparisons will be made between this and other research studies undertaken on various aspects of work careers (in general), and the teaching career (in particular) surveyed in Chapter 2 (ways of conceptualizing occupational careers) and Chapter 3 (the teaching career). The chapter concludes with some suggestions regarding fruitful future research directions on the rather vexed topic of teachers' careers.

The School Teaching Career

Tasmanian state school teachers tend to occur within families in that a large proportion of those in the survey population had relatives who were teachers. For example, over a third had a spouse who was a teacher and close to a half had either a brother or sister who were teachers. Despite this fact two thirds would not encourage a son or a daughter to become a teacher, although they would be more encouraging of a daughter. Many of those who would not actively encourage a son or daughter to become a teacher were concerned with what they regarded as being the declining status of the occupation in society and the increasingly difficult nature of the job. Many saw it as a 'dead end' occupation for the young due to the paucity of employment and promotion opportunities available. Those who would recommend the occupation to a son did so because of the *potential* security it offered; while for daughters they believed that it suited 'a woman's maternal temperament' and combined well with home duties.

Promoted teachers in Tasmania mainly came from the homes of

professional/managerial/white collar workers (42.6 per cent), over a third from the homes of manual workers (36.4 per cent) and the remainder had fathers who were farmers, farm labourers or unemployed. The vast majority (82.1 per cent) had mothers who were not employed outside the home.

Teachers perceived school teaching to be an occupation that offered a career in the sense in which the term is used by Hughes (1952), Pavalko (1971), Ritzer (1972), Huberman (1989), Prick (1989), Butt and Raymond (1989) and others: that is, it implies a commitment on the part of a person to obtaining promotion through the status hierarchy that exists according to some time schedule. However, in terms of those surveyed in this study, men had a greater commitment to a teaching career in these terms than did women. The overwhelming majority (90.8 per cent) of promoted teachers indicated that their career in teaching was important to their overall personal satisfaction in life.

Teaching was also found to be a career which offered incumbents highly structured and orderly career patterns (Wilensky, 1961; Glaser, 1968), a major reason for this being that teachers work careers were built within a bureaucratic-type organization. All teachers were conscious of the fact that their career moves were patterned, and generally planned, rather than random (e.g. Hilsum and Start, 1974; Lyons, 1981; Department of Education, 1982; Huberman, 1989).

A distinction is drawn in the literature between organisational and occupational careers. Most teachers in this study saw their careers first and foremost in terms of the organisation in which they were employed : as being primarily 'Education Department' teachers rather than as members of the teaching profession. School teaching has been found here to have an occupational culture which, as Charters (1970) has pointed out, confronts its practitioners with more or less standardised ways for them to pursue their career within it.

Teachers found working conditions, in the form of economic security and long holidays, the most satisfying aspect of their employment, while their main dissatisfactions related to more professional criteria, such as the size of classes, pressure of work and the extent of extra currricula duties such as playground supervision. In terms of satisfactions associated with teaching there were some differences between males and females, with men placing a greater emphasis on economic and security of employment considerations while women emphasised contact with students and parents. There was no substantial differences between males and females regarding main dissatisfactions with teaching.

This research confirms the view that teachers conceive of the teaching career as consisting of a number of distinct and identifiable stages, but for the teachers surveyed these differed markedly (in both number and content) to those identified in earlier studies (e.g. Morrison and McIntyre, 1973; Tisher et al., 1979; and McArthur, 1981; Huberman,

Discussion of Results and Conclusions Drawn

1989) as being the main stages in the teaching career. The main difference between the stages in the teaching career identified in this study, and those identified by others, is that teachers indicated four additional stages: the achievement of promotion; the movement of a teacher into non-school promotion positions; the achievement of an optimum or most desired work location (which was often achieved in mid career through horizontal rather than vertical mobility); and, temporary exit from the occupation (or leave without pay).

A key reason why these additional stages in the teaching career were identified by the teachers surveyed in this study, but not by those in earlier research, could be that as a result of the contraction in the opportunity structure in teaching that has occurred in recent years teachers have had to rethink the range of career options available to them, and to re-evaluate their careers in ways which encourage them to seek out further stages and additional mechanisms, apart from promotion, to satisfy their occupational needs.

This study shows that identifiable career pathways exist, and career patterns develop, in the teaching career. In addition, not only did these pathways and patterns occur in terms of an 'objective reality' that was created by the actual behaviour of teachers, but teachers were also aware of their existence and explicitly sought them out as they pursued their careers. For example, the career histories of directors and school principals were analysed to identify the career pathways that existed, and were created by, individuals in different types of promotion positions. It was found that the range and variety of career pathways varied according to the particular promotion position occupied. In the case of directors there was basically one main pathway, there being little variation between individuals in the career pathways adopted. For secondary and primary principals a variety of pathways led to the same promotion position. Thus, although those who occupied the same type of promotion position followed similar career pathways, there were often a variety of pathways that could lead to the same promotion position.

The promotion system that exists in teaching was clearly of importance to the vast majority of teachers at some stage in their teaching career; but a wide variation occurred between individuals with regard to the extent to which vertical mobility seemed to be more important, and for a longer period of time, for particular groups of teachers, such as men compared to woman; and various explanations (such as family responsibilities, and freedom to move between schools) have been considered as to why this is so. For those concerned with gaining and maximising promotion in their career, such a career perspective appeared to have an important effect on the way in which they directed their energies, and perceived their role as teachers, whether it was within the individual school or the system as a whole.

Forty-two per cent of teachers rated their chances of gaining further promotion within the Education Department as being either good or excellent, a third rated their chances as fair, and the remainder felt that their chances were not good. This was a surprising finding because at the same time as they were expressing an optimistic view about personally gaining further promotion, they indicated an overall concern about the reduced promotion opportunities and mobility within the teaching service that was occurring due to a contraction in the school system. It could well be that although teachers felt that the promotion opportunities available to the group as a whole were contracting, that they had a positive self image about their own ability to succeed in this difficult climate.

Men were more optimistic about gaining further promotion than were women, which was not surprising given the underrepresentation of women in promotion positions. For those working in schools, the higher a teacher's position in the promotions hierarchy, the better they rated their chances of gaining further promotion. In addition, those in the primary sector (e.g. senior masters/mistresses) were particularly optimistic. This undue optimism may have occurred because they had inaccurately read the opportunity structure in the Education Department, in which case more should be done to communicate the real situation to teachers, perhaps through staff development seminars. If this is not done, and teachers maintain unrealistically high expectations despite the difficult current situation, morale may suffer further when these expectations are not satisfied.

Although promotion within teaching did appear to be of concern to most teachers at some stage in their teaching career, most did not avidly seek promotion over the full length of their working lives. In view of this it is important to recognize that this concern was not sufficiently important to explain what motivated most teachers, most of the time, in their careers. As a result, it could be argued that the Education Department needs to modify the reward structure in teaching to take account of this situation.

In the objective sense teaching was found to be an occupation that offered a variety of different types of careers, both in schools and in various non-school advisory, supervisory and administrative positions. However, the majority (59.2 per cent) of promoted teachers in schools did not perceive this to be the case, and mainly thought about the teaching career in terms of the range of positions available in schools, there being no substantial difference between males and females regarding this matter. For those in advisory, supervisory and administrative positions, the majority mainly considered their future careers in terms of non-school positions.

Those individuals who did come to view teaching as an occupation that offered a range of careers generally did so during mid career. These

Discussion of Results and Conclusions Drawn

perspectives may help explain why there were found to be two main types of careers in teaching, that in schools and that in non-school positions; and why they occurred in parallel, there being little cross over of teachers backwards and forwards between the two careers.

It was also found that the particular type of career a teacher chose depended very much upon their values and motives for becoming a teacher. The difference in outlook and perspective between those who pursued these different types of careers was well illustrated when the main satisfactions and dissatisfactions teachers associated with their current employment position were examined. In terms of satisfactions, those employed in non-school positions placed less emphasis on industrial matters, such as economic factors and holidays, and more upon those satisfactions that were linked to the specific content of the work being undertaken, such as consultation with staff in schools, opportunity to practice own ideas, and time to pursue academic interests. They stressed autonomy and the opportunity for professional development through the pursuit of personal interests. There was a greater similarity between those in school and non-school positions with regard to dissatisfactions with their employment, both stressing pressure at work and curricular commitments.

The majority of teachers (42 per cent) were unsure as to whether they would feel greater loss or gain if they were to leave the classroom for an administrative type position, 30.6 per cent said they would feel greater gain than loss, and just over a quarter (27.4 per cent) greater loss than gain. Women were either more ambivalent about this matter, or felt that they would experience greater loss than gain, than were men.

In terms of the perceptions of individuals, teaching was found to be an occupation that offered a relatively limited promotions hierarchy in the sense that most only considered the range of positions available in schools. However, this matter was complicated by the fact that teachers did not only consider there to be a hierarchy in terms of the range of promotion positions available, but also thought in terms of there being a hierarchy of schools. The latter hierarchy occurred in the sense that some schools were viewed as being more attractive to work in than others, in terms of their size, geographical location and the socio-economic characteristics of the clients they served. This perception, that there was a hierarchy of preferred work locations, appeared to be more important in dictating the career moves of many teachers than was a wish to gain elevation within the promotions hierarchy.

It has been clearly demonstrated by this study that the career movements of teachers, in both the vertical and horizontal mobility sense, are patterned and not random. This has been shown to be the case regardless of the particular sector of the school system in which the teachers were employed, their gender, the promotion position occupied, and whether they worked in school or non-school positions. In addition to the actual behaviour of teachers being patterned rather than random, teachers also perceived this to be the case.

Teachers' careers were analysed to ascertain how long it took them to achieve particular promotion positions. Comparisons were also made between those occupying equivalent promotion positions in different sectors of the school system, and those in school and non-school promotion positions. In addition, for those occupying the same type of promotion position within a particular sector of the school system, comparisons were made between males and females, and between graduates and non-graduates. These comparisons were made to ascertain if there were differences in the time it took the different groups of teachers involved to achieve their particular promotion position.

If the average time it took teachers in particular promotion positions to achieve that position are taken as the guide, it is clear that an age-grade (or experience-grade) system did exist which influences the rate at which the individuals in question achieved vertical mobility. An example can be quoted to illustrate the point: while it took the principals of large primary schools an average of twenty-two years to achieve this position, the time taken by the principals of small primary school to achieve their position was 9.8 years. However, to only consider the average time taken to achieve promotion to a particular position can be misleading in that there was found to be a considerable range around this average in the time taken by teachers to achieve all the promotion positions examined, the extent of this range varying between promotion positions. Thus although it is possible to talk in terms of there being an age-grade system operating with regard to an individual's elevation within the Education Department's promotions hierarchy (if average years of experience when the promotion position was first awarded is used as the criteria) there is also a considerable range in the time taken by particular individuals. It was this that necessitated the distinction to be drawn, for the purposes of analysing teacher career patterns, between 'normal' and 'other' careers. 'Normal careers' were defined as being the middle 50 per cent of any group of teachers surveyed, and so excluded those who had been promoted either unusually quickly or slowly. As a general rule, graduates tended to be promoted earlier than were non graduates, males earlier than females, and those in the secondary school sector earlier than those in primary schools.

In addition to analysing the career patterns of 'normal' teachers (that is, the middle 50 per cent of each group examined), attention was also directed at those teachers who had been unusually fast in terms of the rate at which they had gained promotion. One reason was to identify the personal and professional characteristics of these teachers, and their career strategies, in order to help identify the reasons for their relatively rapid elevation; and whether they experienced any problems in their dealings with fellow teachers which may be a direct result of them being so

Discussion of Results and Conclusions Drawn

successful with regard to the rate and extent to which they had achieved promotion. One problem experienced by these teachers was that of marginality, a situation which arose because they were excluded or shunned by age peers in a way that forced them to operate on the margins of such groups. Such teachers were not privy to conversations between colleagues, and also became the brunt of jokes, often within their hearing. Regarding the actual reasons why these teachers had achieved accelerated promotion, colleagues stressed sponsorship and the 'its who you know, not what you know' factor. As a result these rapidly promoted individuals often found themselves socially isolated, which was one of the penalties they suffered for their unusual success in the promotion stakes.

Career Maps, Strategies and Timetables

It is apparent from the interviews conducted that many promoted teachers planned their career and promotion moves: that is, they were generally not spontaneous. Many spoke about setting goals with regard to the levels of promotion they wanted to achieve, and to working out a plan or strategy of action to try and ensure that they achieved these goals. These career goals and plans for action were time related, in the sense that many teachers set their sights on achieving particular goals within a certain set period of time. Most took care to ensure that the goals and career strategies were realistic, and so achievable, in order (no doubt) to avoid the disappointment and possible loss of face associated with a failure to achieve these things. In making a judgment about what were realistic goals, and in endeavouring to choose a realistic time perspective, teachers 'read' the prevailing opportunity structure operating within the Education Department; and observed the work related behaviour patterns of 'respected colleagues' around them to obtain some guide as to what was achievable, and help identify realistic career goal strategies and timetable norms. They also often modelled their own career plans, strategies and timetables on those which had appeared to work for these successful and respected colleagues.

The career maps and strategies of teachers did not only take account of promotion, but also the types of schools they wanted to work in at various stages in their career. For example, the wish on the part of many to work in a city area when their children were of secondary school age figured in their career map just as clearly as did their wish to occupy a specific promotion position by a particular age. Many of the career plans and strategies developed were age related: that is, they indicated what the teacher in question hoped to achieve by the age of thirty, by forty years of age and so on. Because individuals were keenly aware of the fact that they pursued their careers within an opportunity structure which changed over time, they had to read this structure in a way that enabled them to not only make a judgement about what was likely to be possible at the current time, but to also forecast the future. The most successful teachers in achieving their career goals were those who were best able to read the opportunity structure accurately, to anticipate likely changes in this structure over time, and to take advantage of these ahead of their colleagues.

Largely through observing the behaviour of others, individuals developed 'bench marks' against which they could monitor their own progress in fulfilling career goals. These benchmarks provided the teacher with feedback on their own performance in order that they could adjust their map and strategy if they were not succeeding in the way in which they hoped.

Teachers had no trouble talking about the operation of the promotion system, and their own aspirations, in general terms. However, career maps, strategies and timetables, which were much more specific, were regarded by them as being private, to be discussed with family (and, fortunately, this researcher) rather than colleagues at work. One can speculate that the main reason for this outlook may have been that the teachers did not want to risk the possibility of unachieved career hopes and dreams being open to public scrutiny. Perhaps they also did not want to share their thoughts and career plans with others lest they benefit from these, through increasing the competition the teacher in question may face when developing their own career goals, strategies, and timetables.

Career Anchorage Perspectives

Although some teachers may direct their energies at trying to achieve promotion over the full length of their working life, this was certainly not the norm for the majority of promoted men and women employed in the Education Department of Tasmania. In addition, most interviewees did not seek, for a variety of reasons, to achieve promotion to the top jobs in the promotions hierarchy. In making this point it is important to remember that when it came to considering their career and promotion in teaching most individuals thought almost exclusively in terms of the range of promotion positions available in schools. Yet, if level of salary is taken as the main yardstick, this meant that most teachers did not consider striving after the top positions, because these exist in the non-school advisory, supervisory and administrative areas. In addition, in terms of the range of positions available in schools, most teachers did not consider seeking to become school principals for the same types of reasons that they did not consider non-school promotion positions. That is, both types of promotion positions would largely take them out of the classroom, and so away from the most satisfying aspects of the job that attracted them to becoming school teachers in the first place: contact with children.

Discussion of Results and Conclusions Drawn

This study supports the view advanced by Tausky and Dubin (1965), by Goldman (1978), and others that the 'limited success' career perspective, as explored and illustrated by Whyte (1956) and Mills (1956), and the 'unlimited success' career orientation, as discussed by Parsons (1954), are in fact complementary since both are concerned with considering the same motivational mechanism, that of a 'career anchorage perspective'. In addition, teachers' career anchorage perspectives were found to be not fixed, and unchanging over time, but re-assessed and re-adjusted by the individual at various stages in their career, particularly as personal (and especially family) circumstances changed.

Although many teachers, and particularly men, adopted an 'unlimited success' career perspective early in their careers, for most this became a 'limited success' perspective after they had achieved some promotion and were in mid career. Whereas most women adopted a 'limited success' perspective throughout their career, young male teachers mostly adopted a 'limited success' career perspective up until the time they were married, after which many of them changed to an 'unlimited success' perspective. At this time they were hungry to gain promotion, and willing to move freely between schools and geographical areas to achieve this. However, as their children got older, and they wanted to 'put down roots' in one region of the state, many changed back to a 'limited success' perspective.

In addition to the material gathered about teachers' career anchorage perspectives through interviews, support for the propositions outlined above also appears to come from the career history data collected on the proportion of teachers' job moves that were associated with vertical as against horizontal mobility. For example, a greater proportion of male teachers' job moves, than female teachers' moves, were for vertical rather than horizontal mobility reasons; and the higher a teachers' position in the promotions hierarchy, the greater the proportion of job moves that were associated with vertical mobility. This shift in career perspective tended to be associated with an unwillingness to easily uproot themselves from their place of residence, so that career moves were mainly considered in terms of those work locations which would not necessitate the teacher in question to move their place of residence. This reluctance to move was generally associated with family considerations, such as employment of a spouse, being near family and the education of their own children at the secondary school level.

The main variables that influenced a particular teacher's career anchorage perspective were:

- gender (women were more likely than men to have a 'limited success' career perspective, and to adopt this earlier in their career);
- age (the younger a teacher the more likely they were to adopt an

'unlimited success' perspective in that they were ambitious to gain promotion and were more willing to move between various job locations in search of this. There tended to be a drift to a 'limited success' career perspective as teachers got older); and,
- marital status (in the case of women, their career perspective was less orientated towards gaining promotion and more towards achieving a preferred work location, after they were married. The main reasons were that many women put the needs of their family before their career ambitions, and also viewed their husband's career needs as being more important than their own. Men, on the other hand, become more ambitious to gain promotion after they become married, perhaps because they have a sense of needing additional financial resources in order to support their wife and family).

There appeared to be no correlation with regard to a teacher's qualifications and whether they adopted a limited or unlimited success career perspective.

In summary, with regard to teachers' career anchorage perspectives as outlined by Tausky and Dubin (1965) and others it can be said that most teachers did not consider the full range of promotion positions potentially available to them, both inside and outside schools, when considering promotion in the teaching career. In addition the main value of the career anchorage perspective is that it is useful in helping to direct attention to the way in which the career perspectives of teachers are adjusted and re-assessed over time. It is clear that the limited success and unlimited success career anchorage perspectives are not incompatible as they apply to the teaching career, for teachers are likely to adopt both perspectives, but at different times during their career.

Vertical and Horizontal Mobility, and Career Contingency Factors

Vertical versus Horizontal Mobility

When analysing the career and promotion patterns of state school teachers in Tasmania it was possible to describe and compare the career patterns of various groups of teachers in terms of both vertical and horizontal mobility. For those in the survey population the main form of vertical mobility found to apply to the teaching career was that which Caplow (1954) says occurs when a person is promoted or demoted in the occupation; while horizontal mobility, which Caplow (1954) defines as occurring when an individual moves between different work locations at the same status

Discussion of Results and Conclusions Drawn

level in the promotions hierarchy, was also found to be an important feature of the careers of promoted Tasmanian state school teachers.

The analysis undertaken of the career moves of teachers shows that (in an overall sense) vertical and horizontal mobility are both important within the teaching career. However, the relative weighting of these two aspects of mobility depended upon such things as a teacher's particular position in the promotions hierarchy, for the higher the position the greater was the proportion of career moves associated with vertical rather than horizontal mobility. In addition, the extent to which the dominant feature of a teacher's career pattern was horizontal rather than vertical mobility depended upon their gender, age and level of experience. The trend was for women to place a greater emphasis on horizontal mobility than did men and for teachers to mainly stress vertical mobility early in their careers, with the later emphasis being on horizontal mobility in order to achieve a more desirable work location.

However, one must not assume that all teachers have to choose between these two extremes, for particularly in the case of those who are building their careers at a time when the opportunity structure is favourable, it is often possible to achieve both of these things at the same time: that is, vertical mobility to a preferred work location.

One view contained in the literature is that 'push' factors have a greater influence than do 'pull' factors in affecting a teacher's mobility. In this study it was not possible to disentangle the relative importance of 'push' compared to 'pull' factors in affecting a teacher's horizontal mobility. While some teachers indicated their wish to move to another school or work location because they did not like the characteristics of the particular school or community in which they were currently employed, others focused on where they would like to be working (rather than where they were working) in terms of preferred community and school characteristics.

What is clear is that in their horizontal moves between schools teachers attempted to minimise or keep to a manageable level the potential problems associated with their work in the school and classroom. This meant that they often tried to move to schools where they perceived the teacher's work to be less difficult, and generally attempted to stay away from those schools where they believed the teacher's work to be most demanding or unpleasant. In assessing the desirability of a particular work location, it is clear that many teachers adopted a cost/benefit analysis, in the sense that they weighed up the characteristics of a particular school in terms of such things as: the characteristics of the school's clients in terms of such matters as their social class background, and the likely difficulties associated with dealing with them; the type of community in which the school was located, in terms of whether it was a desirable and pleasant community in which to live, and, if it was not, whether it would be possible for the teacher to live in an adjoining community and commute to school each day. Teachers rated schools using these types of criteria, and then used this to determine which schools they would be willing to work in and which they would like to avoid. There appeared to be a substantial level of agreement amongst teachers about preferred and less preferred work locations.

Due to major changes that have occurred over time in the features and opportunity structure of the school system, in terms of the supply and distribution of promotion positions, it was not possible to undertake an analysis of teacher career histories in order to discover the extent to which teachers prefer to work in large rather than small schools, schools which serve higher rather than lower socio-economic status communities, and schools in city rather than country areas. The only reliable, quantifiable evidence with regard to some of these matters was that which related to teacher demand for the various promotion positions advertised in the Education Department, with much of the evidence on these matters being more qualitative than quantitative in nature since it came from the individual and group interviews conducted with teachers.

The first point to make is that there was considerable agreement amongst teachers regarding the characteristics of a preferred work location. This was regardless of the particular stage in their career, and whether they were mainly stressing vertical or horizontal mobility in the teaching career. In the case of teachers seeking promotion, any school that offered them vertical mobility, and so satisfied their need for this type of reward in their career, was likely to be regarded as being a preferred work location. Different criteria were applied by the second category of teachers: that is, those seeking horizontal mobility. Notwithstanding this point, based upon the material collected in interviews it is possible to say that in terms of their actual behaviour most teachers did prefer to work in city rather than country areas, and in higher rather than lower socio-economic status areas.

This matter was less clear with regard to the size of schools, because it was more difficult to disentangle the influence of school size, as a variable, from that of school location, since the larger schools tended to be located in urban areas and the smaller ones in rural areas. However, having made these observations about certain key characteristics of teachers' preferred work locations, many individuals appeared to be reluctant to admit their preferences regarding this matter, perhaps because it indicated a set of values which they felt uncomfortable displaying, because these cut against the teachers professional ideal of providing an unselfish service to clients.

When deciding upon their preferred work location, from about mid career onwards, many teachers sought to return to that geographical region of the state where their own relatives and family lived. This was likely to be the area in the state where they themselves were born and

Discussion of Results and Conclusions Drawn

grew up as children, and where they completed their own secondary schooling. It seemed that while it was acceptable to many of the teachers (particularly the men) that they be geographically mobile during the early years of their career, when they decided it was time to settle down in one location it was the place where a family support system existed that attracted them the most. This could well be a phenomena peculiar to Tasmanian teachers which is less likely to occur in other education systems in Australia where the population may be more highly mobile in their search for employment opportunities.

The tendency to eventually settle in a part of the state where they were raised and completed their own secondary schooling was more apparent in the case of men rather than women teachers, the latter being more likely to set up home in a location that best suited their husband's career needs. However, all else being equal, women also indicated a preference to settle in a part of the state where their family and relatives lived. This substantiates the earlier finding of Jay (1966) in his study of teachers in England and Wales. But this trend was mainly ascertained through the interviews conducted, rather than through an analysis of career histories, and so needs to be treated with some caution.

A trend emerged with regard to how a teacher's own 'social characteristics' affected their preferred work location. Teachers from lower socio-economic backgrounds, for example, seemed more willing and motivated to teach in working class areas, perhaps because they identified with the children attending these schools or because they felt they had special insights, given their own working class background, to offer such children. In a similar way, teachers who themselves attended country schools, and had lived in country areas during their own schooling, were more drawn to work in these areas than were those educated in city schools. However, this trend may be simply a function of the fact that these teachers simply wanted to return to an area of the state where they themselves were brought up and/or educated. This finding could be useful in affecting the recruiting policy and pattern of the Education Department, at a time when they are experiencing considerable difficulty in staffing schools in country, isolated and lower socio-economic areas.

This study substantiates Becker's (1954) finding that although teachers may move between positions which are at the same level in the status hierarchy, these positions are not equal in all ways. Tasmanian teachers found that some work locations were easier or more rewarding to work in than were others, and these became what may be called their 'preferred work location'. Teachers were found to be generally agreed about the characteristics of a preferred work location, these being schools in urban areas, and in 'middle class' neighbourhoods. Others, as Berlowitz (1971) found elsewhere, generally tried to avoid working in those schools where they perceived the teacher's work as being most difficult. Thus individual teachers were found to employ a decision making framework (Pederson, 1972) based upon a consideration of the costs and related benefits (in both economic and sociological terms), when reviewing alternative employment and mobility possibilities.

Horizontal mobility was found to be particularly important to teachers at a time of reduced promotion opportunities. The reason appears to be that many teachers are becoming increasingly concerned about securing a 'desirable work location' where, amongst other things, the day to day problems commonly associated with a teacher's work are kept to a minimum, or at least within manageable limits. To many teachers a desirable or preferred work location was in an urban rather than a country area, where they were teaching 'middle class' rather than 'working class' students. For some the achievement of such a work location was more important than gaining further promotion, and some expressed a willingness to forego their current promotion position if it meant that they were able to achieve their 'preferred work location'.

Career Contingency Factors

An important concern of this study has been to identify the most influential formal and informal career contingency factors with regard to a teacher's achieved promotion in teaching. When the career histories of teachers were analysed, several formal factors were particularly important in determining who was promoted.

Three particularly important career contingency factors for the teacher studies were age, gender and marital status. This was not surprising because in most societies these variables have a far reaching effect on the role differentiation that occurs between individuals in many areas of social activity, including work (Hutt, 1972; Oakley, 1972). As Pavalko (1971) and others such as Prick (1989) have argued age was found to be an important consideration in influencing a person's career pattern. This research substantiates the findings of many other studies (e.g. Jacobs, 1975; Department of Education, 1982; Nias, 1989) in that a teacher's gender was also an important career contingency factor.

As has been found elsewhere (e.g. McIntosh, 1974; Jones and Montenegro, 1983) a major reason why women may be under represented in the various promotion positions in the Education Department of Tasmania is a lack of women applicants for positions. However, even if this is the case, it remains problematical as to why this is so.

While marital status was found to have an important influence on men's and women's work careers, this was found to occur for different reasons. While many women, once married, tended to put family considerations before the pursuit of a work career or promotion in their occupation, men appeared to apply themselves more vigorously to the pursuit of promotion after marriage.

Discussion of Results and Conclusions Drawn

Men were found to have a higher career perspective (Champoux, 1975), and career saliency (Masih, 1967), and were more likely to be strivers (Wilensky and Edwards, 1959) in their orientation to work, than were women. This may help explain why they were more committed to the achievement of vertical mobility than were women.

A teacher's age/level of experience and gender were clearly important in influencing their vertical mobility as were their academic and professional qualifications.

Gender seems to be particularly influential in affecting the careers of women. It appears from the evidence gathered in this study that women were under represented in most promotion positions in the Education Department, be they school or non-school positions. In addition women took longer, on average, than did men to reach equivalent promotion positions. This situation may be partly due to the fact that women were less likely to apply for promotion than were men, and that once married they were less mobile than men in terms of geographical mobility. Women who did gain extended and/or rapid promotion were more likely than those women who did not achieve these things to be unmarried and, in the case of those who were married, to have smaller families. One reason for this appears to be that for many women the responsibilities of marriage and a family make it difficult for them to pursue promotion in teaching. Another possible explanation is that the satisfactions a woman gains from marriage and a family are such that they are less motivated than are men to look for other types of rewards, such as promotion in their occupation, outside the family. In addition, in many families a husband's career is still put before that of his wife. Another possibility, which it was beyond the scope of this study to test in any detail, is that the promotions system may have a formal or informal bias which favours the promotion of men rather than women.

It has been found in this research that the most successful teachers in gaining promotion had the following characteristics compared to their less promoted colleagues:

- they had spent a shorter period of time, on average, in the various schools/job locations in which they had worked, compared to less promoted teachers;
- they had worked in a greater number of schools or job locations;
- they had spent a greater proportion of their time in the less preferred work locations such as schools in country, isolated, and lower socio-economic status areas;
- they were not more likely to have undertaken further study;
- they were more likely than were the other teachers to have involved themselves in a wide variety of in-school and out-of-school, non-teaching type professional activities. It is not perfectly clear whether this was simply an outcome of their natural

enthusiasm for the job, or a pre-meditated attempt to bring themselves to the attention of those who were able to influence promotion;
- they had a higher career saliency outlook;
- they were more likely than were the other teachers to have developed a clear career perspective, to have set career goals, and to have developed a career strategy, which was linked to a career timetable;
- they were more likely to consider their career in organizational, rather than occupational, career terms;
- they were most likely, in the case of secondary school teachers, to have specialised in history, the humanities or languages in their degree qualifications; and
- they were more likely to be employed in the secondary rather than the primary school sector of the education system.

In addition to examining the characteristics of those who were the most promoted teachers with regard to the level achieved in the school system, it was also of interest to examine the characteristics of those teachers who were unusually rapid in the rate at which they were promoted. The evidence indicates that, in general, promotion came earlier for men that it did for women, and earlier for graduates than non-graduates, although as was noted in earlier chapters there were some exceptions to this situation.

In addition to examining the most promoted, and most rapidly promoted teachers, this study also examined those teachers who were unusually slow in gaining promotion, in order to identify and better understand the strategies which such teachers adopted to help cope with their relative lack of success. One of the difficulties faced when undertaking this analysis was that it was virtually impossible to differentiate between those teachers who had sought promotion and failed, and those who had in fact not chosen to seek promotion. Thus, perhaps one of the most effective strategies adopted by such teachers to cope with their lack of promotion was their refusal to admit, at least to an outsider such as this researcher, that their relatively slow or limited rate of promotion was in fact due to failure: instead, they indicated that it was due to choice.

However, many of these teachers did perhaps reveal their true feelings in an indirect manner when they explained away the success of others in achieving promotion as being simply due to their willingness to conform to the views of those with power in determining who gets promoted, and in their ability to attract and maintain a sponsor. Such teachers spoke about a particular teacher's ability to plug into the 'golden circle': that is, the small group of individuals in the state who they believed affected, to a large extent, who was promoted. These were

Discussion of Results and Conclusions Drawn

mainly the superintendents and directors, who have a great affect on a teacher's promotion prospects.

In order to ascertain whether there were differences in the career patterns of those employed in different sectors of the school system, and in equivalent promotion positions, comparisons were made between the career histories of groups of teachers in different promotion positions. While there was little difference between the average level of experience of principals in different types of large schools, for medium sized schools promotion came earliest for those in special schools and primary schools. Senior masters/mistresses took less time, on average, to achieve their promotion position than did senior teachers; while those in the services areas took longer, on average, to achieve their promotion position than did those in equivalent promotion positions in schools.

There have been changes in the distribution of, and competition for, promotion positions over time. As an example of how the opportunity structure in teaching has changed over time, it was noted that there has been a substantial reduction in the number of promotion positions advertised between 1970 and 1989. The greatest reduction has occurred in the number of positions advertised in the services and secondary school sectors. Over the same period a greater proportion of the promotion positions were advertised in what many teachers saw as being the less desirable work locations: that is, schools in isolated and country regions of the state. It is likely that partly because of this fact, there was a reduction over the period examined in the amount of competition for the promotion positions advertised, particularly for those in isolated regions of the state. Competition amongst men for promotion was greater than it was for women, and this did not change over the time span examined.

Evidence has also been presented, using principals in different types of schools as examples, that the rate at which promotion has occurred for teachers who joined the Education Department between 1940–1974 changed (often substantially) over time. When senior masters/mistresses and senior teachers were examined, it was found that on average a greater proportion of the job moves of males than females were for promotion rather than horizontal mobility reasons.

Most teachers believed that factors such as length of teaching service, and various aspects of getting along well with those who were the 'power brokers' in the promotions system (such as superintendents and principals), were more important in favouring a person's promotion than were various aspects of being a good classroom teacher. There was substantial agreement between men and women, and those occupying different promotion positions, regarding this matter.

Teachers' views regarding the factors that *ought* to favour promotion were very different to those factors which they believed actually did influence promotion. In indicating what ought to influence promotion they placed a much greater stress on the importance of administrative ability, and on items relating to aspects of being an effective classroom teacher and productive member of a school staff. Getting along well with the 'power brokers' in the promotions system, and acquiring a sponsor, were not seen as factors that ought to affect whether or not a teacher was promoted, and their rate of promotion. There was substantial agreement between males and females and those in different promotion positions regarding this matter. Thus there was almost a total reversal in what teachers thought did actually influence promotion, and what they thought ought to influence promotion.

Principals and superintendents, who wrote the teacher reports upon which the Promotions Committee largely based their judgments, and who were therefore important gatekeepers in determining who was promoted in the opportunity structure, were also asked to indicate their views regarding the factors that did, and those that ought to, influence promotion. There was substantial agreement between their views, and those expressed by promoted teachers as a whole, in that they indicated that there was a substantial mismatch between those factors that did, and those that ought to, influence promotion. They also identified conformity with views of advisors as being an important factor in determining who was promoted, while they felt that factors related to teaching ability and being a co-operative staff member ought to be given greater emphasis.

For each category of promoted state school teachers examined in this study the number of years of experience the person had within the Education Department at the time they were awarded their current promotion position was calculated. The average time it took teachers to achieve their particular position was determined, as was the time it took the middle half of the promoted teachers (25th + 75th percentiles), the latter group being referred to as 'typical' or 'normal' teachers in the sense that their rate of promotion was neither unusually fast or slow.

If the average number of years of experience when promoted teachers were awarded their current school or non-school promotion position is examined the trend was that, in general, the higher the promotion position in the promotions hierarchy, the greater the average length of experience before this position was awarded. In addition, the trend was for the principals in larger schools to have more years of experience when they achieved this position than did those principals in the smaller schools. Thus a clear age grade system appeared to exist for promoted teachers in the Education Department. However, for virtually all the promoted positions examined, when the middle 50 per cent of teachers were examined there was a substantial range in the number of years of experience when the promotion position was awarded.

Males, on average, generally achieved their promotion position earlier than did females, this being true for all promotion positions in primary schools and secondary schools (with the exception of vice princi-

Discussion of Results and Conclusions Drawn

pals in medium sized schools). There were so few women in non-school positions that comparisons of career histories according to gender would not have proved fruitful.

Graduates on average, generally achieved their current promotion position earlier than did non-graduates, the exceptions being the principals of large primary schools, principals and vice principals in district schools and the vice principals of medium sized secondary schools. In the case of the principals of large primary schools, and the principals and vice principals in district schools, a possible explanation for this situation is that these were amongst the oldest members of the primary teaching force, undertaking their training at a time when it was virtually unknown for a primary school teacher to be a graduate. An explanation for graduates taking longer than non-graduates to become the vice principals of medium sized secondary schools is that quite a few of these positions were occupied by non-graduate women, who took less time, on average, than men to achieve this particular promotion position.

One of the propositions to be tested was whether the most promoted teachers had moved more frequently between schools than had the others. From the information presented a general trend did emerge where there was a positive correlation between the number of times a teacher moved between schools or work location and the extent of their promotion within the promotions hierarchy. This was not generally the case for principals in terms of the number of times they moved between schools, and whether they were in charge of a large, medium or small school. In addition, promotion did appear to come earlier for those who moved their job location more frequently than the average. Senior teachers had moved more times, on average, than had senior masters/mistresses, with the most mobile group being male senior teachers.

A disproportionately large number of promotion positions in both school and service branch positions in the Education Department of Tasmania were occupied by male (75.7 per cent) rather than female (24.3 per cent) teachers, the majority of full time teachers being female (59.8 per cent) and only 40.2 per cent male. In addition, the trend was that the higher a teacher's status within the promotion hierarchy the more likely it was that the person concerned would be a man rather than a woman. The higher status, better paid positions were generally held by men and this was true for both school and service positions.

Promoted teachers were a relatively youthful group of individuals with almost three quarters (73.9 per cent) being in their 40s or younger. Although an age grade and experience grade system operated within the Education Department, so that there was a positive correlation between the location of a promotion position within the status hierarchy and the average age of incumbents, there was often a considerable variation around the mean when it came to the age of teachers occupying the different promotion positions. When the average level of experience of

205

those in equivalent promotion positions in school and service branches who achieved promotion was compared, one found that promotion came earlier for those employed in schools.

A greater percentage of women than men in promotion positions were single, while promoted women had smaller families than did men. In addition, the higher a woman's promotion position the more likely it was that she would be single, but this was not true for promoted men. Men had moved their place of residence as a result of gaining promotion many more times than had women. The trend emerged that, for those employed in schools, frequency of move of residence was positively correlated with the level achieved in the promotions hierarchy. As clear a trend did not emerge for service personnel.

A surprising finding, however, was that half the promoted men had never moved their place of residence, or else had only moved once. When this finding is put beside those that relate to frequency of moves between school or job locations, it is apparent that many teachers at some stage in their career restrict their move between work locations to within a particular geographical region in order that they do not need to move their place of residence.

The vast majority of promoted teachers (81.6 per cent) were not studying for any further qualification relevant to their career, while most of those who were undertaking further study were studying for a Bachelor's or Master's degree in education. Over half (63.3 per cent) the promoted teachers held a degree from a university or college of advanced education, with the greatest proportion of graduates being employed in the secondary school (80.3 per cent) rather than the primary school, sector. With few exceptions, the higher a teacher's position in the promotions hierarchy the more likely it was that they were a graduate. A disproportionately large number of graduates in promotion positions had qualifications in the humanities/social science/humanities areas with a minority being qualified in maths/science.

The higher a teacher's position within the promotions hierarchy the more likely it was that they would be spiralists (Mann, 1973) or career transients (Keown, 1971) rather than locals (Mann, 1973). In addition, men displayed a greater willingness, than did women, to move between various geographical areas in an attempt to secure promotion in their employment.

Because the school teachers in this study were employed in a formal organization, one would expect that formal criteria and processes of selection would be most important in determining who gained promotion (Hall, 1946; Hughes, 1958; Glaser, 1968). Although a formal pattern of selection and promotion was found to exist within the Education Department of Tasmania, so that certain regular and recurrent promotion patterns occurred according to objective criteria such as an individual's age, length of service and qualifications, it was also found that certain

Discussion of Results and Conclusions Drawn

informal factors (Hall, 1946; Dalton, 1951) were of importance in affecting the shape and time patterns of an individual's career. The main informal factor that was found to have some importance in influencing the careers of those in this study was sponsorship, and conformity to the views of advisors. Certainly teachers believed this to be the case. It was not possible to test for the teachers studied whether other informal factors, such as social characteristics, were of any importance in influencing promotion.

In terms of teachers' perceptions regarding the factors that influence the extent to which, and rate at which, a teacher achieves promotion, the following were believed to be important:

- Gender: the view that males were more promoted than females.
- Qualifications: Having a degree, preferably from a University.
- Movement between schools: It was believed that teachers were unlikely to gain promotion within the one school. As a result movement between schools was important, with the most successful teachers spending no more than approximately five years in the one school.
- Geographical mobility: A willingness to move between different regions in the State.
- Further study was believed to favour promotion.
- Career goals, a strategy and a timetable were regarded as being the hallmark of those who were successful in achieving promotion.
- A changing opportunity structure, from which a teacher benefited in terms of 'being in the right place at the right time'.
- Making a contribution outside the classroom, through extra-curricula activities, involvement in the local community, and at the state level in the Education Department.
- Overall length of service in the Education Department.
- A willingness to work in unpopular work locations, such as schools in isolated, country, or lower socio-economic areas.
- The ability to attract and maintain a sponsor: this was seen as being achieved through being involved in extra-curricular activities, and at the systems level; and by conforming to the view of advisors not threatening their authority.
- Being a competent classroom teacher, and also acquiring administrative experience.

In identifying teacher perceptions regarding the factors that have an important effect on an individual's promotion prospects within the Education Department, the extent to which the analysis of teacher career histories supports teacher views will also be examined.

Many teachers were not satisfied with the way in which the promotion system operated. This was partly reflected by the fact that there was a big disparity between what they believed affected whether a teacher was promoted, and what they believed ought to influence who gets promoted. There was a feeling that sponsorship was a major factor in affecting who was promoted, particularly to the top jobs. Many felt that this was both unreasonable and unfair, and did not work in the interests of ensuring that those who were promoted were the most competent teachers in the system.

If the morale of the teaching service is not to suffer, particularly at a time of reduced promotion opportunities, then the Education authorities need to do more to allay teachers' fears and concerns in this controversial area. This could be achieved through a careful examination, and if necessary modification, of the promotion criteria and procedures adopted in the Education Department.

One question which this study sought to answer was: why do teachers seek promotion? The answer to this question was not straight forward, for teachers seek promotion for a wide variety of different reasons and these motivations can change over the length of their career. It is therefore important that the reward structure developed in teaching takes account of these various motivations and that it is not assumed that most teachers simply seek promotion for the extra money and power involved. In fact many other motivations, such as a wish to maximise their job satisfaction, and to establish new challenges, were also found to be of considerable importance.

Structural and Phenomenological Perspectives in Studying the School Teaching Career

One important aim of this study was to ascertain teacher perceptions regarding the factors that influence promotion within their occupation, and to examine the extent to which these perceptions matched up with the actual work behaviour of teachers.

It was speculated in this research that teachers would be more agreed upon about what does affect promotion, rather than upon what ought to affect promotion, in the education system. This was found not to be the case. A substantial mismatch was found to occur between what teachers believed actually did influence promotion and what they felt ought to influence promotion in the Education Department. Although there was some difference of emphasis regarding this matter when it came to the views of different groups of teachers, such as men compared to women, those in different promotion positions, and teachers employed in different sectors of the school system, overall there was substantial agreement between teachers.

One aim of this study was to match teacher perceptions about the teaching career against their actual behaviour in order to ascertain the extent to which there was a match between the two. An interesting finding is that although there is a match in some areas, there was a complete mismatch between what teachers perceived to be the case and what the career history data analysis showed to actually be the case in terms of behaviour.

The data collected shows that most teachers perceived the teaching career as having both an internal and an external aspect to it in the sense that although teacher careers occur in systems individuals must also make their way in the system in which they are employed. The emphasis between an individual's stress on the external versus the internal aspects of their career depended very much on how promotion minded they were.

Concluding Comments

Using a research framework derived from the sociology of occupations, the study reported upon in this book has aimed to achieve an improved understanding of teachers as an occupational group by undertaking a case study of the promotion and career patterns of state school teachers in one Australian state, that of Tasmania.

The theoretical assumption upon which the study was based is that the career movements of teachers are not random: rather they move in patterned ways between competing positions; and the research methodology adopted was one which blended together quantitative (structural) and qualitative (phenomenological) data. Information on the career histories of teachers was obtained from Education Department records, while data on individual perceptions about the school teaching career was obtained through a questionnaire and by conducting semi-structured individual and group interviews.

It has described and explained differences and similarities in the career patterns of those occupying different promotion positions (men and women teachers, graduates and non-graduates, and those employed in different types of schools and sectors of the school system); and indicated their perceptions regarding a career and promotion in teaching.

Although the focus has been upon aspects of teachers as an occupational group, the findings also contribute to an improved understanding about the operation of the Tasmanian school system as a whole. The reason is that the way in which individuals pursue (or don't pursue) a career in teaching has an important impact on the nature and functioning of the overall school system, the particular schools in which they are employed, and so upon the educational experiences of the children attending these schools. This impact occurs in a variety of ways, such as through influencing teacher turnover rates and teacher morale. Teacher perceptions regarding the structure of rewards that exist in the occupation, and their definitions of success and failure, influence how they allocate their time and deploy their energies between competing tasks in the school and classroom, and help explain why some schools can readily attract teachers while others have difficulty in obtaining experienced staff.

Education policy makers and others concerned with improved teacher effectiveness have much to gain as a result of studying teachers' careers, for as Huberman (1989, p. 343) says:

> On the practical level, studies of the teacher career have an obvious relevance. For example, recent work on 'school improvement' shows that many of the key determinants are career-related: how administrators and teachers view implementation of new practices is closely related to how they construe next steps in their careers. In the same vein, work on 'staff development' or 'workplace conditions' have been shown to be closely tied up with career-related variables. Clearly, issues of personnel policy are contingent of an understanding on the contours and dynamics of the professional career cycle of teachers.

This study has also shown how the Tasmanian school system rewards those teachers who are most prepared to serve the system in terms of (for example) such things as a willingness to move between schools, work in the least popular schools, and conform to the views of advisors.

The findings presented in this book refer to a case study of promoted teachers in one state education system in Australia, that of Tasmania. In view of this, generalisation beyond this group cannot be assumed: that is, it cannot be assumed that they also hold true for unpromoted teachers in the Tasmanian education system, or for Australian State school teachers as a whole. However, it could be argued that there is a need for further research which takes up the types of points raised in this analysis of career and promotion in teaching, and tests these for other populations of school teachers and other occupational groups. If this be the case, it is hoped that this research has contributed to the framing of hypotheses which other studies may seek to test.

There is a need for further research which examines more closely the disparity between teacher views regarding the factors that influence promotion, and those which they believe ought to influence promotion. This is a particularly important area to examine because it was not just the teachers themselves who believed that this disparity existed, but also some of the gatekeepers in the promotions system: the principals and superintendents who wrote the reports about teachers which had a great influence on their promotion prospects. It would also be valuable to undertake additional research on the career patterns and promotion of

Discussion of Results and Conclusions Drawn

women teachers, in order to examine in greater detail why many of their careers are so very different to those of the majority of men. Other research could focus more detailed attention on: those in the 'top' promotion positions; the particularly fast promoted teachers; and, teachers who are not interested in seeking promotion at all. In addition, since this book mainly examines those who have actually achieved promotion, there could be merit in examining those who have yet to be promoted, but who are keen to achieve this.

In addition to further research on the careers of state school teachers in Tasmania, it would be of interest to undertake research which examines the careers of other populations of teachers. For example, it could prove fruitful to undertake studies which examine the career and promotion patterns, and career perceptions, of state school teachers in other state and territory education systems in Australia, and also those teachers employed in the private school sector. These could follow up the types of questions and issues raised in the study reported on in this book, and so help test whether the findings presented here are also true for promoted teachers in other parts of Australia. In doing this the similarities and differences between teachers in various parts of Australia, with regard to career and promotion in their occupation, would become apparent.

It would be particularly helpful if such research studies had a 'policy orientation' in the sense that they sought to discover solutions to the types of problems identified in this research as currently being associated with careers and promotion in teaching. It is, for example, important to explore ways of restructuring the reward system in teaching so that teachers are provided with a variety of ways (in addition to promotion and mobility) of satisfying career needs. This is particularly important at a time of contracting promotion opportunities and mobility in the teaching service and school system.

Research which examines how the gatekeeping devices that exist in the opportunity structure of teaching influence who gets promoted, with particular reference to the part played by sponsorship, could prove helpful. For example, if sponsorship is a major determinant of who is successful in gaining promotion in the teaching career, it could be interesting to examine the extent to which this encourages conformity amongst those seeking promotion, and, if this is so, the likely implications of this state of affairs for the functioning of the school system.

It would be fruitful to study other groups of teachers (and lecturers) in the Australian (and overseas) education systems, such as those employed in the private school sector, universities, colleges of advanced education, technical and further education. These studies would be useful at the current time since, as is the case with school teachers employed in state education systems, there has been a great reduction in promotion opportunities and mobility within these sectors of the Australian education system over the past decade.

Such research could either adopt the same type of research framework and approach outlined in this study, or else test the usefulness of other approaches. For example, a longitudinal study could be undertaken which follows a particular group of teachers (whether they be employed at the school or tertiary level) over a substantial period of their work career in order to identify and explain such things as: changes over time in their career anchorage perspective; the formation and modification of career timetables, maps and strategies; satisfactions and dissatisfactions with their occupation; and, the relative importance of horizontal versus vertical mobility in their career.

In addition, the research framework developed for the study reported on here could be utilized and tested for research about other (roughly) comparable occupational groups in society, such as nurses, accountants or librarians.

Further research approaches could also be adopted and tested to determine their usefulness. For example, in a study of the careers of school teachers, a single or number of schools could be used as the unit of analysis, with a survey being undertaken of those employed in these schools over time. Comparisons could be made between schools with clients from different socio-economic backgrounds, small and large schools, and schools in different types of geographic locations.

The suggestions for further research briefly outlined above are but a few of the many possibilities that are available. As has been argued throughout this book, the study of career patterns and promotion is a rich and fruitful area of inquiry for the researcher since, in the words of a founding father of the sociology of occupations, Everett Hughes, it provides important insights into the individual, the occupation, the organization, and the society as a whole.

Bibliography

ABBOTT-CHAPMAN, J., HULL, R., MACLEAN, R., MCCANN, H. and WYLDE, C. (1991) *Student Images of Teaching-Factors Affecting Recruitment.* Canberra: Australian Government Publishing Service.
ADAMS, R. (1982) 'Teacher development: A look at changes in teachers' perceptions across time', *Journal of Teacher Education.* **23** (4), 40–43.
AHAMAD, B. and BLAUG, M. (Eds) (1973) *The Practice of Man-power Forecasting.* Amsterdam: Elsevier.
ALSPAUGH, J.W. (1969) 'An index of teacher horizontal mobility', *Journal of Experimental Education.* **38**, 5–8.
ANDERSON, N. (1923) *The Hobo: The Sociology of the Homeless Man.* Chicago: University of Chicago Press.
ANTI-DISCRIMINATION BOARD. (1979) *Examination of a Practice in the New South Wales Secondary Teaching Service.* N.S.W.: Anti-Discrimination Board.
ASSISTANT MASTERS AND MISTRESSES ASSOCIATION (AMMA) (1985) 'Women teachers' career prospects', *Assistant Masters and Mistresses Association*: London.
AURAND, G.H. and BLACKBURN, R.T. (1973) 'Career patterns and job mobility of college and university faculty', *Journal of Research in Music Education.* **21**, 162–168.
AGPS. (1980) *National Inquiry into Teacher Education Report.* Canberra: A.G.P.S. (Auchmuty Report).
AUSTRALIAN BUREAU OF STATISTICS. (1986, 1988) *Australian Labour Force Statistics.* Canberra: Australian Government Publishing Service.
AUSTRALIAN COUNCIL FOR EDUCATIONAL RESEARCH. (1972, 1973) *Career and Salary Structures of Teachers in Government Schools in the Australian States.* Hawthorn: A.C.E.R.
AUSTRALIAN COUNCIL FOR EDUCATIONAL RESEARCH. (1975) *Career and Salary Structures of Teachers in Government Schools in Australian States.* Hawthorn: A.C.E.R., 4th Edition.
AUSTRALIAN EDUCATION COUNCIL WORKING PARTY REPORT. (1978) *The Supply of and Demand for Teachers in Australian Primary and Secondary Schools 1978–1985.* Canberra: Australian Government Publishing Service.
BALL, S. and GOODSON, I. (1985) Understanding teachers: concepts and cultures, in BALL, S. and GOODSON, I. (Eds) *Teachers' Lives and Careers.* Lewes: Falmer Press.

Bibliography

BALL, S. and GOODSON, I. (Eds) (1985) *Teachers' Lives and Careers*. Lewes: Falmer Press.
BARDWICK, J.M. (Ed.) (1972) *Readings on the Psychology of Women*. New York: Harper and Row.
BARKER, D.L. and ALLEN, S. (1976) *Dependence and Exploitation in Work and Marriage*. London: Longman.
BASSETT, G.W. (1946) 'Reasons for choice of teaching as a career', *Forum of Education*. **5**, 29–35.
BASSETT, G.W. (1958) 'Occupational background of teachers', *Australian Journal of Education*. **11**, 79–90.
BASSETT, G.W. (1980) *Teachers in Australian Schools, 1979*. Melbourne: The Australian College of Education.
BECKER, H.S. (1951) 'The professional dance musician in Chicago', *American Journal of Sociology*. **57**, 136–144.
BECKER, H.S. (1952) 'The career of the Chicago public school teacher', *American Journal of Sociology*. **57**, 470–477.
BECKER, H.S. (1960) 'Notes on the concept of commitment', *American Journal of Sociology*. **66**, 32–40.
BECKER, H.S., GEER, B., HUGHES, E. and STRAUSS, A. (1961) *Boys in White*. Chicago: University of Chicago Press.
BECKER, H.S., GEER, B., RIESMAN, D. and WEISS, R.S. (Eds) (1968) *Institutions and the Person*. Chicago: Aldine Publishing Coy.
BECKER, H.S. and STRAUSS, A.L. (1956) 'Careers, personality and adult socialization', *American Journal of Sociology*. **62**, 253–263.
BECKER, H.S. (1971) *Sociological Work*. London: Allen Lane, The Penguin Press.
BEHRENS, N. et al., (1978) *School, Community and Work: Urban and Rural Aspects*. Canberra: A.G.S.
BELSON, W. (1981) *The Design and Understanding of Survey Questions*. Aldershot: Gower.
BELSON, W. (1986) *Validity in Survey Research*. Aldershot: Gower.
BENDIX, R. et al., (1952) 'Social origins and occupational career patterns', *Industrial and Labour Relations. Teacher*. **7**, 246–261.
BENET, C. (1983) 'Paints, pots or promotion: Art teachers' attitudes towards their careers', in BALL, S. and GOODSON, I. (Eds) 1985. *Teachers' Lives and Careers*, Lewes: Falmer Press.
BENOIR-SMULLYAN, E. (1944) 'Status, status types and status interrelations', *American Sociological Review*. **9**, 151–161.
BERLOWITZ, M.J. (1971) Teachers: Professionals or Estranged Labour? A study of the career patterns of Buffalo School Teachers during the period 1956–63. Unpublished doctoral dissertation: State University of New York at Buffalo.
BERLOWITZ, M.J. (1971) 'Career patterns of teachers in an urban area', *Urban Education*. **6**, 261–266.
BERNBAUM, G. (1973) 'Headmasters and schools: Some preliminary findings', *Sociological Review*. **21**, 463–484.
BETZ, M. (1973) 'Inter-generational mobility rates of public school teachers', *Journal of Educational Research*. **67**, 3–8.
BETZ, M. and GARLAND, J. (1974) 'Intergenerational mobility rates of urban school teachers', *Sociology of Education*. **47**, 511–522.

BIKLEN, S.K. (1985) 'Can elementary schoolteaching be a career? A search for new ways of understanding women's work', *Issues in Education*. **3** (3), 215–231.
BIKLEN, S.K. (1986) 'I have always worked: Elementary schoolteaching as a career', *Phi Delta Kappa*. March, 504–508.
BONNEY, N. (1986) 'More equal than others', *The Times Higher Education Supplement*. (13 October), 17.
BOOTH, C. (1902) *Life and Labour of the People of London*. London: Macmillan.
BOREHAM, P., PEMBERTON A. and WILSON, P. (Eds) (1976) *The Professions in Australia*. University of Queensland Press.
BOWMAN, M.J. (1966) 'The human investment revolution in economic thought', *Sociology of Education*. **39**, 111–137.
BRIM, O.G., JR. (1976) 'Theories of the male mid-life crisis', *The Counselling Psychologist*. **6** (1), 2–9.
BROOM, L. and LANCASTER-JONES, F. (1976) *Opportunity and Attainment in Australia*. Canberra: A.N.U. Press.
BRYNE, E. (1978) *Women and Education*. London: Tavistock Publications.
BURDEN, P. (1985) 'Teachers' perceptions of their personal and professional development', in SHULMAN, L. and SYKES, F. (Eds) *Handbook of Teaching and Policy*. New York, Longman.
BURDON, J.R. (1983) 'Mobility of elementary teachers', *College Student Journal*. **17**, 183–189.
BURTON, C. (1985) 'The politics of merit and the exercise of power: Issues in the promotion of academic women to positions of influence'. *Conference Report: The Way Forward — Women in Higher Education Management in Australia*. Australian College of Education, June.
BURTON, C. (1987) 'Merit and gender: Organizations and the mobilisation of masculine bias', *Australian Journal of Social Issues*, May.
BURKE, G. (1979) 'Manpower forecasting for teachers: Performance and problems', *Australian Bulletin of Labour*. **5**, 16–33.
BURKHARDT, G. (1975) 'Teacher mobility: A source of instability in a school system', *Australian Educational Researcher*. **2**, 21–24.
BURKHARDT, G. (1976). 'Teacher turnover and mobility — Implications for recruitment policy', *A.C.E.A. Bulletin*. **4**, 11–14.
BURKHARDT, G. (1976) 'Aspects of teacher mobility in the Interim ACT Schools Authority', in *Papers on ACT Education, 1976*. Canberra College of Advanced Education. pp. 33–34.
BUTT, R. et al., (1985) *Individual and Collective Interpretations of Teachers' Biographies*, Lethbridge, Canada: University of Lethbridge.
BUTT, R. (1984) 'Arguments for using biography in understanding teacher thinking', in HALKES, R. and OLSON, J.K. (Eds), *Teacher Thinking*, Lisse, Holland: Swets and Zeitlinger.
BUTT, R. and RAYMOND, D. (1989) 'Studying the nature and development of teachers' knowledge using collaborative autobiography', *International Journal of Educational Research*. **13** (4), 403–419.
CAMPBELL, D.T. (1975) *Being a Teacher in Australian State Government Schools*. Canberra: A.G.P.S.
CAMPBELL, D.T. and STANLEY, J.C. (1966) *Experimental and Quasi Experimental Designs for Research*. Chicago: Rand McNally.

Bibliography

CAPLOW, T. (1954) *The Sociology of Work*. Toronto: McGraw-Hill Book Company.
CARLSON, R.O. et al., (1972) 'Occupations, personnel and careers in education: An overview', *School, College and University*. University of Queensland Press. pp. 115–137.
CARLSON, R.O. (1979) *Orderly Career Opportunities*, (Eric Document No. ED 196129).
CARR-SAUNDERS, A.M. (1933, 1964) *The Professions*. Oxford: Clarendon Press.
CHAMPOUX, J.E. (1978) 'Perceptions of work and non-work', *Sociology of Work and Occupations*. **5**, 402–423.
CHAPMAN, J. (1985) 'Women principals in Australia'. *Paper Presented to the joint A.C.E./A.C.T. Schools Authority Conference*, Canberra.
CHARTERS, W.W. (1956) 'Survival in the profession: A criterion for selecting teacher trainees', *Journal of Teacher Education*. **7**, 253–255.
CHARTERS, W.W. (1963) 'The social background of teaching', in GAGE, N.L. (Ed.) *Handbook of Research on Teaching*. Chicago: Rand McNally and Company.
CHARTERS, W.W. (1967) 'Some obvious facts about the teaching career', *Educational Administration Quarterly*. **3** (i), 183–193.
CHARTERS, W.W. (1970) 'Some factors concerning teacher survival in school districts', *American Educational Research Journal*. **7**, 1–27.
CHINOY, E. (1955) *Automobile Workers and the American Dream*. Boston: Beacon Press.
CLEVERLEY, J. and LAWRY, J. (Eds) (1972) *Australian Education in the Twentieth Century*. Melbourne: Longman.
COLLINS, J.M. (1973) 'Structural changes in the Australian teaching workforce — A female takeover bid?' *Australian Journal of Education*. **17**, 18–24.
COMMONWEALTH DEPARTMENT OF EDUCATION. (1985) *Women in Australian Education: Vol. 3 — Women as Teachers*. Research and Statistics Branch, Canberra.
COMMONWEALTH TERTIARY EDUCATION COMMISSION. (1977, 1982, 1986) *Selected Advanced Education Statistics*. A.G.P.S., Canberra.
CONNELL, R.W. (1985) *Teachers' Work*. Sydney: Allen and Unwin.
COTTRELL, W.F. (1940) *The Railroader*. Stanford University Press.
COULTER, F. (1971) 'The Socialisation of Male, Beginning Teachers into the Teaching Profession'. Unpublished Doctoral Dissertation: Monash University.
COULTER, F. (1972) 'Commitment to teaching and occupational mobility among beginning teachers', *Australian Journal of Education*. **16**, 238–245.
COUNTS, G.S. (1925) 'The social status of occupations', *The School Review*. **33**, 16–27.
COVERDALE, G.M. (1973) 'Some determinants of teacher morale in Australia'. *Educational Research*. **16**, 34–39.
COX, L.A. (1975) *Career '74: Survey of Employment Destinations of 1974 Graduates of Colleges Affiliated with the Victorian Institute of Colleges*. Melbourne: Victorian Institute of Colleges.
CRANE, A.R. (1947) 'Reasons for choosing teaching as a career', *Forum of Education*. **6**, 32–38.
CREED, P. (1987) *Women in the Ministry of Education (Schools Division) in Victoria, 1987*. Policy and Planning Unit, Ministry of Education, Melbourne.

Bibliography

CRESSY, P.G. (1932) *The Taxi-Dance-Hall*. Chicago: University of Chicago Press.
CULBERT, S. and MCDONOUGH, J. (1980) *The Invisible War: Pursuing Self-interests at Work*, New York: Wiley.
DALTON, M. (1951) 'Informal factors in career achievement', *American Journal of Sociology*. **56**, 407–415.
DAVIS, D.J. (1976) *Teachers and their Career Intentions: The New South Wales Case*. Sydney: Centre for the Advancement of Teaching, Macquarie University. Education Monograph No. 16.
DAVISON, R.G. (1971) 'Work satisfaction and teacher mobility', *Clearing House*. **45**, 265–272.
DEEM, R. (1978) *Women and Schooling*. London: Routledge and Kegan Paul.
DE MANN, H. (1929) *Joy in Work: The Manual Worker*. New York: Henry Holt and Company.
DELONG, T.J. (1984) 'A comparison of the career orientations of rural and urban educators', *Educational Review*. **36**, 67–74.
DEPARTMENT OF EDUCATION. (1982) *Teacher Career and Promotion Study*. Wellington, N.Z.: Department of Education.
DEPARTMENT OF EDUCATION AND SCIENCE. (1974) *Teacher Turnover*. DES Report on Education, London, HMSO.
DEPARTMENT OF EDUCATION AND SCIENCE. (1975) *Reports on Education*. London: H.M.S.O.
DIMMOCK, C. (1983) 'Problems of teacher supply, demand and immobility in England, Wales and the USA', *Education Today*. **33**, 19–27.
DONOVAN, F.R. (1920) *The Woman Who Waits*. Boston: R.G. Badger.
DONOVAN, F.R. (1930) *The Saleslady*. Chicago, Ill: University of Chicago Press.
DONOVAN, F.R. (1938) *The Schoolma'am*. New York: Frederick Stokes Company.
DORAN, G.A. (1982) 'Reverse discrimination as justice in the senior promotion of female teachers', *Australian Journal of Social Issues*. **17**, 3–11.
DREYFUSS, (1938) *Occupation and Ideology of The Salaried Employee*. Columbia University: Department of Social Science.
DUBERMAN, L. (1975) *Gender and Sex in Society*. New York: Praeger.
DUBIN, H. (1958) *The World of Work: Industrial Society and Human Relations*. Englewood Cliffs, N.J.: Prentice-Hall.
DUGGAN, E.P. and STEWART, W.A.C. (1970) *The Choice of Work Areas of Teachers*. The Sociological Review Monograph No. 15: University of Keele.
DURKHEIM, E. (1933; orig. 1893) *The Division of Labour*. Glencoe, I11: The Free Press.
EBERTS, R.W. and STONE, J.A. (1985) 'Male-female differences in promotions', *Journal of Human Resources*. **20**, 504–521.
EDUCATION DEPARTMENT OF TASMANIA. (1942) *The Tasmanian Area School*. Hobart: Tasmanian Government Printer.
EDUCATION DEPARTMENT OF TASMANIA. (1977) *Movement of Teachers: Survey Report No. 66*. Hobart: Education Department.
EDUCATION DEPARTMENT OF TASMANIA. (1980) *Report for the Year 1979*. Hobart: Tasmanian Government Printer.
EDUCATION DEPARTMENT OF TASMANIA. (1981) *White Paper on Tasmanian Schools and Colleges in the 1980s*. Hobart: Tasmanian Government Printer.

Bibliography

EDUCATION DEPARTMENT OF TASMANIA. (1930–1965) *The Educational Record*. Hobart: Tasmanian Government Printer.
EDUCATION DEPARTMENT OF TASMANIA. (1930–1952) *Education Reports*. Hobart: Tasmanian Government Printer.
EDUCATION DEPARTMENT OF TASMANIA. (1959–1988) *Classification Lists*. Hobart: Education Department.
EDUCATION DEPARTMENT OF TASMANIA. (1975–1988) *Alphabetical List of Schools and Principals*. Hobart: Education Department.
EDUCATION DEPARTMENT OF TASMANIA. (1930–1988) *Regulations*. Hobart: Tasmanian Government Printer.
EDWARDS, A.L. (1957) *Techniques of Attitude Scale Construction*. New York: Appleton–Century–Crofts.
ENCYCLOPEDIA OF SOCIOLOGY. (1974) Guilford, Conn: Deushkin Publishing Company.
EPSTEIN, C.F. (1970) 'Encountering the male establishment: Sex limits on women's careers in the professions', *American Journal of Sociology*. **75**, 965–982.
EPSTEIN, L.K. (1975) *Women in the Professions*. Lexington, Mass: Lexington Books.
EQUAL OPPORTUNITIES COMMISSION. (1985) *Equal Opportunities and the Woman Teacher: Guidlines for the elimination of Sex and Marriage Discrimination and the Promotion of Equality of Opportunity in Teacher Employment*. London: E.O.C.
ESLAND, G., SALAMAN, G. and SPEAKMAN, M.A. (Eds) (1975) *People and Work*. Milton Keynes: Open University Press.
ETZIONI, A. (Ed.) (1969) *The Semi Professions and their Organization*. New York: Free Press.
EVANS, T. (1982) 'Being and becoming: Teacher's perceptions of sex roles and actions towards their male and female pupils', *British Journal of Sociology of Education*. **3**, 2, 127–143.
EVETTS, J. (1986) 'Teachers' careers: The objective dimension', *Educational Studies*. **12**, 225–244.
EVETTS, J. (1987) 'Becoming career ambitious: The career strategies of married women who became primary headteachers in the 1960s and 1970s', *Educational Review*. **39**, 15–29.
EVETTS, J. (1988) 'Returning to teaching: The career breaks and returns of married women primary headteachers', *British Journal of Sociology of Education*. **9**, 81–96.
FEIMAN-NEMSER, S. (1985) 'Learning to teach', in SHULMAN, L. and SYKES, F. (Eds) *Handbook of Teaching and Policy*, New York, Longman.
FENWICK, P.R. (1982) *Sex Differences in Teachers' Careers and Promotions: A Review of the Literature*. Wellington: Department of Education.
FENWICK, P.R. and SHEPHERD, M. (1982) *Sex Differences in Applicants for and Appointees to Senior Primary Teaching Positions*. Wellington: Department of Education.
FETT, I. (1974) 'Australian medical graduates in 1972', *Medical Journal of Australia*. **1**, 689–698.
FETT, I. (1975) Australian Medical Graduates 1920–1972: A Sociological Analysis. Unpublished doctorial dissertation: Monash University.
FINLAY, J. (1963) 'Two plans for promotion', *The Secondary Teacher*. **91**, 18–20.

FLITTIE, E.G. and NELSON, Z.P. (1968) 'The truck driver: A sociological analysis', *Sociology and Social Research*. **53**, 205–210.
FLODEN, R.E. and HUBERMAN, M. (1989) 'Teachers' professional lives: The state of the art', *International Journal of Educational Research*. **13** (4), 455–466.
FOGARTY, M.P, ALLEN, A.J., ALLEN, I. and WALTERS, P. (1971) *Women in Top Jobs*. London: George Allen and Unwin Ltd.
FOGARTY, M.P., RAPAPORT, R. and RAPAPORT, R.N. (1971) *Sex, Career and Family*. London: George Allen and Unwin.
FORM, W.H. (1968) *Industrial Sociology: The Sociology of Work Organisations*. New York : Harper and Row. Second Edition.
FORM, W.H. and MILLER, D.C. (1949) 'Occupational career pattern as a sociological instrument', *American Journal of Sociology*. **54**, 317–329.
FORM, W.H. (1962) 'Social reference basis of job satisfaction', *American Sociological Review*. **27**, 228–237.
FOX, R.B. (1961) 'Factors influencing career choice of prospective teachers', *Journal of Teacher Education*. **12**, 427–432.
FREEMAN, R.B. (1971) *The Market for College Trained Manpower*. Cambridge, Mass: Harvard University Press.
FRIEDMAN, N.L. (1972) 'Career stages and organisational role decisions in two public junior colleges, in PAVALKO, R.M. (Ed.) *Sociological Perspectives on Occupations*. Itasca, ILL: F.E. Peacock.
FREIDSON, E. (Ed.) (1973) *The Professions and Their Prospects*. London: Sage Publications.
FULLER, F. (1969) 'Concerns of teachers: A developmental perspective', *American Educational Research Journal*. **6**, 207–226.
GALLOP, R. and GAGG, M. (1972) 'Teachers and promotion in further education', *Vocational Aspect*. **24**, 53–66.
GEER, B. (1966) 'Occupational commitment and the teaching profession', *The School Review*. **74**, 31–47.
GEHRKE, N.J. and SHEFFIELD, R.C. (1985) 'Career mobility of women and minority high school teachers during decline', *Journal of Research and Development in Education*. **18**, 39–49.
GILES, J. (1987) 'Valuing women's expertise: Towards a merit based career structure for teachers', in *Women Teachers: The Merit of Classroom Teaching*. Report of the SAIT Women's Conference. 23, May 9–14.
GLASER, B.G. (1964) *Organizational Scientists: Their Professional Careers*. New York: The Bobbs-Merrill Coy. Inc.
GLASER, B.G. (Ed.) (1968) *Organizational Careers: A Sourcebook for Theory*. Chicago: Aldine Pub. Coy.
GLASER, B.G. and STRAUSS, A. (1968) *The Discovery of Grounded Theory*. London: Weidenfeld and Nicolson.
GOFFMAN, E. (1952) 'On cooling the mark out: Some aspects of adaptation to failure', *Psychiatry*. **15**, 451–463.
GOLDMAN, D.R. (1978) 'Career anchorage: Managerial mobility motivations — A replication', *Sociology of Work and Occupations*. **5**, 193–208.
GOLDSTEIN, J. (1976) 'Professional mobility in Israel's secondary schools: Results of a survey of attitudes', *Educational Administration Quarterly*. **12**, 51–67.
GOODE, W.J. and HATT, P.K. (1952) *Methods in Social Research*. Kogakusha: McGraw-Hill.

Bibliography

GOULDNER, A.W. (1957) 'Cosmopolitans and locals: Towards an analysis of latent social roles', *Administrative Science Quarterly*. **2**, 281–306.

GREEN, B.F. (1954) 'Attitude measurement', in LINDZEY, G. (Ed.) *Handbook of Social Psychology*. Cambridge, Mass,: Addison–Wesley Publishing.

GREENBERG, D.H. and MCCALL, J. (1973) *Theories of Teacher Mobility*. Washington: Department of Education Monograph.

GREENBERG, D. and MCCALL, J. (1974) 'Teacher mobility and allocation', *Journal of Human Resources*. **9**, 480–502.

GREENWOOD, M.J. (1975) 'Research on internal migration in the United States: A survey', *Journal of Economic Literature*. **13**, 397–433.

GROSS, N. and TRASK, A.E. (1976) *The Sex Factor and the Management of Schools*. New York: Wiley.

GUBA, E.G., JACKSON, P.W. and BIDWELL, G.E. (1959) 'Occupational choice and teaching career', *Educational Research Bulletin*. **38**, 1–12.

GUSKEY, T.R. (1989) 'Attitude and perceptual change in teachers', *International Journal of Educational Research*. **13** (4), 439–453.

HALL, O. (1946) 'The informal organisation of the medical profession', *Canadian Journal of Economics and Political Science*. **12**, 30–44.

HALL, O. (1948) 'The stages of a medical career', *American Journal of Sociology*. **53**, 327–336.

HALL, O. (1949) 'Types of medical careers', *American Journal of Sociology*. **55**, 243–253.

HALL, O. (1965) *Utilization of Dentists in Canada*. Ottawa: Queen's Printer.

HALL, R.H. (1975) *Occupations and the Social Structure*. Second Edition. Prentice-Hall.

HALL, D.T. (1976) *Careers in Organizations*, Santa Monica: Goodyear.

HAMMOND, P.E. (1966) *The Campus Clergyman*. New York: Basic Books.

HANSEN, M.H., HURWITZ, W.N. and MORDON, W.G. (1953) *Sample Survey Methods and Theory*. New York: Wiley.

HARNISCHFEGER, A. (1975) *Personal and Institutional Characteristics Affecting Teacher Mobility: Schools Do Make a Difference?* Stanford University: Research and Development Monograph No. 136.

HATT, P.K. (1950) 'Occupation and social stratification', *American Journal of Sociology*. **55**, 533–543.

HAUSER, P.M. (1951) 'The labour force as a field of interest for the sociologist', *American Sociological Review*. **16**, 530–544.

HAVINGHURST, R. and NEWGARTEN, B. (1957) *Society and Education*. Boston: Allyn and Bacon.

HEBERLEIN, T.A. and BAUMGARTNER, R. (1978) 'Factors affecting response rates to mailed questionnaires: A quantitative analysis of the published literature', *American Sociological Review*. **43**, 447–460.

HILSUM, S. and START, K.B. (1974) *Promotion and Careers in Teaching*. Slough: National Foundation for Educational Research.

HOLLINGSHEAD, A.B. (1949) *Elmtown's Youth*. New York: John Wiley and Sons.

HOPKINS, K.D. and GLASS, G.V. (1978) *Basic Statistics for the Behavioural Sciences*. Englewood Cliffs : Prentice-Hall Inc.

HOYLE, E. (1969) 'Professional stratification and anomie in the teaching profession', *Paedagogica Europaea*. 60–71.

HUBERMAN, M. (1988) 'Teacher careers and school improvement', *Journal of*

Curriculum Studies. **20** (2), 119–132.

HUBERMAN, M. (1989) 'The professional life cycle of teachers', *Teachers College Record*, **3**.

HUBERMAN, M. (Ed.) (1989) 'Research on teachers' professional lives', *International Journal of Educational Research*, **13** (4).

HUBERMAN, M. (1989) 'On teachers' careers: Once over lightly, with a broad brush', *International Journal of Educational Research*. **13** (4), 347–362.

HUGHES, E.C. (1937) 'Institutional office and the person', *American Journal of Sociology*. **63**, 404–413.

HUGHES, E.C. (1949) 'Queries concerning industry and society growing out of a study of ethnic relations in industry', *American Sociological Review*. **14**, 211–220.

HUGHES, E.C. (1952) 'The sociological study of work: an editorial introduction', *The American Journal of Sociology*. **57**, 423–426.

HUGHES, E.C. (1958a) *Men and Their Work*. Glencoe: Free Press.

HUGHES, E.C. (1958b) 'The study of occupations', in MERTON, R.K., BROOM, L. and COTTRELL, L. (Eds) *Sociology Today*. New York: Basic Books.

HUGHES, E.C. (1971) *The Sociological Eye*. Chicago: Aldine-Atherton Inc.

HUGHES, P. (1982) *Review of Efficiency and Effectiveness of the Tasmanian Education Department*. Volumes I, II. Hobart: University of Tasmania Centre for Education.

HUTT, C. (1972) *Males and Females*. Harmondsworth: Penguin.

HYMAN, H.H. (1954) *Interviewing in Social Research*. Chicago: University of Chicago.

HYAMS, B.K. (1973) State School Teachers in South Australia 1847–1950. Unpublished doctoral dissertation: Flinders University of South Australia.

INGVARSON, L. and GREENWAY, P.A. (1984) 'Portrayals of teacher development', *Australian Journal of Education*. **28** (1), 45–65.

JACKSON, J.A. (Ed.) (1970) *Professions and Professionalization*. Cambridge: Cambridge University Press.

JACOBS, J.E. (1975) 'Women and work: A selected annotated bibliography', *Educational Horizons*. **53**, 142–144.

JAMES, R.J. and JARMAN, P.F. (1985) 'A structural approach to reduced career prospects for teachers', *Educational Management and Administration*. **13**, 37–44.

JAY, L.J. (1966) The mobility of teachers, *Education. (UK)*. **128**, 372.

JECKS, D. (1969a) 'The employment pattern of a selected group of female teachers (1948–1967)', *Western Australian Teachers' Journal*. **59**, 460–466.

JECKS, D. (1969b) 'Male teacher career patterns (1948–1967)', *Western Australian Teachers' Journal*. **59**, 525–533.

JOHNSON, T.J. (1972) *Professions and Power*. London: Macmillan.

JOHNSTON, G.L. (1962) Fifty Years of State Secondary Education in Tasmania: 1913 to 1962. Unpublished Master of Education Dissertation: University of Tasmania.

JOHNSTON, G.L. (1964) 'Tasmania's Technical Schools 1919–1962: An obituary'. *Australian Journal of Education*. **8**, 105–110.

JONES, E.H. and MONTENEGRO, X.P. (1983) 'Factors predicting women's upward career mobility in school administration', *Journal of Educational Equity and Leadership*. **3**, 231–241.

Bibliography

KAHN, R.L. and CANNELL, C.F. (1957) *The Dynamics of Interviewing, Theory Techniques and Cases.* New York: Wiley.
KALE, P. (1970) 'The Career of the Secondary School Teacher in Poona, India. Unpublished doctoral dissertation: University of Wisconsin.
KARMEL, P. (Chair) (1985) *Report of the Quality of Education Review Committee,* A.G.P.S., Canberra.
KAUFMAN, P.W. (1984) *Women Teachers on the Frontier,* New Haven, CT: Yale University Press.
KELSALL, R.K. (1954) 'Self recruitment in four professions', in GLASS, D.U. (Ed.) *Social Mobility in Britain.* London: Routledge and Paul.
KELSALL, R.K. (1960) *Sociological Research in Great Britain.* Sheffield: Sheffield University Press.
KELSALL, R.K. (1963) *Women and Teaching.* London: H.M.S.O.
KENT COUNTY COUNCIL. (1987) *Career Development for Women Teachers.* K.C.C. United Kingdom.
KEOWN, P.A. (1971) 'The career cycle and the step wise migration process', *New Zealand Geographer.* **27**, 175–184.
KLEINERT, J. (1968) Teacher turnover in the affluent school district, *Clearing House.* **42**, 297–299.
KNUDSEN, D.D. and THOMAS, S. (1965) 'Some social factors to consider in non-promotion', *Theory Into Practice.* **4**, 99–102.
KUNDSIN, R.B. (Ed.) (1974) *Women and Success: The Anatomy of Achievement.* New York: Morrow.
KYRIACOU, C. (1987) 'Teacher stress and burnout: An international review', *Educational Research.* **29** (2), 146–152.
LACEY, C. (1978) *The Socialisation of Teachers.* London: Methuen.
LADINSKY, J. (1963) 'Careers of lawyers, law practice and legal institutions', *American Sociological Review.* **28**, 47–54.
LANSING, J.B. and MUELLEN, E. (1967) *The Geographical Mobility of Labour.* Ann Arbor: The University of Michigan.
LE PLAY, F. (1877–79) *The European Working Classes.*
LEVY, B. and LOKAN, J. (1986) *A Longitudinal Study of Career Development and Role Commitment.* Melbourne: Education Department of Victoria.
LEWIN, E. and DAMRELL, J. (1978) 'Female identity and career pathways', *Sociology of Work and Occupations.* **5**, 31–54.
LIGHTFOOT, S. (1985) 'The lives of teachers', in SHULMAN, L. and SYKES, F. (Eds) (1985) *Handbook of Teaching and Policy,* New York, Longman.
LINDENFELD, F. (1963) *Teacher Turnover in Public Elementary and Secondary Schools: 1959–60.* Washington: Government Printing Office. Office of Education Circular No. 675.
LIPSET, S.M. and BENDIX, R. (1951) 'Social mobility and occupational career patterns: Stability of job holding', *American Journal of Sociology.* **LV11**, 366–374.
LIPSET, S.M. and ZETTERBERG, H.L. (1956) 'A theory of social mobility', *Transactions of the Third World Congress of Sociology.* **3**, 155–177.
LITTLER, C.R. (Ed.) (1985) *The Experience of Work.* Aldershot: Gower.
LOGAN, L., DEMSTER, N., BERKELEY, G. and WARRY, M. (1990) *Teachers in Australian Schools: A 1989 Profile,* The Australian College of Education, Canberra.
LORTIE, D.C. (1959) 'Layman to lawmen: Law school, careers and socialisation',

Bibliography

Harvard Educational Review. **29**, 352–369.
LORTIE, D.C. (1975) *School Teacher: A Sociological Study.* Chicago: University of Chicago Press.
LOWYK, J., CLARKE, C. and HALKES, R. (Eds) *Teacher Thinking and Professional Action*, Lisse, Holland: Swets and Zeitlinger.
LYONS, G. and MCCLEARY, L. (1980) 'Careers in teaching', in HOYLE, E. and MEGARRY, J. (Eds) *World Yearbook of Education: Professional Development of Teachers.* London: Kegan Paul.
LYONS, G. (1981) *Teacher Careers and Career Perceptions in the Secondary Comprehensive School.* Slough: National Foundation for Educational Research.
MACLEAN, R.D.I. (1974) Women Students and the Bachelor of Education Programme: A Case Study in Equality of Opportunity. Unpublished Master of Education Dissertation: University of Bristol.
MACLEAN, R.D.I. (1981a) 'Principals' views on promotion', *The Tasmanian Teacher.* **32**, 6.
MACLEAN, R.D.I. (1981b) 'Careers in education project: Preliminary results', *The Tasmanian Teacher.* **32**, 6–7.
MACLEAN, R.D.I. et al., (1984) *Teacher Mobility Study.* Hobart: Tasmanian Teachers Federation.
MACLEAN, R.D.I. (1988) Career and Promotion Patterns of State School Teachers in Tasmania: A Sociological Analysis, Unpublished Ph.D. Thesis: University of Tasmania.
MACLEAN, R.D.I. (1989) *Women Teachers' Careers*, Tasmanian Teachers Federation, Hobart.
MACLEAN, R.D.I. in press, *Profile of Tasmanian Schools and Colleges, 1930–1986.* Hobart: Tasmanian Teachers Federation.
MACLEAN, R.D.I. and MACKENZIE, P. (Eds) (1991) *Australian Teachers' Careers*, Melbourne: Australian Council for Educational Research.
MCARTHUR, J. (1981) *The First Five Years of Teaching.* Canberra: Australian Government Publishing Service.
MCGREAL, T.L. and HUGHES, C. (1971) Operating in the school job market, *The Clearing House.* 397–403.
MCINTOSH, J. (1974) 'Differences between women teachers who do and who do not seek promotion', *Journal of Educational Administration.* **12**, 28–41.
MCLEISH, J. (1970) *Students' Attitudes and College Environment.* Cambridge: Institute of Education.
MCPHERSON, R.B. (1970) 'Teacher turnover in the inner-city', *Administrations Notebook.* **19**, 1–4.
MADGE, J. (1953) *The Tools of Social Science.* London: Longman.
MAEHR, M. and KLEIBER, D. (1981) 'The graying of achievement motivations', *American Psychologist.* **37** (7), 787–793.
MANN, M. (1973) *Workers on The Move.* Cambridge: Cambridge University Press.
MARSLAND, D. (1975) 'Early career mobility of school teachers', *Durham Research Review.* **7**, 982–991.
MARX, K. (1954; orig. 1867) *Capital: A Critique of Political Economy.* Moscow: Foreign Language Publishing House.
MARX, K. (1961; orig. 1846) *Economic and Philosophical Manuscripts of 1844.* Moscow: Foreign Language Publishing House.

Bibliography

MASIH, L.K. (1967) 'Career saliency and its relation to certain needs, interests and job values', *Personnel Guidance Journal.* **45**, 653–658.

MASIH, L.K. (1969) 'Career saliency for teachers and other occupational groups', *Personnel and Guidance Journal.* **47**, 773–775.

MASLIN, J.S. (1949) *Hagley: The Story of a Tasmanian Area School.* Melbourne: Georgian House.

MASON, W.S. (1961) *The Beginning Teacher: Status and Career Orientations.* Washington: US Govt. Printer.

MASON, W.S., DRESSEL, R.J. and BAIN, R.K. (1959) 'Sex role and the career orientations of beginning teachers', *Harvard Education Review.* **29**, 370–383.

MAYO, E. and LOMBARD, G.W. (1944) *Teamwork and Labor Turnover in the Aircraft Industry of Southern California.* Boston: Harvard University Graduate School of Business Administration.

MIDDLETON, M. (1979) 'The origins of the Matriculation Colleges', *Log: Journal of Hobart Matriculation College.* 84–98.

MILLER, D.C. and FORM, W.H. (1964) *Industrial Sociology: The Sociology of Work Organizations.* New York: Harper and Row.

MILLS, C. WRIGHT. (1956) *White Collar.* New York: Oxford University Press.

MOODIE, G. and ACOPIAN, J. (1988) 'New instrumentalism in higher education: Another axe being ground', *Australian Universities' Review.* **1**, 61–65.

MORGAN, B. (1983) 'An examination of the career structure in Victorian State secondary schools', *Educational Administration.* **20**, 41–48.

MORRIS, C.N. (1957) Career patterns of teachers, in STILES, L.J. (Ed.) *The Teacher's Role in American Society.* New York: Harper and Brothers.

MORRIS. M. (1974) 'Who gets promoted?' *Times Educational Supplement.* No. 3103 (15 Nov.).

MORRIS, R.T. and MURPHY, R.J. (1959) 'The situs dimensian in occupational structure', *American Sociological Review.* **24**, 231–239.

MORRISON, A. and MCINTYRE, D. (1973) *Teachers and Teaching.* Harmondsworth: Penguin.

MOSER, C.A. and KALTON, G. (1971) *Survey Methods in Social Investigation.* London: Heinemann.

MURNANE, R.J., SINGER, J.D. and WILLETT, J.B. (1988) 'The career paths of teachers: Implications for the supply and methodological lessons for research', *Educational Researcher.* **17** (6), 22–30.

MUSGRAVE, P.W. (1979) *The Sociology of Education.* London: Methuen.

MYRDAL, A. and KLEIN, V. *Women's Two Roles: Home and Work.* London: Routledge and Paul.

NADEBAUN, M. (1984) The extent and nature of the impact of declining promotional opportunities on senior masters in government secondary schools in Western Australia. Unpublished Master of Educational Administration dissertation: University of New England.

NASH, J.M. (1984) The promotion of women to the principalship: A case study. Unpublished Master of Educational Administration dissertation: University of New England.

NATIONAL UNION OF TEACHERS. (1986) *Equal Opportunities: A Summary of the National Union of Teachers' Policy*, N.U.T., London.

NATIONAL UNION OF TEACHERS. (1987) *Women in Teaching: A Decade of progress?* N.U.T: London.

Bibliography

NATIONAL UNION OF TEACHERS. (1980) *Promotion and the Woman Teacher*. N.A.T. and Equal Opportunities Commission.
NIAS, J. (1989) *Primary Teachers Talking: A Study of Teaching as Work*, London: Routledge.
NIAS, J. (1989) 'Subjectively speaking: English primary teachers' careers', *International Journal of Educational Research*. **13** (4), 391–402.
NOSOW, S. and FORM, W.H. (1962) *Man, Work and Society: A Reader in the Sociology of Occupations*. New York: Basic Books.
OAKLEY, A. (1972) *Sex, Gender and Society*. New York: Harper Colophon Books.
OPPENHEIM, A.N. (1966) *Questionnaire Design and Attitude Measurement*. London: Heinemann.
ORLICH, D.C. (1972) 'An analysis of teacher mobility', *Journal of Teacher Education*. **23**, 230–236.
OSIDOW, S.H. (Ed.) (1975) *Emerging Women: Career Analysis and Outlooks*. Ohio: Merrill Publishing Company.
PANKIN, R.M. (1973) 'Structural factors in academic mobility', *Journal of Higher Education*. **44**, 95–101.
PARK, R.E., BURGESS, E.W. et al., (1925) *The City*. Chicago: University of Chicago Press.
PARK, R.E. and BURGESS, E.W. (1925) *Introduction to the Science of Sociology*. Chicago: University of Chicago Press.
PARK, R.E. (1952) *Human Communities: The City and Human Ecology*. Glencoe, Ill: Free Press.
PARSONS, T. (1954) *Essays in Sociological Theory*. Glencoe: Free Press.
PARSONS, T. (1939; 1958) *The Professions and Social Structure*. Indianapolis: Bobbs-Merrill.
PARTINGTON, G. (1981) 'Teaching and promotion among South Australian teachers: 1950–1979', *South Australian Journal of Education Research*, **1**, 44–59.
PAVALKO, R.M. (1971) *Sociology of Occupations and Professions*. Itasia, ILL: F.E. Peacock.
PAVALKO, R.M. (Ed.) (1972) *Sociological Perspectives on Occupations*. Itasia, ILL: F.E. Peacock.
PEART, G.J. and DOBSON, H. (1980) *Beginning Teachers in Tasmanian Schools*. Hobart: Education Department.
PEART, G.J. and MACLEAN, R.D.I. In press, *Statistical Portrait of State School Teachers in Tasmania: 1930–1986*. Hobart: Tasmanian Teachers Federation.
PEDERSEN, K.G. (1970) 'Teacher migration and attrition', *Administrator's Notebook*. **18**, 1–13.
PEDERSEN, K.G. (1972) 'Teacher turnover in the metropolitan setting', *Education and Urban Society*. **4**, 177–196.
PEDERSEN, K.G. (1973) *The Itinerant Schoolmaster: A Socio-Economic Analysis of Teacher Turnover*. Chicago: Midwest Administration Centre, University of Chicago.
PERRUCCI, C.C. and R. (1970) 'Social origins, educational contexts, and career mobility', *American Sociological Review*. **35**, 451–463.
PHILLIPS, D. (1985) *Making More Adequate Provision*. Hobart: Tasmanian Government Printer.
PHILLIPS, S. (1982) 'Career exploration in adulthood', *Journal of Vocational Behaviour*. **20**, 129–140.

Bibliography

PIBAL, D.M.C. (1972) A Career Pattern Study of Nebraska's Secondary Public School Teachers in Selected Rural High Schools, Medium Size High Schools, and a City School System. Unpublished doctoral dissertation: University of Nebraska.

POPHAM, W.J. (1967) *Educational Statistics: Use and Interpretation.* New York: Harper and Row.

POPPLETON, P. (1988) 'Teacher professional satisfaction', *Cambridge Journal of Education.* **18** (1), 5–16.

PORTER, J. (1965) *The Vertical Mosaic: An Analysis of Social Class and Power in Canada.* University of Toronto Press.

PRICK, L.G.M. (1986) *Career Development and Satisfaction Amongst Secondary School Teachers,* Amsterdam: Vrije Universiteit Amsterdam.

PRICK, L.G.M. (1989) 'Satisfaction and stress among teachers', *International Journal of Educational Research.* **13** (4), 363–377.

PROLMAN, S. (1982) 'Gender, career paths and administrative perceptions', *Administrator's Notebook.* **30**, 1–4.

PSATHAS, G. (1968) 'Towards a Theory of Occupational Choice for Women', *Sociological and Social Research.* **52**, 253–268.

PURVIS, J. (1973) 'Schoolteaching as a professional career', *British Journal of Sociology.* **24**, 43–57.

PUSEY, M. (1976) *Dynamics of Bureaucracy.* Sydney: John Wiley.

RABINOWITZ, W. and CRAWFORD, K.E. (1970) 'A study of teacher's careers', *The School Review.* **68**, 377–399.

REEVES, C. (1935) *A History of Tasmanian Education.* Melbourne: A.C.E.R.

REISS, A.J. (1961) *Occupations and Social Status.* New York: The Free Press.

REMPEL, A. and BENTLEY, R. (1970) 'Teaching morale: Relationship with selected factors', *Journal of Personality and Social Psychology.* **40**, 627–634.

RENTSCHLER, R.E. (1970) Teacher mobility between the Major Metropolitan Areas of New York State. Unpublished doctoral dissertation: State University of New York at Buffalo.

RIMMER, C.M. (1985) The career accounts of women principals in Victorian Education Department high schools. Unpublished Master of Educational Administration Dissertation: University of New England.

RITZER, G. (1972) *Man and his Work.* New York: Appleton–Croff.

ROBIN, S.S. (1965) 'A Procedure for securing returns to mail questionnaires', *Sociological and Social Research.* **50**, 24–35.

ROTH, J.A. (1963) *Timetables.* New York: The Bobbs-Universal Coy. Inc.

SAIT. (1987) *Women Teachers: The Merit of Classroom Teachers.* Report of the South Australian Institute of Teachers Women's Conference.

SAMPSON, S.N. (1985) 'Promotion: Factors affecting women and men teachers in Australian Government systems', in *Educational Research: Then and Now.* Collected papers of the Annual A.A.R.E. Conference. Hobart: Australian Association for Research in Education.

SAMPSON, S.N. (1985) 'Women students and promotion: A search for some explanations', *Queensland Teachers' Journal.* **8**, 14–17.

SARROS, A.M. (1983) Aspects of the under representation of women in administrative positions in secondary schools in Victoria, as related to a comparison of male and female career aspirations. Unpublished Master of Education dissertation: University of Melbourne.

SASSER, C.W. (1975) 'What's wrong with rural schools?' *American School Board Journal*. **162**, 35–36.
SCHWARTZ, V. (1984) *Women in the Education Department in Victoria*. Policy Planning Unit, Ministry of Education, Melbourne.
SCOTT, C. (1961) 'Research on mail questionnaires', *Journal of the Royal Statistical Society*. **XXIV**, 143–195.
SDOFER, C. (1970) *Men in Mid-career*, Cambridge, UK: Cambridge University Press.
SHEPHERD, A. (1971) 'Married women teachers, role perceptions and career patterns', *Educational Research*. **13**, 191–197.
SIEGEL, S. (1956) *Nonparametric Statistics for the Behavioural Sciences*. New York: Mcgraw–Hill Book Company.
SIKES, P.J. (1985) 'The life cycle of the teacher', in BALL, S. and GOODSON, I. (Eds) *Teachers Lives and Careers*, Lewes: Falmer Press, 27–60.
SIKES, P.J., MEASOR, L. and WOODS, P. (1985) *Teacher Careers: Crises and Continuities*. Lewes: Falmer Press.
SILVERMAN, D. (1985) *Qualitative Methodology and Sociology*. Aldershot: Gower.
SJAASTED, L.A. (1961) *Income and Migration in the United States*. Chicago: University of Chicago Department of Photoduplication.
SJAASTED, L.A. (1962) *Migration and Population Growth in the Upper Midwest: 1930–1960*. Minneapolis: Upper Midwest Study Group.
SLOCUM, W.L. (1966) *Occupational Careers*. Chicago: Aldine Publishing Company.
SMITH, A. (1937; orig. 1776) *An Inquiry into the Nature and Causes of The Wealth of Nations*. New York: Modern Library.
SMITH, C.H. (1969) *Social Class Origin and the Mobility of Black Inner City School Teachers*. Unpublished doctoral dissertation: North Western University.
SMITH, C.H. (1970) 'Social class origin and mobility of Black inner-city school teachers', *Urban Education*. **5**, 65–83.
SMITH, D.M. (1975a) 'Head teachers' allocation of salary points in English secondary schools', *Educational Studies*. **1**, 113–119.
SMITH, D.M. (1975b) 'The career structure of head teachers in a Midlands city', *Educational Review*. **27**, 31–41.
SMITH, D.M. (1975c) 'Points allocation, secondary schools and teachers', *Educational Studies*. **1**, 163–170.
SOLOMON, D. (1961) 'Ethnic and class differences among hospitals as contingencies in medical careers', *American Journal of Sociology*. **66**, 463–471.
SOLOMON, D. (1968) 'Sociological perspectives on occupations', in BECKER, H.S. *Institutions and the Person*. Chicago: Aldine Pub. Co., pp. 3–13.
SOROKIN, P.A. (1947) *Society, Culture and Personality: their Structure and Dynamics*. New York: Harper.
SOUTH AUSTRALIAN INSTITUTE OF TEACHERS. (1980) *Deployment and Mobility in the Teaching Service*. Adelaide: S.A. Institute of Teachers.
SPAULL, A.D. (Ed.) (1977) *Australian Teachers: From Colonial Schoolmasters to Militant Professionals*. Melbourne: Macmillan.
SPENCER, D.A. (1986) *Contemporary women teachers: Balancing home and school*, New York: Longman.

Bibliography

STEBBINS, R.A. (1970) 'Career: The subjective approach', *Sociological Quarterly.* **11**, 32–49.
STEVENS, J. (1978) Career movements ot Private and State Secondary School Teachers in Tasmania. Unpublished Bachelor of Arts Honours Dissertation, University of Tasmania.
STOUFFER, A.A. et al., (1949) *The American Soldier.* Princeton: Princeton University Press.
STRAUSS, A.L. (1975) *Professions, Work and Careers.* New Brunswick, N.J.: Transaction Books.
STREETS, G.R. (1972) 'Career commitment of teacher graduates', *Administrators' Bulletin.* **3**, 1–4.
STUART, A. (1962) *Basic Ideas of Scientific Sampling.* London: Griffin.
SUPER, D. (1957) *The Psychology of Careers,* New York: Harper and Row.
SUTHERLAND, E.H. (Ed.) (1937) *The Professional Thief. by a Professional Thief.* Chicago: University of Chicago Press.
SWEDISH INTERNATIONAL DEVELOPMENT AUTHORITY. (1985) *Side by Side: A Report on Equality between Women and Men in Sweden.* Stockholm.
SWIFT, D.F. (1967) 'Social class mobility: Ideology and 11 + success', *British Journal of Sociology.* **18**, 165–186.
TALBERT, J.E. (1986) 'The staging of teachers' careers: An institutional perspective', *Work and Occupations.* **13**, 421–443.
TASMANIAN EDUCATION, NEXT DECADE. (1978) *T.E.N.D. Report.* Hobart: Tasmanian Government Printer. Chairman. W.F. Connell.
TAUSKY, C. and DUBIN, R. (1965) 'Career anchorage: Managerial mobility motivations', *American Sociological Review.* **30**, 725–735.
TEACHERS FEDERATION OF VICTORIA. (T.F.V.) (1986) *The Done Thing: Women Speak about their lives in Teaching.* T.F.V: Melbourne.
TECHNICAL TEACHERS' UNION OF VICTORIA (T.T.U.V.) (1988) *Career Restructure for the Post-Primary Section.* Melbourne: T.T.U.V./V.S.T.A.
THEOBALD, M. (1988) *Women, Education and the State in Nineteenth Century Australia.* Paper Presented at the Labour History Conference.
THOMAS, L.E. (1975) 'Why study mid-life career change?' *The Vocational Guidance Quarterly.* **25** (4), 320–328.
THOMAS, L.E. (1979) 'Causes of mid-life change from high-status careers', *The Vocational Guidance Quarterly.* **27** (3), 202–208.
THOMAS, L.E. (1980) 'A typology of mid-life career changes', *Journal of Vocational Behaviour.* **16**, 173–182.
TISHER, R. et al., (1978, 1979) *Beginning to Teach: Volumes I, II.* Canberra: Education Research and Development Committee.
TRONC, K. and EMMS, F. (1969) 'Promotional aspirations and differential role perceptions', *The Alberta Journal of Educational Research.* **15**, 169–183.
TROPP, A. (1957) *The School Teacher.* London: Heineman.
TROWN, A. and NEEDHAM, J. (1980) *Reduction in Part-timer Teaching: Implications for Schools and Women Teachers.* UK: Equal Opportunities Commission.
VEEMAN, S. (1984) 'Perceived problems of beginning teachers', *Review of Educational Research.* **54**, 143–178.
VIEL, P.J. (1971) 'Up the hierarchy!' *The Clearing House.* **46**, 200–202.
WALKER, R. (Ed.) (1985) *Applied Qualitative Research.* Aldershot: Gower.
WALLER, W. (1961; orig. 1936) *The Sociology of Teaching.* New York: Wiley.

Bibliography

WARD, S.M., et al., (1959) 'Sex role and the career orientation of beginning teachers', *Harvard Educational Review*. **29**, 370–383.

WARREN, D. (1989) 'Messages from the inside: Teachers as clues in history and policy', *International Journal of Educational Research*. **13** (4), 379–390.

WEBER, M. (1947; orig. 1922) *The Theory of Social and Economic Organization*. trans. HENDERSON, A.M. and PARSONS, T. New York: Oxford University Press.

WEBSTER, S.W. and TORSTEN-LUND, S.E. (1969) 'Defectors and persisters: Teachers of disadvantaged students', *Integrated Education*, **7**, 48–55.

WEINBERG, S.K. and AROND, H. (1952) 'The occupational culture of the boxer', *American Journal of Sociology*. **57**, 460–469.

WEISMAN, C.S., MORLOCK, L., SACK, D. and LEVINE, D. (1976) 'Sex differences in response to a blocked career pathway among unaccepted medical school applicants', *Sociology of Work and Occupations*. **3**, 187–208.

WENTWORTH, R. (1979) 'Career aspirations of male and female teachers', *Journal of the South Pacific Association of Teacher Education*. **11**, 3 and 4, pp. 97–104.

WHITCOMBE, J.E. (1979) *A Comparison of Career Patterns of Men and Women Teachers*. Wellington: Department of Education.

WHITE, K. (1967) 'Social background variables related to career commitment of women teachers', *Personnel and Guidance Journal*. **45**, 648–652.

WHYTE, D.R. (1966) 'Social determinant of inter-community mobility: An inventory of findings', *Canadian Review of Sociology and Anthropology*. **4**, 1–23.

WHYTE, W.F. (1943) *Street Corner Society: The Social Structure of an Italian Slum*. Chicago: University of Chicago Press.

WHYTE, W.H. (1948) *Human Relations in the Restaurant Industry*. New York: McGraw-Hill Book Company.

WHYTE, W.H. (1956) *The Organization Man*. New York: Doubleday Anchor.

WIENS, A.E. (1974) Characteristics of 'Mobile' and 'Stable' Occupational Educators by Specialty and Type of School. Unpublished doctoral dissertation. University of Illinois.

WILCE, H. (1985) 'Pay cake crumbs for women', *The Times Educational Supplement* (3 May).

WILENSKY, H.L. and EDWARDS, H. (1959) 'The skidder: Ideological adjustment of downward mobile workers', *American Sociological Review*. **24**, 215–231.

WILENSKY, H.L. (1961) 'Orderly careers and social participation: The impact of work history on social integration in the middle mass', *American Sociological Review*. **26**, 524–25.

WILENSKY, H. (1964) 'The professionalization of everyone?' *American Journal of Sociology*. **70**, 137–158.

WILLETT, J.B. and SINGER, J.D. (1989) 'Two types of questions about time: Methodological issues in the analysis of teacher career path data', *International Journal of Educational Research*. **13** (4), 421–437.

WILLIAMS, W.M. (Ed.) (1974) *Occupational Choice*. London: Allen and Unwin.

WILLIAMS COMMITTEE. (1979) *Education, Training and Employment*. A.G.P.S. Canberra.

WIRTH, L. (1928) *The Ghetto*. Chicago: University of Chicago Press.

WOODS, P. (1981) 'Strategies, commitment and identity: making and breaking the teacher role', in BARTON, L. and WALKER, S. (Eds) *Schools, Teachers and Teaching*, Lewes: Falmer Press.

Bibliography

WOODS, P. and SIKES, P.J. (1987) 'The use of teacher biographies in professional self development', in TODD, F. (Ed.) *Planning Continuing Professional Development*, London: Croom-Helm.
WORMALD, E. (1968) 'Research report: Careers of teachers', *Education for Teaching*. **77**, 84–86.

Appendices

Appendix 1

Propositions Tested

Propositions to be Tested

Chapter 5 extracts the conceptual aspects of the variables to be considered in the study. The following puts empirical flesh on these conceptual bones by looking at specific propositions with which the empirical side of this book is concerned. The propositions to be investigated were arranged under five headings, each of which relate back specifically to the five aspects of the research framework outlined earlier in Chapter 5.

The *first* section refers to propositions to be tested regarding career pathways and career patterns, including the variables that help explain differences and similarities in those pathways and patterns. Section *two* presents propositions that refer to the career timetables of teachers; and section *three* to propositions that relate to the career anchorage perspective and behaviour of teachers. Section *four* contains propositions relevant to the nature, and relative importance, of horizontal and vertical mobility in the school teaching career, to career contingency factors, and to teacher perceptions regarding promotion in the teaching career. Finally, section *five* presents propositions which relate to the objective/structural and the subjective/internal aspects of teacher careers.

Theoretical support for these propositions is derived from the literature reviewed in Chapters 2 and 3. In some cases the propositions seek to test whether the situation that applies to other occupations also applies to teachers; while others are derived from the available research on school teachers, and seek to test the validity of these finding for state school teachers in Tasmania.

    1 *Propositions Regarding School Teaching as an Occupation that Offers a Career*

Many of the propositions tested under this heading derive their theoretical support from earlier studies of occupational groups in society, of which school

Appendices

teachers are but one group. The research framework developed to guide data collection and analysis began with the proposition that school teaching is an occupation that offers its incumbents both an orderly occupational and organizational career.

The propositions examined were:

1.1 There are identifiable stages in the teaching career, these being (e.g. Hall, 1949; Friedman, 1972; Lortie, 1975; Tisher, 1978):
 - generation of an 'ambition' to become a teacher;
 - pre-service training;
 - induction into teaching;
 - the teaching career proper; and,
 - exit from and/or re-entry to teaching.
1.2 Various types of career pathways exist, and career patterns develop, within teaching which are identifiable and analysable (e.g. Hilsum and Start, 1974; Lyons, 1981; Department of Education, 1982; Burdon, 1983);
1.3 There are fundamental similarities between the career pathways pursued by teachers who currently occupy the same status positions within the promotion hierarchy of the education department (e.g. Hilsum and Start, 1974; Lyons, 1981; Rimmer, 1985);
1.4 Teachers who achieve the greatest and/or fastest promotion mainly view their career in organizational rather than occupational terms (e.g. Glaser, 1968; Lyons, 1981; Department of Education, 1982);
1.5 The promotion system and career patterns that occur in teaching are of central importance and concern to teachers, and have a dominant affect upon such things as the way in which they direct their energies, perceive their roles and develop an occupationally related identity (e.g. Hilsum and Start, 1974; Smith, 1975; Lyons, 1981);
1.6 In terms of teacher perceptions, school teaching is an occupation that offers a relatively limited promotions structure in the sense that most consider the promotions hierarchy in terms of the range of positions available in schools, rather than in terms of the full range of positions which exist within the education department both within and outside schools (e.g. Hilsum and Start, 1974; Lortie, 1975; Department of Education, 1982);
1.7 Most teachers experience difficulty in talking about their career, except under exceptional circumstances. The reason is that they regard this as being a sensitive or taboo topic, and so it is difficult to collect full and reliable data about this area unless a variety of data collection methods is used (e.g. Glaser, 1968);
1.8 The career movements of teachers, in both the horizontal and vertical mobility sense, are not random. Teachers move in patterned ways between competing positions, and this equally applies to those in head office and service branch positions, as it does to those employed in schools (e.g. Caplow, 1954; Hilsum and Start, 1974; Lortie, 1975; Marsland, 1975; Lyons, 1981; Department of Education, 1982);

Appendices

2 Propositions Relating to Career Timetables

Individuals structure the time period through which their work activities occur. There arise from this viewpoint a number of propositions that were tested for the teachers who comprise this study.

2.1   Timetable norms and 'bench marks' develop for teachers. These serve to help individuals internalise time perspectives regarding a career in teaching and provide reference points against which they judge their own progress (e.g. Roth, 1963; Lyons, 1981);

2.2   Teachers develop career maps, and career strategies, which are time orientated, in their attempt to achieve success in their occupation (e.g. Roth, 1963; Lyons, 1981);

2.3   An age-grade system, which influences the rate at which, and the nature of, the vertical mobility achieved by teachers operates within an Education Department (e.g. Roth, 1963; Pavalko 1971; Hilsum and Start, 1975; Department of Education, 1982);

2.4   Individuals whose rate of vertical mobility deviates from the age grade norms that have developed experience problems, such as that of marginality, in their careers and work-related relationships (e.g. Pavalko, 1971);

3 Propositions Regarding Career Anchorage Perspectives

3.1   Most teachers direct their energies at trying to achieve promotion over the length of their working life (e.g. Parsons, 1954; Lipset and Bendix, 1959);

3.2   Most teachers seek to reach a promotion position, as fast as possible, that is as close as possible to the peak of the promotions hierarchy. That is, most are committed to an 'unlimited success' career perspective (e.g. Parsons, 1954; Wilensky and Edwards, 1959);

3.3   The career anchorage perspectives of teachers are not fixed but are reassessed and re-adjusted by the individual at various stages in their career (e.g. Gouldner, 1957; Tausky and Dubin, 1965; Hilsum and Start, 1974);

3.4   The key variables which influence whether a particular teacher adopts a limited or an unlimited success model in terms of career anchorage are: gender, age, marital status and qualifications (e.g. Tausky and Dubin, 1965; Goldman, 1978; Department of Education, 1982);

3.5   The limited success and unlimited success career anchorage perspectives, as they apply to teachers, are not incompatible (e.g. Tausky and Dubin, 1954; Goldman, 1978);

4 Propositions Relating to Horizontal and Vertical Mobility, and Career Contingency Factors

A distinctive feature of the career patterns of teachers is the importance of both horizontal and vertical mobility. The following cluster of propositions regarding

235

Appendices

horizontal versus vertical mobility were tested for the survey population who comprised this study:

4.1 It is possible to describe and compare the career patterns of various groups of teachers in terms of both vertical and horizontal mobility (e.g. Caplow, 1954; Hilsum and Start, 1974; Department of Education, 1982);

4.2 The dominant feature of many teacher's career pattern is horizontal mobility (Becker, 1952);

4.3 For most teachers, horizontal mobility to a 'more desirable work location' is more important than is vertical mobility to a less desirable work location. It is possible to identify the circumstances and extent to which a person will give up vertical mobility due to horizontal mobility considerations (e.g. Becker, 1952; Greenberg and McCall, 1974);

4.4 In their moves between schools teachers attempt to minimize, or keep to a manageable extent, what they regard as being the problems associated with their work as teachers (e.g. Becker, 1952; Behrens, 1978);

4.5 Teachers move between schools in order to maximize rewards and minimize the effort required in their job (e.g. Berlowitz, 1971; Greenberg and McCall, 1974). They will try to avoid working in those schools where they perceive the teacher's work as being most difficult, and in so doing adopt a cost/benefit outlook when considering moves between schools (e.g. Becker, 1952; Berlowitz, 1971; Pederson, 1972);

4.6 In terms of teacher perceptions, 'push factors' have a greater influence than do 'pull factors' in affecting a teacher's horizontal mobility (e.g. Pederson, 1970, 1972, 1973);

4.7 'Pull factors' have a greater influence than do 'push factors' in affecting a teacher's vertical mobility (e.g. Pederson, 1970, 1972, 1973);

4.8 The age and sex composition of staff in schools is important in affecting the horizontal mobility of teachers, and this is particularly true for unmarried female teachers during their first 10 years of teaching (e.g. Pederson, 1972);

4.9 For most teachers the pattern of mobility, in both the horizontal and the vertical sense, is one which attempts to maximize moves from:

(a) country to city schools (e.g. Behrens, 1978; Delong, 1984);
(b) small to large schools (e.g. Peart and Dobson, 1980; Maclean, 1984);
(c) schools in low socio-economic status areas to schools in higher socio-economic status areas (e.g. Becker, 1952; Berlowitz, 1971).

4.10 A teacher's birthplace, and the geographical area where they completed their own secondary schooling, will have an important effect on their pattern of geographical mobility in terms of the area of the state in which they want to teach. In general, teachers seek to work in those parts of the state in which they completed their own secondary schooling (e.g. Jay, 1966);

4.11 A teacher's 'social' characteristics, in terms of such matters as their socio-economic background, will affect the pattern of their horizontal and vertical mobility between schools. For example, those from low socio-economic backgrounds will be more likely to teach in low S.E.S. schools than will those from higher socio-economic backgrounds; and those from country areas will be more willing and likely to teach in country areas than will those from city areas (e.g. Bendix, 1952; Jay, 1966; Smith, 1970; Perrucci, 1970);

A number of propositions relating more specifically to career contingency factors arise that are an extension of those which apply in a more general way to vertical mobility in an occupation. In terms of the research literature the emphasis is upon a comparison between the relative influence of the formal (e.g. age, gender, academic qualifications etc.), and the informal (e.g. ethnicity, religion, political affiliation etc.) career contingency factors. The propositions tested in this study were:

4.12 Both formal and informal career contingency factors can be identified that affect the vertical and horizontal mobility of teachers (e.g. Pavalko, 1971);

4.13 Of the formal career contingency factors that exist, a person's age and gender are particularly important (e.g. Freeman, 1975; Department of Education, 1982; Eberts and Stone, 1985; Sampson, 1985);

4.14 The main informal career contingency factors are: ethnicity; religion; socio-economic background; political affiliations; and, membership of out-of-school organizations such as teacher associations and clubs (e.g. Dalton, 1951; Becker, 1952; Viel, 1971; Pederson, 1970; Gehrke and Sheffield, 1985);

4.15 In relatively small education systems (such as that which occurs in Tasmania) informal rather than formal career contingency factors, and sponsored rather than contest mobility, are particularly important in affecting a teacher's career and promotion pattern (e.g. Hall, 1948);

4.16 It is possible to identify certain factors that explain differences in the work careers of male and female teachers. Some of the most important ones are:

(a) Marital status, which has a greater influence upon a woman's career and promotion pattern as a teacher than it does on a man's (Caplow, 1954; Fogarty et al., 1971; Hilsum and Start, 1974; Department of Education, 1982);

(b) Women are less career orientated and promotion minded than are men (e.g. Hutt, 1972; Hilsum and Start, 1974; Nash, 1984; Rimmer, 1985);

(c) Women who gain promotion are more likely to be unmarried and/or to have fewer children than are women teachers who do not gain promotion (e.g. Fogarty et al., 1971; Hutt, 1972; Eberts and Stone, 1985);

(d) Women do not apply for promotion as often as do men (e.g. Hilsum and Start, 1974; Department of Education, 1982);

Appendices

   (e) Existing promotion criteria and procedures in teaching favour men over women (e.g. Fogarty *et al.*, 1971; Department of Education, 1982; Sampson, 1985);
   (f) Women have lower career expectations than do men (e.g. Oakley 1972; Hilsum and Start, 1974; Department of Education, 1982);

4.17 Teachers who achieve promotion have shared characteristics which are different, in important ways, to those possessed by unpromoted or less frequently promoted teachers of the same age, gender and qualifications (e.g. Fogarty *et al.*, 1971; Hilsum and Start, 1974; Lyons, 1981; Department of Education, 1982). The main variables are:

  (a) They have spent a shorter period of time, on average, in the various schools in which they have worked;
  (b) They have worked in a greater number of schools;
  (c) They have spent a greater proportion of their time in the less 'attractive' schools in the education system, which are: country schools, small schools, and schools in lower socio-economic or isolated regions;
  (d) They are more likely to have undertaken further study towards formal qualifications, and to have attended in-service courses;
  (e) They are more likely to have conspicuously involved themselves in a wide range of in-school and out-of-school, non-teaching type activities;
  (f) They have a higher 'career saliency' outlook;
  (g) They are likely to have a clear career perspective and to have established career timetables early in their careers;
  (h) They identify more strongly with the idea of an organizational rather than an occupational career;
  (i) They are more likely to have specialised in subject areas that are in short supply during their training period;
  (j) They are more likely to be employed in primary rather than secondary schools.

4.18 Those who are not successful in gaining promotion, or who gain promotion at a rate which is slower than the average, adopt particular strategies to cope with this situation (e.g. Pavalko, 1971; Becker and Strauss, 1956; Hilsum and Start, 1975; Lyons, 1981);

4.19 It is possible to identify certain factors that influence the speed at which a person achieves promotion (e.g. Hilsum and Start, 1974; Lyons, 1981; Department of Education, 1982). The main ones are:

  (a) gender (promotion comes earlier for men than women);
  (b) graduate/non-graduate status (promotion comes earlier for graduates);
  (c) type of school in which employed at each status level in the promotions hierarchy (promotion comes earlier for those employed in secondary rather than primary schools);

Appendices

5 *Propositions Relating to the Structural and Phenomenological Perspectives in Studying Work Careers*

Relatively few studies have specifically directed their attention to examining teacher perceptions regarding the factors that influence vertical mobility within their occupation, since most adopt a structuralist perspective when examining teaching careers. Even fewer have examined the extent to which there is a match between teacher perceptions and teacher behaviour regarding their work career.

In relation to this important matter this study sought to test the following propositions:

5.1 Teachers are more agreed about what ought to affect the promotion of teachers than they are about what does affect the promotion of teachers (e.g. Hilsum and Start, 1974; Department of Education, 1982).

5.2 There will be some disagreement between teachers working in different areas of the school system (e.g. primary, secondary, etc) regarding the factors that *do* and those that *ought* to affect promotion (e.g. Hilsum and Start, 1974);

5.3 There will be a substantial match between what teachers believe affects their promotion and what the survey data shows actually does affect their promotion (e.g. Hilsum and Start, 1974);

5.4 Most teachers perceive the teaching career as having both an objective/external dimension, and an internal/subjective dimension to it: that is, teacher careers *occur* in systems, but individuals also *make* careers in these systems. (e.g. Lortie, 1975; Lyons, 1981).

Appendix 2

Stage 1 Data: Information from Education Department Personnel Files

CARD 1

The following information, in the form indicated, was obtained from files in the Personnel Section of the Education Department of Tasmania.

Appropriate coding procedures were adopted when the researcher recorded information on these sheets.

1. TEACHER NAME CODE 1 [ ][ ][ ] 4

2. CARD NUMBER 5 [1]

3. GENDER
   M F
   [1][2]

4. BOND/S EXPIRES Yr. Mth.
   - (Least Recent) 7 [ ][ ] 10
   - 11 [ ][ ] 14
   - 15 [ ][ ] 18
   - (Most Recent) 19 [ ][ ] 22

5. BIRTHDATE Yr. Mth.
   23 [ ][ ] 26

6. CLASSIFICATION

		Yr.	
Class 3	27	[ ]	28
Class 2 (Prov.)	29	[ ]	30
Class 2	31	[ ]	32
Class 1	33	[ ]	34
T.T.C. (A)	35	[ ]	36
T.T.C. (Status)	37	[ ]	38
T.T.C.	39	[ ]	40
T.T.C.	41	[ ]	42
Other	43	[ ]	44

Appendices

7. ADDITIONAL YRS. OF STUDY   Yrs. of Study
                                Shown?

	Yes	No
45	1	2

		Years	
(Least Recent)	46		47
	48		49
	50		51
	52		53
	54		55
	56		57
	58		59
	60		61
	62		63
(Most Recent)	64		65

8. HIGHEST LEVEL OF SECONDARY EDUCATION RESEARCH

	Type	Yr.	
66			68

9. DATE FROM WHICH L.S.L. CALCULATED

	Yr.	Mth.	
69			72

CARD 2

1. TEACHER NAME CODE   1 [   ] 4

2. CARD NUMBER   5 [2]

3. QUALIFICATIONS

		Year Qualif.	DK	T	M	OS	O	P	H	F	
					Place			Results			
(Least Recent)	6		0	1	2	3	0	1	2	3	11
	12		0	1	2	3	0	1	2	3	17
	18		0	1	2	3	0	1	2	3	23
	24		0	1	2	3	0	1	2	3	29
	30		0	1	2	3	0	1	2	3	35
	36		0	1	2	3	0	1	2	3	41
(Most Recent)	42		0	1	2	3	0	1	2	3	47

0 = M indicated

Appendices

4. CAREER HISTORY: NUMBER OF ENTRIES ON CARDS 3-8

                                51 [   ] 52

EXPLANATORY LEGEND:

Place of Qualification: DK = Don't know
                                  T = Tasmania
                                  M = Mainland Australia
                                  OS = Overseas

Results in Course: O = Not indicated in records
                                  P = Pass
                                  H = Honours
                                  F = Not successfully Completed

CARDS 3, 4, 5 AND 6

1. TEACHER NAME CODE   1 [| |] 4

2. CARD NUMBER   5 [3]

3. CAREER/PROMOTION PROFILE:

	Date	School/Place	Promotion Position 9	
6				15
16				25
26				35
36				45
46				55
56				65
66				75

Appendix 3

Stage 2 Data: Questionnaire

Appendix 3(1): Questionnaire-letter to Teachers

Dear

RE: CAREERS IN EDUCATION PROJECT

We write to seek your co-operation in providing information for a research study which is of direct relevance to the work of state school teachers and education administrators in Tasmania.

The research study being undertaken is part of an investigation into the career and promotion patterns of Tasmanian state school teachers and education administrators over their working lives.

This research comes at a time when there is a heightened interest in, and concern about, promotion and careers in teaching, on the part of education departments, teacher unions, and individual teachers. The reason is that owing to the national trends of stabilising participation rates in schools, and falling numbers within the relevant age cohorts, there has been a reduced demand for teachers. One result is that given a stable teacher/pupil ratio there is currently an oversupply of persons seeking employment as teachers, and this is likely to have a substantial effect upon promotion and career patterns in education.

In addition, one legacy of the rapid expansion of school systems that occurred in recent years is that a significant proportion of positions at various levels within the promotions hierarchy are occupied by relatively young teachers, and so this, coupled with a lack of growth in the teaching service, has dampened down the career and promotion opportunities available in teaching. We are still uncertain about the likely effect of these reduced opportunities for advancement on teacher-behaviour and the teaching profession.

This study also comes at a time when there is concern about the high rates of teacher-turnover that exist in most Australian school systems. This trend concerns many education authorities because a widely held (although largely unresearched) belief is that high turnover rates mitigate against teachers developing a stable and enduring relationship with their students, which is seen as being the basis upon which effective learning and teaching is built.

We hope it is clear from what has been said that although the primary focus

Appendices

of this study is upon certain aspects of promotion and career patterns in education, the research findings and conclusions from the study will also help enhance our understanding of the operation of school systems.

This study has the full support of the Director-General of Education and the Tasmanian Teachers Federation. It also enjoys the support of the various Teacher Associations: The Principals, Vice-Principals, Senior Master/Mistresses, and Senior Teachers Associations.

You are one of a sample of Education Department personnel in Tasmania who have been selected to take part in this study. Early next term you will receive a questionnaire by mail. The success of the research, and the validity and usefulness of its results, depend on the co-operation of all those who, like yourself, are being asked to participate in this way. We would therefore be most grateful if you would complete the questionnaire when it reaches you and return it as quickly as possible (preferably within a week), in the stamped addressed envelope provided.

All data will be treated in the strictest confidence. It will be coded onto I.B.M. cards to be used in group comparisons only. In no circumstances will any individual or school be identified to any other individual, school or employing authority. The only information to be published will be anonymous and in summary form.

If you have any questions about the project I will be happy to answer them by mail or telephone [(002) 23 0561, extn 644 or 375; private (002) 34 5884]; and I hope that in any case you will use the space provided in the questionnaire to express your own (anonymous) opinions.

With many thanks,

Yours sincerely,

Rupert Maclean,
Chief Investigator,
Careers in Education Project.

Appendices

Appendix 3(2): Questionnaire

STRICTLY CONFIDENTIAL

CAREERS IN EDUCATION PROJECT

FACULTY OF EDUCATION

UNIVERSITY OF TASMANIA

Appendices

STRICTLY CONFIDENTIAL

For office use

CAREERS IN EDUCATION PROJECT

Instructions

(a) For each question where a choice is offered, please choose the appropriate answer and put a circle around the number which corresponds with it. Please circle only one number unless otherwise instructed.

FOR EXAMPLE: A person who has a son and two daughters should answer the following question as shown:—

How many children do you have?   0   1   2   ③   4   5   6 or more

(b) For all other questions please answer in the spaces provided.

(c) Please answer all questions.

(d) Space is provided on the last page for you to include any further information or comments you would like to add.

Ref. No. *1-4*

Card *5*
P.P. *6-7*
Type *8-10*
Size *11*

SECTION ONE: CAREER FACTORS

1. **As at the current time how many times have you needed to move your place of residence** directly as a result of you achieving promotion?(Do not include moves made for other reasons e.g. because a member of your family changed jobs.)

    Number of times moved residence _____

    12

2. Which of the following best represents your estimate of your chances of gaining further promotion?

Excellent	1	Poor	4	
Good	2	No chance at all	5	
Fair	3			

    13

3. Please indicate

    (a) The promotion position in the Education Department you would **like to occupy** 10 Years from now (please be as specific as possible e.g. Principal, Class IA Primary School).

    Position: _____

    14-19

    (b) The promotion position in the Education Department you would **expect to occupy** 10 years from now (please be as specific as possible).

    Position: _____

    20-25

4. Indicate which of the following statements best coincides with your own overall view:

    When I think about my own career and promotion within the Education Department, I mainly think in terms of the range of positions that are available **in schools**. 1

    When I think about my own career and promotion within the Education Department, I mainly think in terms of the range of positions that are available **outside schools**, such as head/regional office or specialist positions (e.g. consultant, superintendent, research branch). 2

    When I think about my own career and promotion within the Education Department, I think in terms of both the range of positions in **schools**, **and outside schools**. 3

    26

5. Some people think that it would be (or was) a genuine loss for them to leave the classroom to enter more administrative-type positions in or outside schools. Others are attracted by the notion of taking on a more administrative type role. Which of the following comes closest to expressing *your* overall feelings on the matter?

    I would (did) feel much greater **loss** than gain if (when) I left the classroom for an administrative-type post 1

    I would (did) feel greater **loss** than gain if (when) I left the classroom for an administrative-type post 2

    I would (did) feel equal **loss and gain** if (when) I left the classroom for an administrative-type post 3

    I would (did) feel greater **gain** than loss if (when) I left the classroom for an administrative-type post 4

    I would (did) feel much greater **gain** than loss if (when) I left the classroom for an administrative-type post 5

    27

1

Appendices

For office use

SECTION TWO: RELEVANT ATTITUDES

6. One facet of a person's life is his or her career, which may be defined as a long-term paid involvement in a particular profession or occupation. Given this definition, how important to your overall personal satisfaction is the pursuit of a career?

    Very important 1
    Important 2
    Uncertain of its importance 3
    Unimportant 4
    Very unimportant 5

28

7. Please indicate the extent to which you personally agree or disagree with the following general statements:

(a) Most teachers prefer to work in city rather than country schools.

    Strongly agree 1
    Agree 2
    Uncertain 3
    Disagree 4
    Strongly disagree 5

29

(b) I would prefer to work in a city rather than a country school.

    Strongly agree 1
    Agree 2
    Uncertain 3
    Disagree 4
    Strongly disagree 5

30

(c) Most teachers prefer to work in large rather than small schools.

    Strongly agree 1
    Agree 2
    Uncertain 3
    Disagree 4
    Strongly disagree 5

31

(d) I would prefer to work in large rather than small schools.

    Strongly agree 1
    Agree 2
    Uncertain 3
    Disagree 4
    Strongly disagree 5

32

(e) Most teachers prefer to work in schools in 'middle class' rather than 'working class' type areas.

    Strongly agree 1
    Agree 2
    Uncertain 3
    Disagree 4
    Strongly disagree 5

33

(f) I would prefer to work in schools in 'middle class' rather than 'working class' type areas.

    Strongly agree 1
    Agree 2
    Uncertain 3
    Disagree 4
    Strongly disagree 5

34

Appendices

For office use

8. Below is a list of possible sources of satisfaction or dissatisfaction concerned with teaching in schools. Select (a) *up to five* items you personally consider *most satisfying*, and (b) *up to five* items you personally consider *most unsatisfying*, and write the appropriate codes in the panels provided at the foot of the list.

ITEM	CODE	ITEM	CODE
Promotion prospects	01	Status of the profession in society	22
Opportunity to pursue further qualifications	02	Effect of part-time teachers on staff relationships	23
Economic security	03	Contribution of part-time teachers to school management	24
Working hours	04		
Holidays	05	Extent of 'duties' allocated, (e.g. playground supervision)	25
Time to pursue personal interests	06	Allocation of 'free' periods	26
Time to pursue academic interests	07	Size of classes – general	27
School/classroom accommodation	08	Size of classes – examination groups	28
Staffroom accommodation	09	Influence of internal examinations	29
Equipment – 'hardware' (e.g. tape recorders, projectors, etc.)	10	Influence of external examinations	30
Equipment – textbooks	11	Opportunity to practise own ideas	31
Consultation between princ. and staff	12	Pastoral care given to individual pupils	32
Staffroom relationships	13	Pupil discipline	33
Consultation between staffs of different schools	14	Interruptions to lessons	34
Relationships with parents	15	Extent of non-professional work required	35
Opportunity to meet parents	16	Extent of extra-curricular commitment	36
Pressure at work	17	Supervision of students' practice teaching sessions	37
Relationships with advisers/superintendents	18	Extent of student teaching practice in schools	38
Staff-pupil relationships	19		
Guidance offered by advisers/superintendents	20		
Guidance offered probationary teachers by other staff	21		

Other item(s). Please Specify _____ 39

(a) Insert in the panel *up to five most satisfying* items ☐☐☐☐☐

(b) Insert in the panel *up to five most unsatisfying* items ☐☐☐☐☐

35-36
37-38
39-40
41-42
43-44

Please include any additional comments in the space below:

45-46
47-48
49-50
51-52
53-54

9. ONLY THOSE NOT EMPLOYED IN SCHOOLS (E.G. DIRECTORS, SUPERINTENDENTS, SUPERVISORS, PRINCIPAL/SENIOR EDUCATION OFFICERS, ETC.) SHOULD ANSWER QUESTION 9.

(a) Please list up to 5 factors which you personally find most satisfying about the work associated with your current promotion position.

i _____
ii _____
iii _____
iv _____
v _____

55-56
57-58
59-60
61-62
63-64

Appendices

For office use

(b) Please list up to 5 factors which you personally find most unsatisfying about the work associated with your current promotion position.

i _____ 65-66
ii _____ 67-68
iii _____ 69-70
iv _____ 71-72
v _____ 73-74

10. The following list contains factors which may influence promotion prospects in the Tasmanian state school system. In the panels provided below the list please write the codes of:—

Ref. No. *1-4*
Card   *5*

(a) five main factors which in your view generally favour promotion *at present;* and
(b) five main factors which you believe *ought* generally to favour promotion.

FACTOR	CODE	FACTOR	CODE
Length of teaching experience	01	Good relationship with Principal	21
Long service in a particular school	02	Good relationship with other staff	22
Experience in a variety of schools	03	Having a strong personality	23
Service in country schools	04	Being married	24
Service in isolated schools	05	Being a parent	25
Being a graduate	06	Being a man	26
Higher degree qualifications in Education	07	Being a woman	27
		Being younger than 40	28
Having expertise in a particular subject or method	08	Being native to area where post advertised	29
Concern for welfare of individual pupils	09	Having taught in area where post advertised	30
Qualification in subject for which there is a teacher shortage	10	Willingness to move to other areas	31
Successful experience with examination candidates	11	Experience in education apart from teaching	32
Ability to control pupils	12	Experience outside education, e.g. industry	33
Flexibility in teaching methods	13	Participation in civic activities, e.g. councillor, community service	34
Administrative ability	14	Religious affiliation	35
Attendance at in-service courses	15	Political affiliation	36
Participation in extra-curricular activities	16	Membership, Tasmanian Teachers Federation	37
Familiarity with new ideas in education	17	Membership, Australian College of Education	38
Participation in innovative practices	18	Social class background	39
Conformity with views of advisers and/or superintendent	19	Ethnic background	40
Personal/social contacts with people who can influence promotion	20		

Other factor(s). Please Specify _____ 41

(a) Five factors which *do* favour promotion *at present.* (use codes) [ ][ ][ ][ ][ ] 6-7
(b) Five factors which *ought* to favour promotion (use codes)   [ ][ ][ ][ ][ ] 8-9

Please include any additional comments in the space below:

10-11
12-13
14-15
16-17
18-19
20-21
22-23
24-25

4

249

Appendices

For office use

11. ONLY THOSE NOT EMPLOYED IN SCHOOLS (E.G. DIRECTORS, SUPERINTENDENTS, SUPERVISORS, PRINCIPAL/SENIOR EDUCATION OFFICERS ETC.) SHOULD ANSWER QUESTION 11.

   (a) Please list **5 main factors** which in your view generally **favour promotion at present** to the type of promotion position you currently occupy.

      i _____   *26-27*
      ii _____   *28-29*
      iii _____   *30-31*
      iv _____   *32-33*
      v _____   *34-35*

   (b) Please list **5 main factors** which in your view **ought** generally to favour promotion to the type of promotion position you currently occupy.

      i _____   *36-37*
      ii _____   *38-39*
      iii _____   *40-41*
      iv _____   *42-43*
      v _____   *44-45*

12. (a) If you had (have) a son, would (did) you encourage him to become a teacher?   *46*

     Strongly encourage 1
     Encourage 2
     Neither encourage nor discourage 3
     Discourage 4
     Strongly discourage 5

   (b) If you had (have) a daughter would (did) you encourage her to become a teacher?   *47*

     Strongly encourage 1
     Encourage 2
     Neither encourage nor discourage 3
     Discourage 4
     Strongly discourage 5

SECTION THREE: TEACHER QUALIFICATIONS AND TEACHING SUBJECTS

13. Which one of the following age ranges of pupils were you primarily trained to teach during your initial teacher training?   *48*

   Infant 1
   Primary 2
   Secondary 3
   Primary/Secondary 4
   Not trained for specific age range 5
   Untrained 6
   Others (please specify) _____ 7

14. Which one of the following Tasmanian Education Department categories apply to you?
(Take account of both your academic and professional training: for example, a 3 year degree plus Dip.Ed. = 4 year trained).

   1 year trained teacher 1   *49*
   2 year trained teacher 2
   3 year trained teacher 3
   4 year trained teacher 4
   Untrained teacher 5
   Other (please specify) _____ 6

Appendices

For office use
50

15. At the current time are you studying for a qualification relevant to your career?

Not studying for further qualification	1
Matriculation	2
Bachelors degree	3
Masters degree	4
Doctorate	5
Diploma/Certificate	6
Other (please specify) _____	7

16. The following subjects are each given a code. By means of these codes please indicate, in the panels below, the main subjects in which you specialised:

   (a) during your first degree (if any)
   (b) during your teacher training (if any) i.e. teaching method areas
   (c) if neither (a) nor (b) apply, other subject areas of specialisation (if any) e.g. Business College, Trade courses, etc.

   If there were no specialist subject/s in your course/s use **Code 62**.
   You may insert one, two or three codes, but only if they refer to your **main** subjects.

   EXAMPLE: If you had not taken a first degree, and your specialist subjects during teacher training had been Maths and Science, you would answer:

   (a) | 61 | |
   (b) | 30 | 47 |
   (c) | | |

Subject	Code	Subject	Code	Subject	Code
Agriculture/Rural Science	01	Geography	18	Political Science	38
Ancient Civilizations	02	Geology	19	Primary Method	39
Art/Design/Visual Arts	03	German	20	Psychology	40
Biology/Botany/Zoology	04	Greek	21	Public Administration	41
Chemistry	05	Health & Recreation	22	Religious Studies	42
Commerce	06	History	23	Rural Science	43
Computer Studies	07	Home Economics	24	Russian	44
Crafts/Woodwork/Metalwork	08	Indonesian	25	Secondary Method (general)	45
Dance/Drama	09	Infant Method	26	Secretarial Studies/Shorthand/Typing	46
Dutch	10	Italian	27	Science	47
Economics	11	Japanese	28	Social Psychology	48
Education (this code applies only to degree subject)	12	Latin	29	Social Science	49
		Maths	30	Sociology	50
Engineering	13	Music	31	Spanish	51
English	14	Needlecraft	32	Speech & Drama	52
Environmental Studies	15	Philosophy	33	Statistics	53
French	16	Photography	34		
General Studies	17	Physical Education	35		
		Physics	36		
		Polish	37		

Other subject(s) (please specify) _____ 54

Not trained 60   **No degree** 61   **No specialist subject in course** 62

(a) Subject(s) first degree (if any) | | |
(b) Subject(s) teacher training (if any) | | |
(c) Subject(s) of other qualifications if (a) or (b) not applicable | | |

Please include any additional comments in the space below:

51-52
53-54
55-56

57-58
59-60
61-62

63-64
65-66
67-68

251

Appendices

	For office use

17. ONLY THOSE EMPLOYED IN SCHOOLS SHOULD ANSWER QUESTION 17.

Please refer to question 16, and, in the panel below, write the code(s) of the *main* subject(s) you teach in your school.

NOTE:
(a) If your teaching did not involve 'specialist' subjects (e.g. as in infant or primary schools) or if your teaching was spread across a variety of subjects (e.g. as with a teacher of 'General Subjects' in a Secondary school), use CODE 70.
(b) If your time-table involved less than 20% teaching (e.g. that of a non-teaching principal, or of a school counsellor), use CODE 71.

Main subject(s) taught :   (codes as for Question 16)

69-70
71-72
73-74

SECTION FOUR: PERSONAL BACKGROUND DATA

18. Marital status
    Single 1
    Married 2
    Separated/divorced 3
    Widowed 4
    Other (please specify_____) 5

75

19. How many children, if any, do you have?   (Please circle the appropriate number)
    0   1   2   3   4   5   6 or more

76

20. Describe your father's normal occupation at the time you left school. Please state both grade and nature of the occupation.

    For example —   Foreman in a manufacturing industry
                        Solicitor in private practice
                        Teacher in a state secondary school

Please do not simply use terms such as clerk, public servant, teacher, etc.

Father's occupation: _____

77-78

21. Describe your mother's occupation at the time you left school in a similar way.

Mother's occupation: _____

79-80

22. Which of the persons listed below are, or have been, teachers. Circle all appropriate numbers and delete the plural form when it is not applicable.

    Your own mother 1
    Your own father 2
    Your own brother(s) 3
    Your own sister(s) 4
    Your brothers' daughter(s) 5
    Your brothers' son(s) 6
    Your sisters' daughter(s) 7
    Your sisters' son(s) 8
    Your own daughter(s) 9
    Your own son(s) 10
    Your own husband/wife 11
    Mother's mother 12
    Mother's father 13
    Mother's sister(s) 14
    Mother's brother(s) 15
    Cousin(s) on your mother's side 16
    Cousin(s) on your father's side 17
    Father's mother 18
    Father's father 19
    Father's sister(s) 20
    Father's brother(s) 21
    Other relative(s) (e.g. step-relatives; please specify)
    _____ 22

Ref. No. *1-4*
Card   5

6-50

23. What is your
    (a)   Sex: Male 1
                   Female 2

51

                   Year
    (b)   Date of birth 19 ☐☐

52-53

Appendices

SECTION FIVE: ADDITIONAL INFORMATION *For office use*

24. Is there any other information that appears to you to be relevant and which you would like to add to your answers or this questionnaire? If so, please comment below.

Thank you very much for your co-operation in completing this questionnaire. Please return it in the reply-paid addressed envelope provided.
CAREERS IN EDUCATION PROJECT
C/- FACULTY OF EDUCATION
THE UNIVERSITY OF TASMANIA
G.P.O., BOX 252C,
HOBART
TASMANIA 7001.

Appendix 4

Stage 3 Data: Interview Schedules

Appendix 4(1): Careers in Education Project: Individual Interview Schedule

1 *Preamble*:
Thank you for agreeing to be interviewed.

I would like to make it perfectly clear from the outset that your comments will be treated in the strictest confidence. When the data collected from interviewers is written up in a research report no individual or school will be identifiable: the published information will be anonymous.

2 *Explanation Regarding Careers in Education Project*:
As I indicated on the telephone when inviting you to be interviewed, the aim of this study is to gain an improved understanding of State School teachers in Tasmania by finding out more about their careers and promotion in teaching. We want, for example, to be able to explain differences and similarities in the career patterns of various groups of teachers who occupy differing positions within the promotions hierarchy; and to identify those factors that influence teacher careers and promotion. Some of this information has already been collected through the questionnaire which you and other teachers filled in some time ago.

The purpose of conducting interviews is to obtain more detailed information than was possible through the questionnaire: to survey more fully the opinions and attitudes of teachers regarding various aspects of careers and promotion within the Education Department of Tasmania.

Do you have any questions you would like to ask about the research project? (If so, answer these).

In the interests of improved accuracy, would you mind if I tape recorded the interview? I assure you that comments made will be treated in the strictest confidence.

3 *Questions*:

(a) Looking back over your time with the Education Department of Tasmania what do you regard to be the *most satisfying* aspects of *teaching* in schools?

Why do you feel this?

Appendices

(b) What do you find to be the *most satisfying* aspects of the work associated with your *current promotion position*?

Explain to me why you feel this.

(c) What are the main reasons why you have sought promotion within the Education Department of Tasmania?

How important is gaining promotion to you? Why?

To what extent, and in what ways, have your motivations changed over your time with the Education Department?

(d) What are the main factors which, in your view, generally *favour promotion at present*, in the Tasmanian State School system?

Why do you think that these factors are important?

(e) What are the main factors which, in your view, generally *ought to favour promotion* in the Tasmanian State School system?

Why do you believe that these factors should be important?

[If a mismatch occurs between the answers to questions (d) and (e), ask question (f). If not, go straight to question (g).]

(f) Why, in your opinion, is there a difference between your views regarding the factors that *do influence promotion* at present and those that *ought to influence* promotion?

(g) When deciding upon whether or not to seek promotion in the Education Department what have been the main considerations you have taken into account?

Explain how and why each of these have been important to you.

(h) It has been said that for some teachers it is more important to obtain a 'more desirable work location' at their current promotion level than it is to obtain promotion to a 'less desirable work location'. What are the characteristics of your preferred work location? How important is this to you? Explain why you feel this way.

(i) If an ambitious person asked your advice on how they could best achieve the greatest promotion in the Education Department of Tasmania in the shortest time, what would you say?

In terms of your promotion in the Education Department, what are the types of things you have done (in terms of career tactics) to increase your chances of gaining promotion?

(j) What, in your opinion, are the personal and professional characteristics of the *most promoted* teachers in the Tasmanian Education system?

Appendices

What do you believe are the characteristics of the *least promoted* teachers in the system?

(k) Do you regard yourself as having been successful in your career as a teacher in the Education Department of Tasmania? What criteria do you apply when judging this, and why choose these?

(l) Various researchers talk about the careers of teachers consisting of a number of different, and distinct, "stages". What do you regard to be the main stages in the teaching career, and what are the characteristics of each stage?

(m) How satisfied are you with the way in which the promotions system operates?

What changes, if any, would you like to see in the promotions system and procedures adopted?

(n) It is widely recognised that there are reduced promotion opportunities and mobility within the Tasmanian Education system due to there being a contraction in the system in terms of student enrolments and government funding for education.

What influence do you think this has on the behaviour and morale of most teachers you know? What affect does it have on your own behaviour and morale?

What do you believe could be done to reduce the possibly adverse effect of a contracting education system, on teacher behaviour and morale?

4 *Conclusion*
Are their any other comments you would like to make which are relevant to this study? If so, please feel free to make them.

Thank you very much for your time and interest in being interviewed.

N.B. Interviews were semi-structured in format and so the questions listed above are those covered with all interviewees. In addition, each interview also covered various other facets of careers and promotion in teaching, depending upon the particular interests and responses made by individual interviewees.

Appendix 4 (2): Careers in Education Project; Group Interview Schedule

1 *Preamble*:
The results of the individual interviews conducted with teachers throughout the state for the Careers in Education Project have been written up in summary form, and these were distributed as background reading to all teachers, like yourselves, who have been invited to attend a group interview.

Appendices

I propose to go through each of the questions asked in the individual interviews, in turn, and would like all of you, both as individuals and as members of this group interview session, to discuss your response to the views given by the individual teachers interviewed. In doing this I would like you to indicate the extent to which you personally believe that the teacher responses reported upon are representative of the views held by teachers employed by the Education Department of Tasmania.

2 *Questions*:
Go through each question contained in the Individual Interview Schedule: See Appendix 4(1).

Appendix 5

Career Profiles of Promoted Teachers: Statistics

Table 5.1 Promoted teachers in primary schools: years of teaching experience when status awarded

	Lge. Schls. (N = 47)	Principals Med. Schls. (N = 45)	Sm.Schls. (N = 50)	*Vice Princ. (N = 30)	S.T.'s (N = 77)
Mean Exp.	22.5	17.3	9.8	14.3	11.2
25th Centile	17	13	6	9	7
75th Centile	28	17	12	18	14
Range	11–35	9–33	3–29	5–30	3–25
Mode	15	17	8	10	8

* The position of V.P. only exists in large primary schools

Table 5.2 Promoted teachers in primary schools, males and females: years of teaching experience when status awarded

	Principals* (Med./Small Schools)		V.P.'s		S.T.'s	
	Males (N = 87)	Females (N = 8)	Males (N = 23)	Females (N = 7)	Males (N = 22)	Females (N = 55)
Mean Exp.	13.2	13.8	13.7	16.1	8.6	12.3
25th Centile	6	10	11	13	5	8
75th Centile	12	12	12	18	10	15
Range	3–23	4–29	5–30	9–24	4–22	3–25
Mode	8	12	11	17	5	12

* There were no female principals in large schools.

Appendices

Table 5.3 Promoted teachers in primary schools, graduates and non-graduates: years of teaching experience when status awarded

	Principals		V.P.'s		S.T.'s	
	Grad. (N = 26)	Non-grad. (N = 114)	Grad. (N = 4)	Non-grad. (N = 26)	Grad. (N = 8)	Non-Grad. (N = 68)
Mean Exp.	17.7	16.0	11.8	15.0	8.5	11.5
25th Centile	15	10	8	11	7	7
75th Centile	23	23	11	18	9	16
Range	4–33	3–35	6–22	5–30	4–18	4–25
Mode	15	22	N/A	9	8	12

Table 5.4 Promoted teachers in secondary schools: years of teaching experience when status awarded

	Principals		V.P.'s		S.M.'s
	Lge. Schls. (N = 38)	Med. Schls. (N = 4)	Lge. Schls. (N = 50)	Med. Schls. (N = 12)	(N = 167)
Mean Exp.	21.4	21.8	17.1	15.2	9.3
25th Centile	18	22	14	13	6
75th Centile	24	22	19	17	12
Range	10–35	21–22	9–30	6–23	2–25
Mode	18	22	13/17	16	9

Table 5.5 Promoted teachers in secondary schools, males and females: years of teaching experience when status awarded

	Principals Males Females	V.P.'s Males (N = 41)	(Lge. Schls) Females (N = 9)	V.P.'s Males (N = 7)	(Med. Schls) Females (N = 5)	S.M.'s Males (N = 121)	Females (N = 44)
Mean Exp.	There were	16.5	18.7	15.9	14.2	8.9	10.1
25th Centile	no women	13	17	16	10	6	7
75th Centile	principals in	19	24	17	16	11	13
Range	sec. schools	10–30	9–28	13–19	6–23	2–25	3–24
Mode		13	17	13	16	6	5

Appendices

Table 5.6 Promoted teachers in secondary schools, non-graduates and graduates: years of teaching experience when status awarded

	Principals (Lge. Schls.)		Principals (Med. Schls.)		V.P.'s (Lge. Schls.)		V.P.'s (Med. Schls.)		S.M.'s	
	Grad. (N = 33)	Non-grad. (N = 5)	Grad. (N = 3)	Non-grad. (N = 1)	Grad. (N = 44)	Non-grad. (N = 6)	Grad. (N = 6)	Non-grad. (N = 6)	Grad. (N = 91)	Non-grad. (N = 74)
Mean Exp.	20.7	26.2	20.8	22.0	16.3	21.7	15.5	14.8	7.4	11.6
25th Centile	18	21	N/A	N/A	13	18	15	10	5	8
75th Centile	23	27	N/A	N/A	19	25	17	18	9	15
Range	10–33	19–35	21–22	N/A	9–28	17–30	13–19	6–23	2–20	3–25
Mode	18	N/A	22	N/A	13	17	13	16	6	12

Table 5.7 Promoted teachers in secondary schools, different school types: years of teaching experience when status awarded

	Principals		V.P.'s (Lge. Schls.)		V.P.'s (Med. Schls.)	S.M.'s	
	H.S. (N = 36)	Sec. Coll. (N = 6)	H.S. (N = 44)	Sec. Coll. (N = 6)	H.S. (N = 12)	H.S. (N = 132)	Sec. Coll. (N = 33)
Mean Exp.	21.5	21.3	17.3	15.2	15.2	9.8	7.2
25th Centile	19	19	13	14	13	6	6
75th Centile	24	22	18	17	17	12	10
Range	10–35	18–20	9–30	12–17	6–23	6–25	5–16
Mode	19	18	13	17	16	6	5/10

Appendices

Table 5.8 Promoted teachers in district schools*: years of teaching experience when status awarded

	Principals			V.P.'s (N = 15)	S.T.'s (N = 9)	S.M.'s (N = 25)
	Lge. Schls. (N = 4)	Med. Schls. (N = 14)	Sml. Schls. (N = 3)			
Mean Exp.	24.3	20.4	11.4	15.4	10.1	9.4
25th Centile	14	18	N/A	12	7	5
75th Centile	26	22	N/A	16	11	11
Range	10–33	13–33	7–12	8–26	5–22	3–24
Mode	N/A	21	N/A	11	11	5

* Career profile information on teachers in District schools is not divided up according to the sex of the teacher because very few, if any, teachers in such promotion positions are women. For example, there are no women principals, or vice principals; while only 5, or 0.8 per cent of the total number of S.M.'s are women.

Table 5.9 Promoted teachers in district schools, non-graduates and graduates: years of teaching experience when status awarded

	Principals		V.P.'s		S.T.'s		S.M.'s	
	Grad. (N = 16)	Non-Grad. (N = 15)	Grad. (N = 3)	Non-grad. (N = 12)	Grad.	Non-Grad. (N = 9)	Grad. (N = 15)	Non-grad. (N = 10)
Mean Exp.	18.2	15.2	17.0	15.0	—	10.1	6.3	14.0
25th Centile	18	12	N/A	11	—	7	5	9
75th Centile	21	17	N/A	16	—	11	7	16
Range	7–33	6–33	13–24	8–26	—	5–22	3–11	5–24
Mode	18	12	N/A	11	—	11	5	6/24

Table 5.10 Promoted teachers in non-school positions*: years of experience when status awarded

	Directors (N = 8)	Superintendents (N = 18)	Supervisors (N = 14)	PEO's (N = 10)	SEO's (N = 23)
Mean Exp.	28.4	23.2	20.2	20.7	14.6
25th	27	15	18	19	12
75th	30	29	25	23	16
Range	25–33	10–35	11–26	12–37	5–31
Mode	30	31	25	20/23	5

Because of the small number of women in non-school positions (Table p), it is not fruitful to construct separate tables for males and females as was done for the other promotion positions examined.

Appendices

Table 5.11 Number of times principals had moved between schools/work locations during teaching career, according to type and size of school

	Sec.* Coll. (N = 6)	High Schools		Primary Schools			District Schools		
		Large (N = 32)	Medium (N = 4)	Large (N = 49)	Medium (N = 47)	Small (N = 50)	Large (N = 3)	Medium (N = 14)	Small (N = 14)
Mean No of Moves	6.6	7.3	4.8	8.7	7.6	6.1	9.0	6.7	6.8
25th Centile	6	7	4	7	5	4	8	5	6
75th Centile	7	8	6	10	10	6	10	8	7
Range	4–7	2–17	3–7	4–18	3–14	2–11	7–12	4–11	3–16
Mode	7	7	6	8	4	5	8	5	6

N.B.: *All Secondary Colleges are classed as large schools.

Table 5.12 Principals in different types of schools: years of teaching experience when status awarded by size of school

	Sec. Coll.	High. Schl.	Dist. Schl.	Prim. Schl.	Spec. Schl.
Lge.Schls.	(N = 6)	(N = 36)	(N = 20)	(N = 146)	(N = 13)
Mean Exp.	(N = 6) 21.3	(N = 32) 21.5	(N = 3) 20.8	(N = 49) 22.0	—
25th Centile	19	18	14	17	—
75th Centile	22	24	33	28	—
Range	18–30	10–35	10–33	11–35	—
Mode	18	18	N/A	17	—
Med. Schls.					
Mean Exp.	—	(N = 4) 21.8	(N = 14) 20.4	(N = 47) 16.8	(N = 7) 11.6
25th Centile	—	22	18	13	8
75th Centile	—	22	22	17	14
Range	—	21–22	13–33	10–33	6–22
Mode	—	22	22	17	10
Sml. Schls.					
Mean Exp.	—	—	(N = 14) 11.4	(N = 50) 9.8	(N = 6) 8.2
25th Centile	—	—	8	5	9
75th Centile	—	—	15	12	10
Range	—	—	6–19	2–29	4–11
Mode	—	—	12	4	11

Code:
Large Schools: 351+ students (Class 1A & 1)
Medium Sized Schools: 151–350 students (Class 2 & 3)
Small Schools: 8–150 students (Class 4, 5 & 6)

Index

Abbott-Chapman, J. 9
Adams, Henry 6
Adams, R. 38, 41
administration ability 111–12, 115, 170, 172, 204–5
age and promotion, 9, 12, 21–2, 26, 34, 40, 45, 51, 55–7, 60, 78, 158, 167, 171, 193, 195, 197, 200–1, 205–6
   as individual attribute 28–9
   of teachers in case study 90–1
Ahamad, B. 14
alienation 2, 50
ambition 20, 26–7, 41, 43, 156, 159, 168
anchorage perspectives, career 12, 33–5, 75, 78, 80, 171, 194–6, 235
Anderson, N. 2, 7
appeals 72, 175
application 31, 55, 57, 145–7, 175, 200–1
appointment procedures 71–3
aspirations 18, 20, 28, 30–1, 41, 57–8, 102, 127, 168, 172, 194
Auchmuty, ? 43, 46
authority 48, 67, 207
autonomy 16, 29, 102, 191
availability of promotion 9, 26, 30–1, 63, 77, 83, 105, 141, 145, 172, 177–8, 180–1, 187, 190

background
   details of teachers in case study 88–94
   age 90–1
   class, socio-economic 93–4
   marital status/family size 91–2
   occupational inheritance 92–3
   sex 88–90
   socio-economic 48–9, 51
Ball, S. 8, 38
Bardwick, J.M. 30
Bassett, G.W. 8, 30, 40
Becker, Howard S. 3, 8, 17–18, 23–4, 27, 46–9, 52, 54, 62, 75, 79, 199, 236–8
behaviour, teacher 3, 5, 7–10, 15–16, 35, 39, 43, 48, 54, 59, 75, 80, 83, 160, 177, 183–6, 189, 192–4, 198, 208–9
Behrens, N. et al. 49, 236
Bendix, R. 33, 49, 235, 237
Berkeley, G. 8
Berlowitz, M.J. 39, 49–50, 199, 236
Bidwell, G.E. 17
Blaug, M. 14
Booth, Charles 2
boredom 162–3, 178
Boreham, P. et al. 42
Bowman, M.J. 14, 51
Broom, L. 93–4
Burden, P. 38
Burdon, J.R. 234
Burke, G. 14
Burkhardt, G. 56
Butt, R.L. 38, 40, 188

263

Index

Caplow, T. 17, 20–1, 23, 30–1, 52, 78, 196, 234, 236–7
career
  summary and discussion of case study 187–212
    anchorage perspectives 194–6
    maps, strategies and timetables 193–4
    structural and phenomenological perspectives 208–9
    teaching as 187–93
    vertical and horizontal mobility and contingency factors 196–208
  teaching as 76–7, 233–4
Careers in Education Project 74–5
case study
  characteristics of promoted teachers in 88–117
  research design and procedure 74–86
    framework 754–9
    framework drawn together 79–80
    methodology 80–6
Champoux, J.E. 18, 32, 201
characteristics of promoted teachers in case study 88–117
  academic and professional qualifications 94–9
  background details 88–94
  factors and views related to promotion 99–117
Charters, W.W. 19, 188
Chinoy, E. 5
choice 9, 26, 41, 43–4, 46, 159, 202
cities, schools, in 49–50, 108, 110, 119, 141, 143, 147, 155, 193, 198–200
class, social 22, 27–8, 34, 49
  background 158–9, 197, 199
  of teachers in case study 93–4
commitment 15–16, 18, 30, 32, 34–5, 39, 45, 49, 56–7, 156, 164, 173–4, 179–80, 183, 188, 191, 200
competence 22, 29, 68, 83, 162, 170, 172, 180, 185, 207–8
competition 10, 141–5, 165, 182, 185, 194, 203
conceptualization of occupational careers 14–37

attributes of individual 27–35
career structure 20–7
careers in context 18–19
occupation, profession and career 15–18
perceptions of career structure 35–6
conformity 42, 59–60, 111–12, 115, 169, 173, 202, 204, 206–7, 210–11
Connell, R.W. 8
contact
  with children 40, 60–1, 100–1, 112, 117, 156, 188, 194
  social 59–61, 164
Cooper, ? 38
Coulter, F. 43–4
country, schools in 49–50, 108, 112–13, 119, 141, 143, 145, 147, 155, 172, 176–8, 198–201, 203, 207
Crawford, K.E. 30, 46
Cressey, P.G. 2

Dalton, M. 7, 22–3, 29, 42, 207, 237
definitions
  career 17
  career patterns 24–5
  career saliency 32
  graduate 95
  occupation 15
  occupational sociology 4
  profession 16
Delong, T.J. 236
De Mann, H. 2
demotion 20, 26–7, 119, 184, 196
Demster, N. 8
Director General of Education 68, 72, 82, 176
discipline 48, 60–1, 111–12
distribution of promotion positions 58, 141–5, 198, 203
district schools, career patterns of teachers in case study in 129–33
  gender 130–1
  qualifications 131–3
  overall situation 129–30
division of labour 1–2
Dobson, H. 49–50, 236
Donovan, F.R. 2, 7
Doran, G.A. 58

Dreyfuss, ? 2
Duberman, L. 30–1
Dubin, R. 27, 32–5, 78, 195–6, 235
Duggan, E.P. 49
Durkheim, Emile 1–2, 6

Eberts, R.W. 57, 237
education, background 34, 50, 199
Edwards, H. 27, 33, 201, 235
Emms, F. 21, 79
environment, desirable working 17–18, 23, 25, 39–40, 43, 48–9, 52, 79–80, 108–11, 119–20, 155, 160, 172, 176–8, 189, 191, 195–201, 203, 207
Epstein, C.F. 23
Epstein, L.K. 32
ethnicity 22, 27–8, 49–51
Etzioni, A. 16, 30, 41–2
exit from teaching career 9, 160, 189
expectations 21, 26–7, 29, 46–7, 161, 166–7, 180–1, 185, 190
experience 12, 21–2, 29, 41, 44, 49, 51–7, 59–61, 117, 161, 167, 170–2, 192, 197, 201, 203–5
extra-curricula activities 42, 44, 60–1, 101, 103, 166, 169, 172–3, 188, 201, 207

failure 26–7, 77, 161, 193, 202, 210
family 26, 30–2, 56–7, 155, 160–1, 165, 178–9, 189, 193, 195–6, 199–201, 206
  size of, of teachers in case study 91–2
Fenwick, P.R. 57
Fett, I. 92, 117n
Flittie, E.G. 25
Fogarty, M.P. 29–32, 237–8
Form, W.H. 4, 15, 17
framework of case study 11, 76–80
  anchorage perspectives 78
  drawn together 79–80
  horizontal vs vertical mobility 78–9
  Roth's notion of career timetables 77–8
  structural and phenomenological perspectives 79
  teaching as career 76–7

Freeman, R.B. 30, 237
Friedman, N.L. 17–18, 24, 79, 234
further promotion 105–7, 109, 182–3, 189–90
further study 95–6, 206–7

Gagg, M. 61
Gallop, R. 61
Ganguillet, ? 38
Geer, Blanche 3, 46
Gehrke, N.J. 49, 237
gender 12, 28, 34, 45, 51, 60, 78, 120–3, 138, 158–60, 167, 171–2, 176, 187, 207, 209
  application 31, 55, 57, 145–7, 200–1
  background details of teachers in case study 88–90
  and career 155, 163–5
  of district school teachers 130–1
  factors favouring promotion 112–14
  geographical mobility and 104–5
  graduates/nongraduates 96
  infant mistresses 68, 83–4
  marital status 91–2
  of primary school teachers 123–4
  promotion in or out of school 110
  satisfaction and 101–3
  of secondary school teachers 126–8
  and teaching 93
  underrepresentation of women 28, 30–1, 57–8, 127, 190
  women/men 5, 18, 23, 47, 62–3, 190–2, 195–7, 203, 205–6, 208, 211
geographical mobility 25, 31, 50, 76, 104–5, 112, 136, 164–5, 172–4, 176, 179, 195–6, 199, 201, 207
  of teachers in case study 133–6
Glaser, B.G. 4, 18–19, 21–2, 25, 29, 76, 79, 188, 206, 234
Goffman, E. 26
Goldman, D.R. 34–5, 78, 195, 235
Goodson, S. 8, 38
Gouldner, A.W. 25–6, 235
graduates/nongraduates 47, 55, 58–60, 63, 112, 118, 164, 170, 172, 192, 205–6, 209
  definition 95
  of teachers in case study 95–7

Index

Green, B.F. 56
Greenberg, D.H. 14, 23, 49, 236
Greenway, P.A. 8, 38
Greenwood, M.J. 14
Guba, E.G. 17
Guskey, T.R. 8, 35

Hall, Oswald 3, 7, 15, 18, 20–3, 42–3, 76, 206–7, 234, 237
Hall, R.H. 29
Havinghurst, R. 23, 50
hierarchy
  non-school 68
  promotional 9–11, 21, 29, 33–5, 38, 44, 53–4, 57–8, 61, 67–8, 71, 78, 80–3, 89–90, 105–6, 118, 120–1, 130, 133, 149, 155, 159, 170–1, 178, 180–1, 190–2, 194–5, 197, 204–6
  status 15, 20, 27, 32, 43–52, 135, 188
Hilsum, S. 7, 35–6, 39–47, 54–60, 62, 79, 188, 234–9
Hirsch, ? 38
holidays 39, 100–3, 188, 191
horizontal mobility 10–12, 23–5, 35, 43, 49, 62, 75–6, 80–1, 120, 171–2, 176–8, 180, 189, 191, 195, 203
  in teaching 47–52
  /vertical 52–4, 78–9, 196–208, 235–8
  in case study 136–9
hours, working 40, 102–3
Hoyle, E. 42
Huberman, M. 8, 38–9, 41, 43–4, 46, 188, 210
Hughes, Everrett C. 1–3, 5, 7, 17–19, 21, 23, 26, 28, 32–3, 35, 54, 78, 188, 206, 212
Hull, R. 9
Hutt, C. 28, 30–1, 200, 237

ideas 39, 60–1, 102, 111
identity 5–7, 15–16
incentives 18, 34, 50–2, 174, 177, 190, 198, 201, 208, 210–11
induction 9, 43–4, 46, 62, 159
infant mistresses 68, 83–4
influence and promotion 29, 59, 82–3, 157, 162–3, 166, 168, 173, 175, 186, 202–3, 208, 210–11
  factors of promotion 111–17
Ingvarson, L. 8, 38
inheritance, occupational 158–9, 187
  of teachers in case study 92–3
inservice training 16, 56, 60, 112, 115, 165
interview
  promotion 175–6
  use of, in case study 11, 75, 81, 85–6, 154, 209
  format 254–7

Jackson, P.W. 16
Jacobs, J.E. 30, 200
Jay, L.J. 50, 199, 236–7
Jecks, D. 8, 56
Johnson, T.J. 16
Johnston, G.L. 63
Jones, E.H. 31, 200

Karmel, P. 9
Kelsall, R.K. 30
Keown, P.A. 14, 25, 76, 206
Kundsin, R.B. 31

Lacey, C. 7, 46
Ladinsky, J. 7, 17, 25, 38
Lancaster-Jones, F. 93–4
Lansing, J.B. 14
Le Play, Frederick 2
Lightfoot, S. 41, 43–4
limited/unlimited success perspectives 27, 33–5, 75, 78, 167, 171–2, 195–6
Lipset, S.M. 33, 235
locals 25–6, 76, 165, 206
Logan, L. 8
Lombard, G.W. 2–3
Lortie, Dan C. 3, 8, 35–6, 41–4, 46, 57, 59, 76, 234, 239
luck 168, 173
Lyons, G. 7, 17–18, 21, 25–6, 29, 35–6, 39–40, 42, 44, 46–7, 54–5, 57, 59, 62, 79, 188, 234–5, 238–9

McArthur, J. 8, 43–4, 59, 188
McCall, J. 14, 23, 49, 236
McCann, H. 9

McIntosh, J. 31, 57, 200
McIntyre, D. 14, 43, 188
McLeish, J. 14
Mann, M. 14, 25–6, 76, 206
marginality 29, 193
marital status 12, 26, 28, 31–2, 57, 78, 167, 171–2, 176, 179, 195–6, 200–1, 206
  of teachers in case study 91–2
Marsland, D. 7, 234
Marx, Karl, 1–2, 50
Masih, L.K. 32, 56, 201
Mason, W.S. 56
Mayo, E. 2–3
Meason, L. 8, 38, 41
merit 22, 71
methods, teaching 48, 60–1, 111–13, 117
methodology 10–11, 209
  design basis 81–2
    aims 81
    case study of one Australian State Education System 81–2
    teachers in promotion positions 82
  patterns of case study 118–
  procedures for gathering data 84–6
    Education Department records 84–5
    interviews 85–6
    questionnaires 85
  survey population 83–4
migration 25, 39, 48–51, 53, 56–60, 72, 104–5, 156, 160, 178, 205
Mills, C, 27, 33, 50, 78, 195
mobility 7–8, 11–12, 42–3, 45, 54, 133–6, 156, 160, 164, 178, 189–90, 201, 206–7, 210–11
  see also geographical mobility; horizontal mobility; vertical mobility
Montenegro, X.P. 31, 200
morale 183–6, 208, 210
Morris, C.N. 23, 45
Morris, M. 30
Morrison, A. 14, 43, 188
motivation 28–9, 32–5, 119, 156, 160–3, 172, 186, 190–1, 195, 199, 201, 208

Muellen, E. 14

Nadebaun, M. 43
Nash, J.M. 237
Nelson, Z.P. 25
Newgarten, B. 23, 50
Nias, J. 8, 35, 39, 79, 200
Nosow, S. 4, 17
number
  of moves between schools 135–7
  of promotion positions 69–70, 198, 201, 205–6
  of Tasmanian schools 64–5
  of teachers 6, 83–4

Oakley, A. 28–31, 200
occupation, profession and career 15–18
occupational status 188
opportunity 9, 16, 19, 30, 40, 45, 77, 80, 83, 105, 141, 143–5, 158, 160, 165, 172, 176–8, 181–5, 187, 190, 200, 208, 211
  behaviour and morale 183–6
  structure 10, 19, 36, 42–3, 54, 118, 147, 149, 180–1, 189–90, 193–4, 197–8, 203–4, 207
  of Tasmanian teachers 63–73
    appointment and promotion procedures 71–3
    changing structure of promotion system 66
    changing structure of state school system 64
    hierarchy of promotion position 67–8
    number, distribution of promotion positions 69–70
    number, distribution of, and size of schools 64–6
organisational careers 7, 18–19, 21–2, 24–9, 35, 42, 75–6, 154–5, 188, 202
Orlich, D.C. 56

parents 48, 102
Park, Robert E. 2, 36
Parsons, T. 29, 33, 78, 195, 235
part-time teachers 83

Index

pathways, career 8, 10, 156, 158, 163, 180, 189
patterns of teachers in case study, career 118–53
  in district schools 129–33
  distribution of, and competition for, promotional positions 141–5
  horizontal vs vertical mobility 136–9
  methodology for analysis 118–21
  mobility between work locations 133–6
  pathways of Directors, school principals 149–52
  in primary schools 121–2
  rate at which promotion occurs 145–8
  in secondary schools 124–9
  of service personnel 133
  teachers in different sectors of Education Department 139–41
Pavalko, R.M. 5, 15, 20–1, 26, 28, 32, 35, 78–9, 188, 200, 235, 237–8
Peart, G.J. 49–50, 69–71, 236
Pedersen, K.G. 51, 56, 200, 236–7
perceptions 7, 10–12, 36, 43, 46–7, 54, 61–2, 75, 77, 81, 118, 191–2
  of career structures 59–61
  related to promotions 99–117
    benefit/loss of leaving classroom for promotion 104
    characteristics of desirable school 108–11
    factors influencing promotion 111–17
    further promotion, likelihood of 105–17
    migration 104–5
    promotion in or out of school 108–9
    satisfaction of teaching 100–4
    satisfaction of teaching career 99
  of teaching career 154–86
    anchorage perspectives 171
    composite picture of promoted teacher 172–3
    contingency factors 163–71
    further promotion, chances of 182–3
    horizontal mobility 176–8

opportunities, behaviour and morale 183–6
opportunity structure, changes in 180–1
promotionn system, operation of 174–6
reasons for seeking promotion 160–13
stages of career 159–60
teachers not seeking mobility 178–80
teachers not seeking promotion 173–4
teaching as career 154–9
Perrucci, C.C. and R. 237
phenomenological perspectives 11–12, 35–6, 47, 75, 79–80, 154, 208–9, 239
Phillips, D. 42, 63–4
power 7, 18, 29, 33, 53, 68, 78, 82, 182, 208
preservice training 9, 43, 46, 94–5, 98, 159
prestige 7, 17–18, 23, 25, 52, 78
Prick, L.G.M. 8, 38, 40–1, 44, 79, 188, 200
primary schools 39, 96–7, 99, 190
  career patterns of teachers in case study in 121–4
    gender 123–4
    qualifications 124–5
    overall situation 121–2
  /secondary schools 40, 47, 53, 55–6, 58–60, 63, 69–70, 72, 192, 202, 206
  in Tasmania 64–5
principals 38, 48, 53–4, 58–9, 66–7, 69–70, 82–5, 169, 189, 204, 210
  in case study
    age 90–1
    factors favouring promotion 115–16
    further promotion 107, 109
    gender 89–90
    geographical mobility 106
    graduates 96–7
    in district schools 129–32, 147–8, 205
    pathways, career 149–52

268

in primary schools 120–2, 124–5, 135, 147–9, 192, 205
in secondary schools 121, 124–9, 134–41, 147–9, 151
procedures
  appointment 71–3
    appeals procedure 72
    appointments 72
    changes over time 72–3
    promotion committee 71
    promotion criteria 71
    procedures 72
  promotion 83, 118, 175
profession 6, 15–18, 20, 23, 25, 30, 33, 40–3, 155, 185–6, 188
  teaching as 38–62, 155–6
professionalization 16, 21
promotion committee 71, 115, 175
propositions to be tested in case study 233–9
  anchorage perspectives 235
  horizontal vs vertical mobility 235–8
  structural and phenomenological perspectives 239
  teaching as career 233–4
  timetables 235
Purvis, J. 16

qualifications 12, 21, 26, 71, 120, 131–3, 164, 167, 184, 196, 201–2, 206–7
  of teachers in case study 94–9
    age group trained to teach 94–5
    further study 95–6
    graduate/nongraduate status 95–7
    length of training 94–5
    specialism, subject 98–9
    subjects taught in school 99
    see also graduates/nongraduates
questionnaires, use of, in case study 11, 85, 88, 100, 117, 209
  format 243–53

Rabinowitz, W. 30, 46
rate of promotion 21–2, 25–6, 29, 54, 62, 79, 90, 119–20, 123–4, 126, 131, 155, 163–4, 168, 170, 172, 180, 192–3, 201, 203–4, 211
  in case study 145–8
Raymond, D. 40, 188
records, Tasmanian Education Department 11, 75, 84–5, 88, 118, 209
  information on 240–2
re-entrants 45, 56, 59
regulations, selection 21, 28–9, 35, 57
relationships 5, 20, 24, 59–61, 113, 115, 117, 178, 192, 203–4
retirement 40, 44–5, 105, 160
Rimmer, C.M. 234, 237
Ritzer, G. 17, 19, 25, 188
role 4, 7, 15, 17, 31, 34, 82, 189
  differentiation 1–2, 28–30, 200
  social 5–6, 25, 40, 43–4, 77
Roth, Julian A. 3, 24, 29, 46, 54, 75, 235
  notion of career timetables 77–8, 80

salary 23, 42, 51–4, 66–8, 85, 89, 99, 101–2, 119, 122, 161, 163, 182, 186, 191, 194, 205, 208
saliency, career 32, 56, 202
Sampson, S.N. 8, 18, 30, 57, 79, 237–8
Sasser, C.W. 49
satisfaction 32, 34, 39–41, 44, 51, 59, 99–104, 156, 163, 179, 181, 188, 191, 194, 201, 208
schooling, length of 64–5
secondary schools 42, 53–4, 96–7, 99
  career patterns of teachers
    in case study in 124–9
    gender 126–8
    qualifications 128–9
    overall situation 124–6
  /primary schools 40, 47, 53, 55–6, 58–60, 63, 69–70, 72, 192, 202, 206
security 40, 48, 100–1, 158, 187–8
selection 21–2, 71, 176, 206
self-esteem 18, 33, 39, 78
self-questioning 41, 44
senior master/mistress 38, 52–4, 57, 67–8, 70, 82, 84–5, 136–9, 141, 143, 203, 205

269

Index

in case study
  age 90–1
  further promotion 107, 109
  gender 89
  geographical mobility 106
  graduates 97
  in district schools 129–33
  in secondary schools 124–9
senior teachers 67–8, 70, 82, 84–5, 136–9, 141, 143, 203, 205
  in case study
    age 90–1
    further promotion 107, 109
    gender 89
    geographical mobility 106
    graduates 97
    in district schools 130–2
    in primary schools 121–5
seniority 20, 22, 67, 73, 111–12
service, length of 2–3, 21, 56, 60, 71, 73, 90, 112, 115, 165, 170–1, 206–7
service personnel 10, 29, 39, 48, 59–61, 68, 70–2, 76, 82–5, 120, 133, 139, 141–2, 147, 159–60, 171, 174, 176, 190–1, 194, 203–6, 210
  career pathways of directors 149–52, 189
  in case study
    age 90–1
    career patterns 133
    further promotion 107, 109
    gender 89
    geographical mobility 106
    graduates 97
    migration 105
    satisfaction 102–4
    superintendents and factors favouring promotion 115–16
Sheffield, R.C. 49, 237
Shepherd, M. 57
Sikes, P.J. 8, 38, 41
Singer, J.D. 8
size
  of class 40, 101, 188
  of school 49–51, 53–4, 67, 108–11, 121–2, 124, 139–40, 191, 198
    Tasmanian 64–6
  of Tasmanian education system 82–3

Sjaasted, L.A. 14, 51
Slocum, W.L. 19
Smith, Adam 1
Smith, C.H. 49, 237
Smith, D.M. 7, 39, 42, 46, 234
socialization 6, 16, 43–4
socio-economic status of schools 108, 110–11, 172, 176, 178, 191, 198, 200–1, 207
sociology, occupational 1–13, 14–15, 35–6, 38, 62
  case study
    findings 12
    purpose of 10–12
    content of 4
    promotion and career patterns in teaching 7–10
    reasons for studying 5–6
    of school teachers 6–7
Solomon, D. 3, 15
Sorokin, P.A. 6, 21
Spaull, A.D. 42, 45, 57
specialism, subject 40, 58–61, 67–8, 98–9, 183, 202
spiralists 25–6, 76, 206
sponsorship 22–3, 36, 42, 60, 62, 78, 164, 168–71, 175, 193, 202, 204, 206–8, 211
stages, career 9, 12, 17, 20, 24–6, 62, 76, 159–60, 189–90, 195, 198
  in teaching 43–6
Start, K.B. 7, 35–6, 39–47, 54–60, 62, 79, 188, 234–9
statistics of career profiles of promoted teachers 258–62
status 6, 17, 23, 40, 67
  ascribed 156, 158, 187
  decline 45
  hierarchy 15, 20, 27, 32, 43–52, 135, 188
  level 2, 10, 25, 28–31, 54–7, 66, 68, 71, 76, 78, 83, 89, 119–20, 159, 178, 182, 196–7, 199, 205
  marital 12, 26, 28, 31–2, 57, 78, 91–2, 167, 171–2, 176, 179, 195–6, 200–1, 206
  occupational 5, 21–2
  relative 133

Index

socio-economic, of schools 108, 110–11, 172, 176, 178, 191, 198, 200–1, 207
Stone, J.A. 57, 237
Stevens, J. 26, 56
Stewart, W.A.C. 49
strategy, career 12, 77, 167, 171, 173, 176–7, 192–4, 202, 107
Strauss, A. 18, 27, 238
stress 40, 101, 103, 184, 188, 191
structure 17, 35–6, 62
 career 20–7, 155, 163
  failure 26–7
  horizontal mobility 23–4
  patterns 24–6
  promotion criteria 21–3
  stages 20
  timetables 24
  vertical mobility 20–1
 career in teaching 43–55
  career proper 46–7
  horizontal mobililty 47–52
  patterns 54–5
  stages in 43–6
  timetables 54
  vertical and horizontal mobility 52–4
  perceptions 59–61
 structural perspectives 11–12, 35–6, 46, 75, 79–80, 208–9, 239
success 156, 161, 168, 170–1, 181, 190, 194, 201, 207, 210
 see also limited/unlimited success perspective
suitability 21, 71, 83
Sutherland, E.H. 2, 7
Swift, D.F. 27
system
 promotion, operation of 174–6, 194
 Tasmanian school 63–5, 118, 149, 173, 180–1, 184, 209–10

Talbert, J.E. 76
Tasmania
 education system 63–5, 82–3, 149, 173, 180–1, 184, 209–10
 enrolment in 64, 66, 118, 180
 number of schools in 64–6

Teacher Mobility Study 74–5
teaching
 as career 38–62, 154–9
 attributes of school teachers 55–9
 career structure 43
 in context 42–3
 different types of career 156–8
 occupation, profession and career 38–42
 occupational and organisational careers 154–5
 occupational inheritance 158–9
 patterns 155
 teacher perceptions of career structures 59–61
 methods 48, 60–1, 111–13, 117
timetables, career 12, 15, 24, 28–9, 54, 75, 167, 171, 173, 181, 188, 193–4, 202, 207, 235
 Roth's notion of 77–8, 80
Tisher, R. *et al.* 8, 43–4, 46, 59, 188, 234
training 20, 45, 124, 156, 166, 205
 insevice 16, 56, 60, 112, 115, 165
 preservice 9, 43, 46, 94–5, 98, 159
transients 25, 76, 206
Tronc, K. 21, 79
turnover of teachers 49–51, 56, 210

underrepresentation of women 28, 30–1, 57–8, 90, 127, 190, 200

values 7, 18, 48, 156–7, 191, 198
variety of schools 56, 60–1, 82, 139–41, 201
vertical mobility 10–12, 17, 20–2, 25–6, 28–30, 32, 34–6, 44, 55, 57, 61–2, 75–6, 80–1, 120, 153, 171, 176, 180
 /horizontal 52–4, 78–9, 196–208, 235–8
 in case study 136–9
 in teaching 52–4
vice principals 53–4, 58, 66–9, 82, 84–5, 139–42
 in case study
  age 89–90
  further promotion 107, 109
  gender 89–90

271

Index

geographical mobility 106
graduates 97
in district schools 129–32, 205
in primary schools 121–5
Viel, P.J. 42, 237
vocation 16, 155–6

Waller, W. 5, 8, 59, 76
Warren, D. 43
Warry, M. 8
wastage 9, 45, 47

Weber, Max 1–2
Whyte, D.R. 33, 195
Whyte, William F. 3
Wilensky, H.L. 17, 25, 27, 33, 76, 188, 201, 235
Willett, J.B. 8
Wirth, L. 2
Women Teacher's Careers Study 174–5
Woods, P. 8, 38, 41

Zetterberg, H.L. 33

For Product Safety Concerns and Information please contact our EU representative GPSR@taylorandfrancis.com
Taylor & Francis Verlag GmbH, Kaufingerstraße 24, 80331 München, Germany

www.ingramcontent.com/pod-product-compliance
Lightning Source LLC
Chambersburg PA
CBHW051631230426
43669CB00013B/2253